THE MAKING AND MEANING OF A MEDIEVAL MANUSCRIPT

THE MAKING AND MEANING OF A MEDIEVAL MANUSCRIPT

INTERPRETING MS BODLEY 851

Thomas C. Sawyer

D. S. BREWER

© Thomas C. Sawyer 2025

All Rights Reserved. Except as permitted under current legislation no part of this work may be photocopied, stored in a retrieval system, published, performed in public, adapted, broadcast, transmitted, recorded or reproduced in any form or by any means, without the prior permission of the copyright owner

The right of Thomas C. Sawyer to be identified as the author of this work has been asserted in accordance with sections 77 and 78 of the Copyright, Designs and Patents Act 1988

First published 2025
D. S. Brewer, Cambridge

ISBN 978 1 84384 746 5

D. S. Brewer is an imprint of Boydell & Brewer Ltd
PO Box 9, Woodbridge, Suffolk IP12 3DF, UK
and of Boydell & Brewer Inc.
668 Mt Hope Avenue, Rochester, NY 14620–2731, USA
website: www.boydellandbrewer.com

Our Authorised Representative for product safety in the EU is Easy Access System Europe – Mustamäe tee 50, 10621 Tallinn, Estonia, gpsr.requests@easproject.com

A CIP catalogue record for this book is available
from the British Library

The publisher has no responsibility for the continued existence or accuracy of URLs for external or third-party internet websites referred to in this book, and does not guarantee that any content on such websites is, or will remain, accurate or appropriate

*Hoc etiam votum facili bonitate secunda,
hoc nostris superadde bonis: ne transeat istud
ad limam livoris opus; ne sentiat illam
iudicii formam, qua cancellatur honestum,
suppletur vitium; quae verba decentia radit,
turpia subscribit; quae praestantissima scalpro
mordet et omne bonum legit indignante labello.*

The author and publisher are grateful to the New York Medieval Society
for generous financial support towards the costs of this volume.

CONTENTS

List of Illustrations   viii
Acknowledgments   x
List of Abbreviations   xiii
A Note on Transcriptions and Translations   xv

Introduction: How to Read a Medieval Book   1
1   Recomposing Bodley 851   30
2   Misogamist Fragments   84
3   Recomposing Walter Map   118
4   Walter Map's *Piers Plowman*   157
Conclusion: Manuscript Meaning   196

Bibliography   201
Index of Manuscripts   219
General Index   220

ILLUSTRATIONS

Tables

1	Descriptive overview of BodL. MS Bodley 851. Arranged to reflect present day appearance of the manuscript.	6
2	Analytic overview of BodL. MS Bodley 851. Arranged to reflect production of the manuscript over time.	65
3	Comparison of chapter titles in the *De nugis curialium* between the table of contents (inked, Scribe A) and the main text (rubricated, Scribe X).	130

Plates (pp. 70–83)

All plates reproduced from BodL., MS Bodley 851. All photos © Bodleian Libraries, University of Oxford under the Creative Commons licence CC-BY-NC 4.0. Images accessed through the Digital Bodleian at: https://digital.bodleian.ox.ac.uk/objects/0cecbb9e-b126-4360-b514-eb949f851b43/

1 BodL. MS Bodley 851, fol. 6v.
2 BodL. MS Bodley 851, fol. 7r.
3 BodL. MS Bodley 851, fol. 22r.
4 BodL. MS Bodley 851, fol. 71r.
5 BodL. MS Bodley 851, fol. 73r.
6 BodL. MS Bodley 851, fol. 80v.
7 BodL. MS Bodley 851, fol. 81v.
8 BodL. MS Bodley 851, fol. 83v.
9 BodL. MS Bodley 851, fol. 97v.
10 BodL. MS Bodley 851, fol. 117r.

ILLUSTRATIONS

11 BodL. MS Bodley 851, fol. 118v.
12 BodL. MS Bodley 851, fol. 124r.
13 BodL. MS Bodley 851, fols. (row 1) 17vb (detail), 25vb (detail), 26rb (detail); (row 2) 27va (detail), 33vb (detail), 41rb (detail); (row 3) 44ra (detail), 55rb (detail), 59ra (detail); (row 4) 59vb (detail), 63ra (detail), 73va (detail); (row 5) 111vb (detail), 112ra (detail), 119rb (detail); (row 6) 119va (detail), 119vb (detail), and 120ra (detail).
14 BodL. MS Bodley 851, fols. 126v (detail), 128v (detail), 130v (detail), 134r (detail), and 135r (detail).

The author and publisher are grateful to all the institutions and individuals listed for permission to reproduce the materials in which they hold copyright. Every effort has been made to trace the copyright holders; apologies are offered for any omission, and the publisher will be pleased to add any necessary acknowledgment in subsequent editions.

ACKNOWLEDGMENTS

It is a strange thing to publish a first book without immediate professional benefit, and a stranger thing still to realize that I may never again receive research funding to complete a second one. Like many of my generation, I am precariously employed: this counts for no tenure file. It is perhaps a quixotic venture to publish a thing simply because I think it is true. And yet – a dearly held yet! – for me, this book cannot help but signal a kind of wary optimism. Through it, I contribute my vanishingly small part to a great conversation among thinkers known, anonymous, and forgotten. In undertaking to write and publish an academic monograph, I find myself cautiously hopeful: not only that someday *The Making and Meaning of a Medieval Manuscript* will matter professionally, but that it might matter – truly, that it might have some meaningful bearing, however small – for those who read it.

For that hope, and for the training, encouragement, and guidance that ground such optimism, I owe my gratitude to more people than it seems possible to enumerate. I have relied intellectually, emotionally, materially, and imaginatively on more wonderful humans than I could dream of bringing to mind at once, much less listing on paper. Among such a brilliant multitude, I must acknowledge that the debts collected here are bound to be scant, grubby, and incomplete. For those who appear below, and for those whom I have inadvertently omitted: please know that my thanks exceed their expression.

My profoundest thanks to Jessica Rosenfeld, without whom this book would not exist, much less have any hope of persuading. If the central idea is mine, its best formulations are hers. For countless provocations, I thank David Lawton, who has never failed to say exactly what he thinks about a thought or its consequence. For reading a full working draft of the monograph, and for multiplying imaginative avenues for further research, I thank Michelle Karnes.

My writing is deeply indebted to an intersecting array of thoughtful communities gathered in that Midwestern, South-seeming, pot-holed metropolis of St. Louis, Missouri. At Washington University in St. Louis, I was fortunate to find the single best (extended) cohort ever to have tended the towering groves of academe: Josh Brorby, Kelly Caldwell, Katie Collins, Jonathan Koch, John Ladd, Ethan Levinson, Grace Lillard, Dan Normandin, Sam Pergadia, Michael Sanders, Sam Smith, Deborah Thurman, and Mel Walsh. It was a sorry thing to lose our last years together to something so unfit for feasting as a viral plague. The world was more a place because of you.

A separate portion of thanks to John and Jonathan, who read fresh-baked drafts of much of the material here, often in text and DM, and never failed to provide new perspective on an idea I thought I had finally captured.

At WashU, I learned to be a scholar and a critic. My thanks to Jessica and David (not for the last time); to the Faculty in English and the Faculty in Comparative Literature, especially Guinn Batten, Bill Maxwell, Anca Parvulescu, Wolfram Schmidgen, Gerhild Williams, and Steve Zwicker; to members of the Medieval Colloquium, especially Daniel Bornstein, Nancy Pope, Mark Pegg, Bellamy Pope, and Christian Schneider; and to the Early Modern Reading Group, a truly interdisciplinary gathering ever welcoming to this print-curious codicologist. In St. Louis, too, I found conversation and inspiration among the community at Saint Louis University. Notes taken at events put on by the Center for Medieval and Renaissance Studies are scattered throughout this work, and my Friday afternoons would have suffered more than my scansion, were it not for the Latin Reading Group led by Joan Hart-Hasler. Thanks especially to Joan, Ruth Evans, and Tony Hasler for kind encouragement in years when kindness could be hard to come by. I thank Holly James-Maddocks, whose manuscript course at SLU inspired my very first engagement with Bodley 851. Finally, of St. Louisians past, I thank Seth Strickland, my ultimate roommate not related by blood or marriage, for remaining a brilliant interlocutor and conference companion.

The University of Chicago has classified me as "staff," not "faculty" or even an "academic appointee" – a fact easily forgotten amidst the generosity of scholars here. My thanks to the medievalists at the Lexicon project for welcoming me to their events – especially to Julie Orlemanski, who was under no obligation to improve my drafts so, and to Joe Stadolnik, a font of research tools and institutional hacks. My thanks to my colleagues in the Writing Program, whose collective wit is surpassed only by their generosity of spirit. And my thanks to my collaborators in the humanities core, who have improved this work indirectly but substantively. Special thanks to Ben Jeffery, who cares deeply – sometimes startlingly – about the implications of critical thought. In Chicago, too, I have had the great pleasure of inheriting co-organization, with Julie Chamberlin, of the Midwest Medievalist Middle English Reading Group. Thanks to MMERG for reading multiple chapter drafts, especially Ian Cornelius, Zach Hines, Sarah Noonan, Arthur Russell and Liza Strakhov. In fact, to Ian, Zach, and Sarah I owe a double portion of thanks, for their aid in wrangling Chapter 1 into shape.

Much of Chapter 2 and part of the Introduction were previously published in *Studies in the Age of Chaucer* (2022) as "Wicked Wives and the Insatiable Virgin: Reading the Codicological Unconscious in a Fragment of MS Bodley 851." Thanks to the New Chaucer Society for permission to republish here.

Double thanks to NCS for unexpectedly generous financial support of my scholarship at conferences near and far: centers and tangents of the argument below were tested and improved in London, Toronto, and Durham. A section of the introduction was previously published in "Bookish Brains and Visionary Learning in the Apocalypsis goliae episcopi," copyright © 2022 Johns Hopkins University Press, with first appearance in *ELH*, Volume 89, Issue 1, Spring, 2022, pages 1–31. My thanks for permission to reproduce and modify that material here.

Special thanks to Professor Gillian Adler and the New York Medieval Society, whose generous financial support in the final stages of this project facilitated a truly eye-catching cover as well as the inclusion of full-color plates displaying images central to my inquiry.

My thanks to the team at Boydell and Brewer for supporting this project wholeheartedly, and for enduring my countless neurotic queries on process and presentation. My thanks to all anonymous readers for their improvements to the ideas ventured within.

A project of this scope is bound to collect countless miscellaneous debts. By no means comprehensively, for thoughts both included and begrudgingly omitted from the work that follows, I thank Patricia Bart, Neil Cartlidge, Susanna Fein, Andy Galloway, Drew Hicks, Kathryn Kerby-Fulton, Jill Mann, Richard Newhauser, Jo Nixon, Tommy Pfannkoch, Noëlle Phillips, Daniel Sawyer (no relation), Ben Utter, Lawrence Warner, and Sarah Wood.

Thanks to Arthur Bahr for mentorship wholly undeserved. Thanks to Justin Jackson, whose prudent advice ("don't go to graduate school") I am happy to have disregarded. Thanks to Philip Purchase, co-convener of the *Walter Map Reading Group*, for many hours of patient instruction amongst the fruits of Aetna. Thanks to Paul Vinhage for many joyous hours of raucous translation, chief among innumerable scholarly gifts.

Most of all, I thank my family, a category of relation that only sometimes has to do with blood. Love to all the aunts and uncles that put up with my bookish pursuit of invention in childhood and adulthood. Love to my grandmas. Love to my parents, Tom and Tracy, and my adoptive parents, Clay and Judy. (How is it that none of you have stopped me from drinking more coffee and buying more books?) Love to #wonderlfand, especially Alex, Erica, Maureen, Nathan, Steven, and Travis: you never fail to remind me what's important about thinking carefully and caring enough to think. Love to Jon (now you have to write a book). Love to AJ and Sam, interlopers of the tabletariat and interloping brothers. Love to Teddy, brother and friend chief among all. Love to Lauren and Becket, as we embark on ever-more adventures.

It goes without saying that all infelicities that remain within these pages are mine alone. May the collective labor we call learning transform any remaining error to discovery, someday.

ABBREVIATIONS

BL	London, British Library
BodL.	Oxford, Bodleian Library
CCCM	Corpus Christianorum Continuatio Mediaevalis
CCSL	Corpus Christianorum Series Latina
CUL	Cambridge, Cambridge University Library
De coniuge	*De coniuge non ducenda*
DIMEV	*Digital Index of Middle English Verse*. Edited by Linne R. Mooney *et al.* www.dimev.net/
Dissuasio	*Dissuasio Valerii ad Rufinum*
DMLBS	*The Dictionary of Medieval Latin from British Sources*. Edited by R. E. Latham *et al.* London: British Academy, 1975–2013. Accessed via https://logeion.uchicago.edu
Du Cange	*Glossarium mediae et infimae latinitatis*. Edited by Charles Dufresne Du Cange *et al.* Niort: L. Favre, 1883–1887. Accessed via https://logeion.uchicago.edu
EETS	Early English Text Society
EQHF	Richard Firth Green. *Elf Queens and Holy Friars: Fairy Beliefs and the Medieval Church*. Philadelphia, PA: University of Pennsylvania Press, 2016
IMS	Raymond Clemens and Timothy Graham. *Introduction to Manuscript Studies*. Ithaca, NY: Cornell University Press, 2007
James *et al.*	Walter Map. *De Nugis Curialium: Courtiers' Trifles*. Edited by M. R. James, Christopher Brooke, and R. A. B. Mynors. Oxford: Clarendon Press, 1983
JMEMS	*Journal of Medieval and Early Modern Studies*
JMLat	*Journal of Medieval Latin*

MED	*The Middle English Dictionary*. Edited by Hans Kurath *et al.* Ann Arbor, MI: University of Michigan Press, 1952–. https://quod.lib.umich.edu/m/middle-english-dictionary/dictionary
ODNB	*Oxford Dictionary of National Biography*. Edited by Sir David Cannadine *et al.* www.oxforddnb.com/
OED	*The Oxford English Dictionary*. Edited by John A. Simpson *et al.* Oxford: Clarendon Press, 1989–. www.oed.com/
OUMEM	Kathryn Kerby-Fulton, Linda Olson, and Maidie Hilmo. *Opening Up Middle English Manuscripts: Literary and Visual Approaches*. Ithaca, NY: Cornell University Press, 2012
PL	Patrologia Latina
PMLA	*Publications of the Modern Language Association*
SAC	*Studies in the Age of Chaucer*
WMMB	Joshua Byron Smith. *Walter Map and the Matter of Britain*. Philadelphia, PA: University of Pennsylvania Press, 2017
YLS	*Yearbook of Langland Studies*

A NOTE ON TRANSCRIPTIONS AND TRANSLATIONS

When citing from the manuscript, I capitalize the first word of each sentence in translation (according to modern conventions) but do not alter the case of any letters in transcription (according to medieval conventions). I have not modernized **i/j** or **u/v**. Similarly, I have not expanded diphthongs (as **e** to **æ**). I expand and italicize scribal abbreviations, including Tironian *et*. Citations and notes usually refer to parallel lines in modern edition, where available.

Unless otherwise noted, all translations are my own.

INTRODUCTION:
HOW TO READ A MEDIEVAL BOOK

How do you read a medieval book? Answers to this broad methodological question generally fall into two related disciplinary categories, the book-historical and the literary-critical. One way to read medieval books is to study them as material objects. In this, the book-historical (or "codicological") perspective, to read a medieval book is to inquire into the physical components of that book, to understand those components in terms of historicized and geographically localized mechanical processes, and to derive from the features and arrangement of those components information about the people who made the book and books like it.[1] Without significantly addressing textual contents, book historians can uncover an astounding array of information surrounding the economic, social, and political processes that governed

---

[1] Throughout this monograph "codicology" describes "the study of all of the physical aspects of the manuscript book" (Albert Derolez, *The Palaeography of Gothic Manuscript Books: From the Twelfth to the Early Sixteenth Century* [Cambridge: Cambridge University Press, 2003], 10). For accessible and comprehensive overviews of the production, description, and scholarly approaches to medieval books, see Christopher De Hamel, *Scribes and Illuminators* (Toronto: University of Toronto Press, 1992); Raymond Clemens and Timothy Graham, *Introduction to Manuscript Studies* (Ithaca, NY: Cornell University Press, 2007); and Orietta Da Rold and Elaine M. Treharne, eds., *The Cambridge Companion to Medieval British Manuscripts* (Cambridge: Cambridge University Press, 2020). For overviews of manuscript production focused on English books, see Kathryn Kerby-Fulton, Linda Olson, and Maidie Hilmo, *Opening up Middle English Manuscripts: Literary and Visual Approaches* (Ithaca, NY: Cornell University Press, 2012) and Daniel Wakelin, *Designing English: Early Literature on the Page* (Oxford: Bodleian Library, University of Oxford, 2018). Invaluable as general references are essays collected in Richard Gameson, ed., *The Cambridge History of the Book in Britain. Volume 1, c. 400–1100* (Cambridge: Cambridge University Press, 2012) and Rodney M. Thomson and Nigel J. Morgan, eds., *The Cambridge History of the Book in Britain. Volume 2, c. 1100–1400* (Cambridge: Cambridge University Press, 2007); along with those in Jeremy Griffiths and Derek Pearsall, eds., *Book Production and Publishing in Britain, 1375–1475* (Cambridge: Cambridge University Press, 1989); and Alexandra Gillespie and Daniel Wakelin, eds., *The Production of Books in England 1350–1500* (Cambridge: Cambridge University Press, 2011).

medieval manuscript production. We can identify the chemical processes that allowed for the manufacture of parchment or ink, survey the use and variety of medieval bindings, estimate the supply of sheepskin and quills for major cities and remote provinces, and model the circulation of skilled labor, in England and on the continent, by way of paleographic analysis and attention to shifting practices in decoration and illumination.[2] From features of a manuscript such as the size of its pages, the breadth of its margins, how it was prepared for the act of writing, how the writing itself was imposed and corrected, and the overall tactile impression of the object, we can make surprisingly accurate inferences about the kinds of texts it is likely to contain and the audiences it was likely meant to reach.[3] Moreover, any encounter with medieval texts in terms of authorship, readership, and circulation implicitly relies upon some prior scholarly study of medieval books. The hands-on archival work of collating, measuring, and describing manuscript collections that is central to all book history underpins nearly every aspect of academic labor on that vast and complex historical period in Europe caught between antiquity and modernity.

A book might have weight, dimensions, and components; but it might also contain words, thoughts, and concepts. Near the end of *Troilus and Criseyde*, Geoffrey Chaucer addresses his text in bookish terms, memorably encouraging it to "Go, litel bok, go" (V.1786).[4] When Chaucer sends his "litel bok" out into the world, what he describes is the sending of a copy – a material object – and what is important about that object, for him, is that it contains his text, the one he labored to produce, *Troilus*. Few, if any, Chaucerians would read the lines "O moral Gower, this book I directe / To the and to the, philosophical

---

[2] Along with resources given in the previous note, which trend toward English scholarship, classic studies on procedures for manuscript production include A. Gruys and J. P. Gumbert, eds., *Codicologica: towards a science of handwritten books*, 5 vols. (Leiden: E. J. Brill, 1976–80); Marilena Maniaci, *Terminologia del libro manoscritto* (Rome: Istituto centrale per la patologia del libro, 1996); and Denis Muzerelle, *Vocabulaire codicologique* (Paris: CEMI, 1985). For a recent, evocative study of the history of parchment, see Bruce W. Holsinger, *On Parchment: Animals, Archives, and the Making of Culture from Herodotus to the Digital Age* (New Haven, CT: Yale University Press, 2022).

[3] For examples in different areas of study discussing the high- and late-medieval period, see Michael Johnston, *The Middle English Book: Scribes and Readers, 1350–1500* (Oxford: Oxford University Press, 2023), Daniel Sawyer, *Reading English Verse in Manuscript c.1350–c.1500* (Oxford: Oxford University Press, 2020); Julia Boffey, *Manuscript and Print in London c.1475–1530* (London: British Library, 2012); and Christopher de Hamel, *Glossed Books of the Bible and the Origins of the Paris Book Trade* (Cambridge: D. S. Brewer, 1984).

[4] Quotations from Chaucer's works are cited parenthetically from Geoffrey Chaucer, *The Riverside Chaucer*, ed. Larry Benson *et al.*, 3rd ed. (Boston, MA: Houghton Mifflin, 1987).

Strode," as meaning that Chaucer expects Gower and Strode to share a single material codex – "this book," the kind of thing that modern archivists give a shelfmark (V.1856–7). Rather, we understand that Chaucer means for Gower and Strode to receive copies of his text – "this book," the kind of thing that modern scholars give a title. The demonstrative "this" refers to a conceptual object ("book"), rather than a physical object ("book"), to an arrangement of words that can be reproduced endlessly in a proliferation of consumable media, rather than an arrangement of ink and parchment that can only ever be in one place at one time.[5] We nevertheless understand Chaucer to have sent some *thing*: to send the conceptual kind of book, some physical book was necessary as its medium.

Gower and Strode could have read *Troilus* simultaneously without bumping heads. Similarly, modern scholars do not need to read *Troilus* from any of its manuscript copies in order to read *Troilus* at all, nor do we commonly claim that many of the material features of manuscript copies of *Troilus* – say the average size or weight of those physical books – have direct bearing on what their common text says. Instead, as is appropriate to the object of study (Chaucer's "litel bok"), we read edited copies of *Troilus* in a Norton edition, or in the relevant section of the *Riverside Chaucer*, or in one of dozens of other printings. *Troilus* functions conceptually as a book for modern readers, just as it once did for medieval audiences. (When asked, "what are you reading?" the vast majority of readers would respond, "Chaucer's *Troilus*" – and not, "this rectangular object here with a burnt-orange border, having 600 or so thin pages, much taller than it is wide, weighing about half a kilogram.")[6] Through examination of Chaucer's "book," *Troilus and Criseyde*, from the perspective of literary analysis we come to understand the contours of Chaucer's world in myriad contexts, such that the book might function as a repository of culture and personhood, of thought, feeling, identification, and uncertainty.

Accordingly, another way to read medieval books is to study the texts they bear.[7] For the average reader in the humanities, this approach will be more familiar. It encompasses a vast range of critical and theoretical methodologies. Any publication that concerns itself primarily with the analysis or assessment

---

[5] For a wide-ranging study of how scribes and readers arranged these two kinds of "book" in relation to one another, see Daniel Wakelin, *Immaterial Texts in Late Medieval England: Making English Literary Manuscripts, 1400–1500* (Cambridge: Cambridge University Press, 2022). Wakelin prefers "material book" and "immaterial text"; but as he acknowledges, "bok" has a broad range of attested meanings (*MED*, s.v. *bok*).

[6] This being the Norton edition of *Troilus* that happens to be on my shelf: Geoffrey Chaucer, *Troilus and Criseyde*, ed. Stephen Barney (New York: W. W. Norton, 2006).

[7] I understand "text" to include illustrative material, or any "imagetext," as in Jessica Brantley, *Reading in the Wilderness: Private Devotion and Public Performance in Late Medieval England* (Chicago, IL: University of Chicago Press, 2007).

of texts, individually or in groups, might be understood productively in terms of its contribution to how medieval texts function as medieval books. Literary study in particular treats poetry, prose, history, romance, Latinity, vernacularity, devotion, parody, and praise – as a small sampling of appropriate descriptive terms – according to formal, conventional, and thematic markers so diverse and entangled in modes of human experience as to prohibit adequate summary in brief.

What distinguishes the book-historical from the literary-critical approach to reading medieval books, most basically, has to do with some distinction between arrangements of physical material and arrangements of textual material. To clarify this distinction, and to gain a sense of where it can become muddled in practice, we might extend the example of Chaucer's *Troilus* a step further. Of course, there are manuscript objects that contain only *Troilus* – centuries-old books whose physical components begin and end in roughly the same place as the beginning and the ending of *Troilus* – plus or minus margins, flyleaves, bindings, annotations, decoration, and so on. There are also manuscript objects that contain *Troilus* alongside further texts, some Chaucerian, some not. For the better part of literary analysis this distinction has little bearing; for book history, it is foundational.

The Making and Meaning of a Medieval Manuscript: Interpreting MS Bodley 851 insists that fundamental evidentiary distinctions between ways of reading medieval books ought to play a greater role in the dominant methods that guide literary analysis of medieval texts. Of course, there are already excellent instances of scholarship that seek to create productive hybrid forms of book-historical and literary-critical study. I discuss many below. Nevertheless, in all hybrid approaches to books and their texts, or texts and their books, the fact that books and texts are at once inextricably related and categorically distinct forms a fundamental conceptual obstacle and a constant invitation to further inquiry. We cannot guarantee that what a book might signify as an object, on one hand, and what a book might signify as a text, on the other, will have any direct bearing on one another. (As if we might measure the weight of Criseyde's sorrow in kilograms!) To ask how to read a medieval book is to ask how distinct forms of evidence about medieval books in each sense might be brought into meaningful conversation with one another.

A Method for Reading Medieval Books

The Making and Meaning of a Medieval Manuscript proposes a generalizable method for engaging book-historical evidence in literary-critical practice. Schematically, the method begins with an assessment of material evidence for the production of a single manuscript object, then asks how material evidence from a manuscript's production can yield insight into interpretation of that manuscript's textual contents. In this way, the method provides a hermeneutic designed to structure assessments of literary significance without pre-determining those assessments according to any single category for inquiry (e.g., author, genre, topic, or theme).

Over the course of this introduction, I will theorize what I term the "codicological unconscious" in order to describe how mixed-content manuscripts might once have signified for historical agents with expectations and delights at once strikingly unlike those of later readers and resonant for contemporary audiences. A robust definition of the codicological unconscious can be found below. For now, a thin definition: the codicological unconscious describes the range of unstated and obscured meanings that might emerge from close examination of a book and its texts in conversation with one another. Throughout the chapters of *The Making and Meaning of a Medieval Manuscript*, I attend to the construction of a single codex as a functional archive in order to understand what the material book might conceal about the significance of the immaterial books it contains – and indeed represents as material objects of analysis.

We cannot recreate the medieval experience of reading a medieval book. Through a close examination of how any given medieval manuscript was patched and stitched together over time, however, we can outline some of the terms upon which some medieval experiences of reading texts depended, in specific manuscript copy. Just as no two medieval mixed-content manuscript books are identical, so also no two treatments of their production, arrangement, and significance will fully coincide. Evidence from the material production of mixed-content manuscripts by medieval agents can serve as a legend for designating textual groups, as a map for determining effective critical approaches to those groups, and as a guide to defamiliarizing modern perceptions of medieval texts.

To read a medieval manuscript is to travel in the boundary regions between the kinds of books that are designed to be replicated and the kinds of books that are, by definition, singular and irreplaceable. We need not linger over ultimate origins or final destinations – the opacities of authorship and the ever-shifting demands of the present – in order to chart clear pathways for understanding how a given material manuscript might inform the meaning of its collected material texts. Indeed, to travel between one kind of book and the other requires attention to forms of agency and reception that may have been invisible to any single contributor, even for the production of a single manuscript. We can capture an idea of how books have been read through attention to how books have been made and re-made over time.

The production of a single composite manuscript thus informs a shifting archive of textual relations, in which material compilation continuously alters the horizons of literary meaning. Because medieval manuscripts model the accretion and loss endemic to all processes of collection, they may also yield new insight into the construction of material archives further afield. One theoretical corollary to the codicological unconscious is that close attention to the production of any delimited material archive can provide competing perspectives on the significance of the texts that archive contains. The archival medium itself is worth studying, not as identical with its message, but as evidence for how message was conveyed along the broad highways and backwater footpaths that so often characterize the fortunes of literary history. The message is in the making of the medium.

MS Bodley 851 and Books Like It

In arguing for a generalizable codicological method that produces wholly singular critical results, I will give sustained attention to a single book-object: Oxford, Bodleian Library MS Bodley 851. This mixed-content manuscript produced in England contains over twenty texts, largely of unknown origin and primarily in Anglo-Latin, written in at least eight different scribal hands, mostly transcribed and decorated in the second half of the fourteenth century, and finally compiled and bound in the middle of the fifteenth century. For an overview of the manuscript's current arrangement, see Table 1.

Table 1. Descriptive overview of BodL MS Bodley 851. Arranged to reflect present-day appearance of the manuscript. **Rigg No.** refers to the item numbers used by Rigg in his description, as modified in Chapter 1. **Title** gives the edited title of the work, or else the first line. **Scribe** gives the scribe responsible for inked text; **Added No.** gives an estimate of chronological order in which texts were likely copied. **Dec.** enumerates decorative schemes present within the text as described on pp. 38–9. **Folios** gives the range of folios on which the text appears; and **Collation** provides quires discussed approximately where they occur, with constitutive folios in parenthesis.

Rigg No.	Title	Scribe	Added No.	Dec.	Folios	Collation
Part I						
1	De nugis curialium	A	10	1,2,3	7ra–73va	iii$^{12(-2)}$ + iv–viii^{12} (7–77)
2	Fall of Carthage	A	11	3	73va–vb	
3	Epistola sathanae	X	12		74ra–va	
4	Execution of Archbishop Scrope	Y	22		74va–75rb + 76va	
5	Convocatio sacerdotum	Dod	20		75va–76rb	

INTRODUCTION 7

	Part II					
6	Ave virgo mater christi	B	1	2	78ra–80rb	ix[12] (78–89)
7	De coniuge non ducenda	B	2	1,2,3	80va–81va	
8	Debate between heart and eye	X	13	2	81va	
9a	Michael of Cornwall, First Invective	C	3	1,2	81vb–83va	
9b-c	Michael of Cornwall, Second and Third Invectives	A	4	1,3	83va–89ra	
10-11	Fall of Troy	A	5	1,3	89ra–90rb	x[12] (90–101)
12a	Bridlington Prophecy	A	6	1,3	90rb–94va	
12b	Cambri carnaruan	A	7	3	94va	
13	Babio	A	8	3	94vb–97va	
14	Speculum Stultorum	A	9	1,3	97vb–115vb	xi[12] + xii[10] (102–123)
15	Battle of Neville's Cross	X	16		116ra–116vb	
16	Battle of Crécy	X	17		116vb–118rb	
17	Untitled verse (three lines)	X	18		118rb	
18	Apocalypsis goliae episcopi	X	14	3	118va–120vb	
19	Untitled riddle	X	19		120vb	
20	Geta	Dod	21		120vb–123ra	
	Part III					
21(a)	Piers Plowman: Z-text	X	15	3	124r–139r	xiii–xiv[8] (124–139)
21(b)	Piers Plowman: A-text (cont.)	Q	23		139r–140v	
21(c)	Piers Plowman: C-text (cont.)	Q	24		141r–208r	xv[6]–xvii[6], xviii[8], xix[10], xx[8]–xxiii[8] (140–208)

Chapter 1 provides a thorough account of the production of Bodley 851 through the work of Scribe X; and Table 2 (pp. 65–6) provides one representation of how the manuscript came to be modified over time by premodern agents.

The specific manuscript, Bodley 851, is both theoretically incidental to the expression of the method I present and functionally essential to the deployment of this monograph: in order to explore the codicological unconscious, a codex is required. It matters to *The Making and Meaning of a Medieval Manuscript*, therefore, what sort of manuscript Bodley 851 is. Two of the texts present in Bodley 851 survive uniquely within its bindings and are widely known to medieval scholars: the much-contested Z-text of *Piers Plowman* and the full text of Walter Map's *De nugis curialium* ("On courtiers' trifles"). Although one agent saw fit to compile Map and *Piers* together, and although some small number of readers may have encountered them together, no modern literary scholar has read these two texts in conversation with one another. Nor, in modern scholarship, is either text commonly read in conversation with the popular Anglo-Latin poems compiled in the same manuscript collection, such as the *De coniuge non ducenda* ("On the necessity of avoiding marriage"), the Bridlington *Prophecy*, or the *Apocalypsis goliae episcopi* ("The revelation of the bishop Golias"). No single topical or thematic category is sufficient to describe the variety of textual material that Bodley 851 contains. As the genres preserved within Bodley 851 range among dream-vision, Marian devotion, anti-marital satire, anti-ecclesiastic comedy, and military paean, so the present study gathers together an array of topics frequently isolated from one another in contemporary scholarship.

Because Bodley 851 is best known for its unique texts, the *De nugis curialium* and the Z-text of *Piers Plowman*, both of which are infamously difficult to categorize, the manuscript might appear to preclude fruitful comparison with other late-medieval manuscripts of the same type, or indeed to raise the question of whether Bodley 851 corresponds to a "type" at all. If we begin with the question, "what kind of manuscript contains Walter Map and *Piers Plowman*?" – or, more broadly, "what kind of manuscript contains longform Anglo-Latin prose alongside longform Middle English alliterative poetry?" – or more descriptively, "what kind of manuscript contains a snarky collection of historical witticisms and fantastic tales alongside experimental personification allegory for exploring problems of theology, social justice, and the human condition?" – our search will be doomed from the outset. In this sense, what Bodley 851 is like must be overshadowed by careful attention to what it represents.

Every medieval manuscript was handmade by human agents possessing varying degrees of aptitude and knowledge of their craft; and mixed-content manuscripts form a remarkable sub-category of medieval manuscripts on the whole, insofar as they preserve texts in quantities and arrangements nowhere else present in the surviving material record. Yet, even by the standards of singularity we use to assess mixed-content medieval manuscripts, we can find few satisfactory parallels for the assortment of most remarkable texts present within Bodley 851. If every medieval manuscript is in some way unique, and if the likeness between unique, mixed-content manuscripts is commonly described by way of shared texts, then the most famous texts in Bodley 851 – those we now attribute to Map and Langland – would seem to preclude comparison with other manuscripts.

Bodley 851, however, does bear fruitful comparison with mixed-content collections in more capacious terms. As A. G. Rigg demonstrated at length in his sequence on "Medieval Poetic Anthologies," the textual material compiled between Map and Langland in Bodley 851 resembles a type of Latin miscellany common to monastic and university contexts in fourteenth- and fifteenth-century England. Over the course of four publications and more than a decade of descriptive research, Rigg detailed textual links between seven manuscripts, including Bodley 851, that frequently contained a wide array of Latin verse commonly read in some combination, including (from Bodley 851) the *De coniuge*, the two poems Rigg grouped together as "The Fall of Troy," the Bridlington *Prophecy*, *Babio*, *Speculum stultorum*, the *Apocalypsis goliae episcopi*, and Vitalis of Blois's *Geta*.[8] Throughout his bibliographic descriptions, Rigg suggested further representative manuscripts in insular and continental repositories, some of which I discuss below; for a quick comparison,

---

[8] A. G. Rigg, "Medieval Latin Poetic Anthologies (I)," *Mediaeval Studies* 39 (1977): 281–330; "Medieval Latin Poetic Anthologies (II)," *Mediaeval Studies* 40 (1978): 387–407; "Medieval Latin Poetic Anthologies (III)," *Mediaeval Studies* 41 (1979): 468–505; "Medieval Latin Poetic Anthologies (IV)," *Mediaeval Studies* 43 (1981): 472–97. In sum, Rigg provided descriptive accounts of BL Cotton MSS Titus A.20, and Vespasian E.12; BodL. MSS Rawl. B.214, Rawl. G.109, Digby 166, Bodley 603, and Bodley 851. To these we should add Rigg's "Glastonbury Miscellany," interest in which originally directed him toward these books: A. G. Rigg, *A Glastonbury Miscellany of the Fifteenth Century: A Descriptive Index of Trinity College, Cambridge, MS.O.9.38* (London: Oxford University Press, 1968). The "Medieval Latin Poetic Anthologies" sequence has been extended three times: David Townsend and A. G. Rigg, "Medieval Latin Poetic Anthologies (V): Matthew Paris' Anthology of Henry of Avranches (CUL MS. Dd. 11.78)," *Mediaeval Studies* 49 (1987): 352–90; Peter Binkley, "Medieval Latin Poetic Anthologies (VI): The Cotton Anthology of Henry of Avranches (B.L. Cotton Vespasian D.V., Fols. 151–184)," *Mediaeval Studies* 52 (1990): 221–54; Greti Dinkova-Bruun, "Medieval Latin Poetic Anthologies (VII): The Biblical Anthology from York Minster Library (MS. XVI Q 14)," *Mediaeval Studies* 64 (2002): 61–109. Although none of these latter three entries share much in the way of material with the original nucleus of texts that prompted Rigg's inquiry, all are helpful for considering the range and purpose available to late-medieval compilers of mixed-content manuscripts containing large quantities of Latin verse in late-medieval England.

the chart at the end of "Medieval Latin Poetic Anthologies (III)" is especially useful.[9] Still, Rigg's research was by no means comprehensive. To begin with any grouping or pairing of relevant texts inevitably leads the researcher far afield into ever-different assortments of medieval manuscript collections. A list of manuscripts like Bodley 851 – in textual, topical, or thematic terms – and a list of surviving mixed-content medieval manuscripts collecting Anglo-Latin verse with or without Middle English verse might, in the end, be one and the same list.

We can nevertheless designate some specific influences evident within this manuscript's bindings. Thirteenth-century and fourteenth-century manuscripts associated with monastic learning, with the schools, and with the universities frequently share interest in the specific grouping of texts given above. Along with poems by Walter of Châtillon and poems by Hildebert of Lavardin, Bodley 851's Latin materials were compiled frequently in late-medieval England. While the *De coniuge* and the *Apocalypsis goliae episcopi* – a common pair – form one basis for many of the manuscripts Rigg selected, they also appear together in grammatical or schools manuscripts (manuscripts organized around "schools texts"), such as Cambridge, Gonville and Caius College MS 385, largely a collection of writings of John of Garland that includes the unique copy of Alexander Neckham's *Sacerdos ad altare*.[10] Social satire and household drama form a rough generic parameter for Lincoln Cathedral Library MS 105, which contains two copies of *Babio* – the latter copied from the former, in an early modern hand – alongside a copy of *Speculum stultorum* and the section of Guido delle Colonne's *Historia* dealing with the destruction of Troy. And Troy itself, as a figuration of London, often acts as a thematic bond in mixed-content manuscripts containing material similar to that filling Part II of Bodley 851, as in Lincoln Cathedral MS 105, just described, or BodL. MS Lat. misc. c. 75 part 1, an early fourteenth-century booklet from the library of John Bale, that contains the first "Fall of Troy" poem, *Speculum stultorum*, a further Troy-poem, and the second "Fall of Troy poem" in that order. One striking manuscript, the Bekynton Anthology (BodL. MS Add. A.44), contains copies of the *De coniuge*, the *Apocalypsis goliae episcopi*, and the *Geta* along with debate poems of a type famously deployed in Michael of Cornwall's *Invectives* (preserved in Bodley 851) – and possibly parodied throughout Map's *De nugis curialium* – as well as a text of Walter Map's *Dissuasio Valerii ad Rufinum* ("Valerius Dissuades Rufinus";

---

[9] Rigg, "Medieval Latin Poetic Anthologies (III)," 502–3.

[10] On common schools texts, see Marjorie Curry Woods, *Weeping for Dido: The Classics in the Medieval Classroom* (Princeton, NJ: Princeton University Press, 2019); Nicholas Orme, *Medieval Schools: From Roman Britain to Renaissance England* (New Haven, CT: Yale University Press, 2006); and Tony Hunt, *Teaching and Learning Latin in Thirteenth-Century England*, 3 vols. (Cambridge: D. S. Brewer, 1991).

also present in the *De nugis curialium*) and a text now found among the flyleaves of Bodley 851, the *Miles gloriosus*.[11] While the above manuscripts do not contain any materials that compare directly with the *De nugis curialium* or *Piers Plowman* in terms of breadth or style, they nevertheless give some sense of how many of the texts preserved within Bodley 851 circulated through diverse textual networks and among distinct medieval readerships.

Alongside Rigg's list of *comparata* governed by a loose affiliation with institutions of Latin learning in the Middle Ages, we might also consider broader arrangements of Latin verse-material collected for personal or communal use. A fuzzier class of Latin miscellany manuscript has gained scholarly interest in recent years, as exemplified by Houghton MS Lat 300, a continental collection of Latin verse edited by Jan M. Ziolkowski, Bridget K. Balint, and their graduate students as the *Carmina Houghtoniensia*.[12] The Houghton Songs demonstrate an interest in arranging superficially unlike textual contents of satirical bent in a way reminiscent of Bodley 851 along with many of Rigg's "anthologies," already noted. Although MS Lat 300 shares no texts with Bodley 851, it does share texts with several other manuscripts in Rigg's group – most commonly with Rawlinson G.109 and Cotton Titus A.20 – and references to items such as the *Debate between heart and eye*, the "Fall of Troy" poems, and the *Speculum stultorum* recur throughout the detailed notes to the edition. The quantity and density of texts present in the Houghton manuscript far exceed Bodley 851, however. Its editors detail ninety-six items in only eleven folios, as compared with the just over twenty items evident within the approximately 140 folios of Bodley 851 discussed in this study. While both contain a mixture of Latin texts, the quality of their separate "Latinities" differs a great deal.[13]

A disciplinary difficulty does arise when addressing the broad category of medieval manuscript collections containing Middle English verse alongside Latin verse.[14] Of course, some famous trilingual collections are widely known.

---

[11] See A. G. Rigg, *A History of Anglo-Latin Literature, 1066–1422* (Cambridge: Cambridge University Press, 1992), where the Bekynton is "the anthology par excellence of this – perhaps of any – period of Anglo-Latin" (152–3).

[12] Jan M. Ziolkowski and Bridget K. Balint, eds., *A Garland of Satire, Wisdom, and History: Latin Verse from Twelfth-Century France (Carmina Houghtoniensia)* (Cambridge, MA: Houghton Library of the Harvard College Library, distributed by Harvard University Press, 2007).

[13] On the status of Latin as a vernacular, see especially Christopher Cannon, "Vernacular Latin," *Speculum* 90.3 (2015): 641–53 and Nicholas Watson, "The Idea of Latinity," in *The Oxford Handbook of Medieval Latin Literature*, eds. Ralph J. Hexter and David Townsend (Oxford: Oxford University Press, 2012), 124–48.

[14] For the vast array of translations, commentaries, and annotations that are most often discussed in scholarship on collocations of Latin and vernacular texts, see Jane

Few manuscripts can compete with Harley 2253, for example, which Derek Pearsall once declared (alongside the *Pearl* manuscript) the "most important single MS of Middle English poetry."[15] Nor can many manuscripts lay claim to the breadth of canonical material preserved in BL Harley MS 978, which collects not least among its treasures goliardic verse, French romance including the most complete collection of the *Lais* of Marie de France, and unparalleled musical material alongside the celebrated Middle English "Summer is I-cumen in" (itself lyrical). Overall, Daniel Birkholz voices what seems to be scholarly consensus in naming "multilinguality" as the least contestable "aspect of the miscellany" as encountered *c*.1250–1350.[16] But whether and how "miscellaneity" can be a useful category for critical inquiry remains a subject of significant debate.

Similar manuscripts to Bodley 851 are infrequently discussed in terms of what their Latinity has to do with their English contents. This situation may have resulted from how our archival tools are organized most commonly around linguistic principles that serve to separate, rather than unite, the full picture of shared manuscript contexts. For example, even so astoundingly useful a resource as the *Digital Index of Middle English Verse* remains agnostic about the existence of non-English materials in its manuscripts. (The entry for Harley 978, for example, lists only the single Middle English lyric.)[17] And even so enduring a guide to Latin verse writings as Hans Walther's *Initia Carminum* provides only shelfmarks (increasingly out of date) to manuscript descriptions (likewise) from a broad European tradition that may or may not provide a full account of textual contents within.[18] Most scholars familiar with questions of Latinity and vernacularity in England could, of course, name further manuscripts of the type that Bodley 851 presents. Few, however, could confidently generate a robust handlist. Accordingly, scholars lack structured access to compilations of Latin and Middle English verse outside of sustained interest in single authors and celebrated objects.

In sum, it would be difficult for the modern reader of Bodley 851 to discover many of the sporadic thematic trends that critics have found peppered across the disparate texts within a manuscript like MS Lat 300, Harley 2253, or many purely English compilations (e.g., BodL. MS Laud misc. 108). In order

---

Gilbert and Sarah Harris, "The Written Word," in *Medieval British Manuscripts*, eds. Da Rold and Treharne.

[15] Derek Pearsall, *Old English and Middle English Poetry* (London: Routledge, 1977), 120.

[16] Daniel Birkholz, *Harley Manuscript Geographies: Literary History and the Medieval Miscellany* (Manchester: Manchester University Press, 2020), 22.

[17] *DIMEV* s.v. "London, British Library Harley 978" for DIMEV 5053.

[18] Hans Walther and Alfons Hilka, *Initia Carminum Ac Versuum Medii Aevi Posterioris Latinorum* (Göttingen: Vandenhoeck & Ruprecht, 1959).

to understand a manuscript like Bodley 851 – and to map approaches to more complex manuscripts with contents at once similar and far afield – it is necessary to consider its production over time, and so to discover the routes by which its material components came to bear its component texts in relation to one another.

The Whole Book and Fragmented Practice

Method addresses media. In the Middle Ages, as in every historical period, material media played a large role in the construction and transmission of textual meaning. Moreover, in manuscript cultures of the Middle Ages, every textual object was hand-crafted by human agents who practiced varying degrees of attention, competence, and care. Book historians know more than ever about how medieval manuscripts were produced, the audiences who read them, and the prevailing tastes, trends, and themes that informed their composition and modification over time.[19] Scholars have attended especially closely to miscellany manuscripts, individually, in groups (according to any number of principles of selection), and at scale.[20] Indeed, the precise taxonomic

---

[19] Apart from the resources given in notes 1–3, see: Michael Johnston and Michael Van Dussen, eds. *The Medieval Manuscript Book: Cultural Approaches* (Cambridge: Cambridge University Press, 2015); Kathryn Kerby-Fulton *et al.*, eds., *New Directions in Medieval Manuscript Studies and Reading Practices: Essays in Honor of Derek Pearsall* (Notre Dame, IN: University of Notre Dame Press, 2014); Carol M. Meale and Derek Pearsall, eds., *Makers and Users of Medieval Books: Essays in Honour of A. S. G. Edwards* (Cambridge: D. S. Brewer, 2014); M. T. Clanchy, *From Memory to Written Record: England, 1066–1307*, 3rd edition (Malden, MA: Wiley-Blackwell, 2013); Margaret Connolly and Linne R. Mooney, eds., *Design and Distribution of Late Medieval Manuscripts in England* (York: York Medieval Press, 2008); Derek Pearsall, ed. *New Directions in Later Medieval Manuscript Studies: Essays from the 1998 Harvard Conference* (York: York Medieval Press, 2000); A. S. G. Edwards *et al.*, eds., *The English Medieval Book: Studies in Memory of Jeremy Griffiths* (London: The British Library, 2000). For resources pertaining to paleography in particular, see Chapter 1 of the present monograph.

[20] See, e.g., Julia Boffey and John J. Thompson, "Anthologies and Miscellanies: production and choice of texts," in *Book Production and Publishing*, eds. Griffiths and Pearsall, 279–316; Stephen G. Nichols and Siegfried Wenzel, eds., *The Whole Book: Cultural Perspectives on the Medieval Miscellany* (Ann Arbor, MI: University of Michigan Press, 1996), especially Ralph Hanna, "Miscellaneity and Vernacularity," 7–22 and Julia Boffey, "Short Texts in Manuscript Anthologies," 37–52; Stephen Kelly and John J. Thompson, eds., *Imagining the Book* (Turnhout: Brepols, 2005); Richard Beadle and Colin Burrow, eds., *Manuscript Miscellanies, c. 1450–1700* (London: British Library, 2011); Margaret Connolly and Raluca L. Radulescu, eds., *Insular Books: Vernacular Manuscript Miscellanies in Late Medieval Britain* (Oxford: Oxford

significance of the word "miscellany" remains under constant interrogation – as distinct from, e.g., "anthology," "commonplace book," "household book," or simply "compilation."[21] Nevertheless, the continuing proliferation of essay collections,[22] monographs,[23] and journal articles[24] analyzing miscellaneous manuscripts and theorizing "miscellaneity" signals an enduring interest in

---

University Press, 2015); and Arthur Bahr, "Miscellaneity and Variance in the Medieval Book," in *Medieval Manuscript Book*, eds. Johnston and Van Dussen, 181–198.

[21] While I prefer "collection" or "mixed-content manuscript" throughout this study, Connolly and Radulescu report only the term "multi-text manuscript" as sufficiently neutral for describing these objects as to avoid contention among scholars who study them (*Insular Books*, 1).

[22] For example: Susanna Fein, ed., *Interpreting MS Digby 86: A Trilingual Book from Thirteenth-Century Worcestershire* (York: York Medieval Press, 2019); Susanna Fein, ed., *The Auchinleck Manuscript: New Perspectives* (York: York Medieval Press, 2016); Susanna Fein and Michael Johnston, eds., *Robert Thornton and His Books: Essays on the Lincoln and London Thornton Manuscripts* (York: York Medieval Press, 2014); Wendy Scase, ed., *The Making of the Vernon Manuscript: The Production and Contexts of Oxford, Bodleian Library, MS Eng. Poet. a. 1* (Turnhout: Brepols, 2013); Kimberly K. Bell and Julie Nelson Couch, eds., *The Texts and Contexts of Oxford, Bodleian Library, MS Laud Misc. 108: The Shaping of English Vernacular Narrative* (Boston, MA: Brill, 2011); Susanna Fein, ed., *Studies in the Harley Manuscript: The Scribes, Contents, and Social Contexts of British Library MS Harley 2253* (Kalamazoo, MI: Medieval Institute Publications, 2000); Derek Pearsall, ed., *Studies in the Vernon Manuscript* (Cambridge: D. S. Brewer, 1990).

[23] For monographs on one or more mixed-content manuscripts, see: Arthur Bahr, *Fragments and Assemblages: Forming Compilations of Medieval London* (Chicago, IL: University of Chicago Press, 2013); Brantley, *Reading in the Wilderness*; Andrew Taylor, *Textual Situations: Three Medieval Manuscripts and Their Readers* (Philadelphia, PA: University of Pennsylvania Press, 2002); Myra Seaman, *Objects of Affection: The Book and the Household in Late Medieval England* (Manchester: Manchester University Press, 2021); Keith Busby, *Codex and Context: Reading Old French Verse Narrative in Manuscript* (New York: Rodopi, 2002); Elizabeth Wilson Poe, *Compilatio: Lyric Texts and Prose Commentaries in Troubadour Manuscript H (Vat. Lat. 3207)* (Lexington, KY: French Forum, 2000).

[24] Journal articles and essays in collections themed around other topics regularly discuss one or more miscellany manuscripts in terms of their texts; but the class of object is more frequently discussed at special conferences and in their resultant collections than in special issues – a situation leading to an endearing proliferation of statements comparing the miscellaneity of modern critical productions and medieval literary ones, e.g., "Ironically most scholarship on miscellanies has itself been published through the miscellany format of the modern essay collection, with many pieces on individual manuscripts now available though in disparate locations" (Margaret Connolly, "The Whole Book and the Whole Picture: Editions and Facsimiles of Medieval Miscellanies and Their Influence," in *Insular Books*, eds. Connolly and Radulescu, 294).

the creation, use, modification, and availability of mixed-content manuscripts and their mixed texts.[25] It is not enough, in this increasingly common view, to harvest medieval texts from their medieval books, which were so often miscellaneous in material construction. It is necessary to examine, as Stephen G. Nichols and Siegfried Wenzel influentially put it, the "whole book."[26] Each manuscript acts not only as a textual repository but as an index of the total processes of its making.

It is also necessary to acknowledge from the outset that examinations of the "whole book" in a miscellaneous setting *may* run the risk of imposing meaning, rather than discovering meaning. Derek Pearsall has argued that "miscellanies… have played a disproportionately large part in English manuscript studies," since the modern literary search for order in apparent disorder too easily can transform into a modern fabrication of ahistorical literary significance.[27] To examine the "whole book" or any arbitrary collection of its parts might potentially have the effect of introducing unity under the guise of discovering unity. Moreover, Ralph Hanna III has argued that, for emergent vernacular texts "in a precanonical period, exemplar poverty motivates much of the literary record," since "manuscript compilers… were constrained to make the fullest imaginable use of any book that came to hand, and their planned core selections would come to coexist with other items."[28] Indeed, for vernacular collections specifically, even if coherent organizing interests may possibly have informed the production of a given manuscript, there is no guarantee such interests can be recovered by modern criticism.

My own approach historicizes the relationship between material evidence and textual significance by grounding literary interpretation in manuscript production. If mixed-content manuscripts can exhibit varying degrees of coherence and unity according to economic, circulatory, and personal

---

[25] "The dominance of miscellaneity is a unique feature of manuscript culture" (Johnston and Van Dussen, eds., *Medieval Manuscript Book*, 5); "These interrelated matters of terminology and taxonomy together constitute the most fundamental issue connected with the comprehension of medieval miscellany manuscripts" (Connolly and Radulescu, eds., *Insular Books*, 5). For taxonomic discussions of "miscellaneity" and its limitations, see Theo Stemmler, "Miscellany or Anthology? The Structure of Medieval Manuscripts: MS Harley 2253, for Example," *Studies in the Harley Manuscript*, 111–21; and Derek A. Pearsall, "The Whole Book: Late Medieval English Manuscript Miscellanies and Their Modern Interpreters," in *Imagining the Book*, eds. Kelly and Thompson, 17–29.

[26] "Arguing that the individual manuscript contextualizes the text(s) it contains in specific ways, materialist philology seeks to analyze the consequences of this relationship on the way these texts may be read and interpreted" (Nichols and Wenzel, *The Whole Book*, 2).

[27] Pearsall, "The Whole Book," 17.

[28] Hanna, "Miscellaneity and Vernacularity," 47.

pressures now lost, how is the literary critic to discern which manuscripts and which of their texts merit close literary attention, and on what terms? How do we distinguish textual groupings that can bear the weight of close analysis from those groupings that are accidental, misleading, or simply invented? What manuscript features signal the existence of a material unit suitable for literary analysis?

Of particular importance for understanding the production of many mixed-content manuscripts (including Bodley 851) are developments in booklet theory first developed by Pamela Robinson and subsequently modified by Ralph Hanna, Alexandra Gillespie, and Erik Kwakkel, among others.[29] Most basically, booklet theory accounts for the frequent use of unbound and limp-bound quires, not intended for or requiring immediate binding, in the transmission of late-medieval literature and in the production of late-medieval books. What "distinguishes the booklet from other forms of production," writes Hanna, is "the postponement of any overall plan for a finished book, in some cases until after production has ceased."[30] The circulation of booklets afforded a great deal of flexibility to scribes, compilers, and other users in an economy of copying characterized by scarcity. For the purpose of compiling collections of texts, these units were invaluable, being relatively cheap, highly portable, and physically extensible.

Robinson's original criteria identified booklets solely according to their material features: leaf dimension, handwriting, decoration, patterns in catchwords, quiring, wear on outer leaves, blank terminal leaves, and so on. Gillespie's added criterion, which asks whether there is a distinctive method of stitching or binding, follows this pattern.[31] One fundamental premise of booklet theory, in this view, is that material units can be identified without consideration of textual content. Indeed, the distribution of texts, without consideration of their contents, can itself form key evidence for patterns of scribal production.[32] So, for example, while the study of paleography (Robinson's

---

[29] Pamela Robinson, "The 'Booklet': A Self-Contained Unit in Composite Manuscripts," *Codicologica* vol. 3, 46–69; Ralph Hanna, "Booklets in Medieval Manuscripts: Further Considerations," in *Pursuing History: Middle English Manuscripts and Their Texts* (Stanford, CA: Stanford University Press, 1996), 23–34; Alexandra Gillespie, "Medieval Books, Their Booklets, and Booklet Theory," in *Manuscript Miscellanies, c. 1450–1700*, eds. Beadle and Burrow, 1–29. See also Gumbert, "Codicological Units," and Erik Kwakkel, "Towards a Terminology for the Analysis of Composite Manuscripts," *Gazette Du Livre Médiéval* 41.1 (2002): 12–19.

[30] Hanna, "Booklets in Medieval Manuscripts," 30.

[31] See the list at Gillespie, "Booklet Theory," 2; along with her proposed addition to the list, 18.

[32] Hanna seems to misunderstand this point, even as he astutely emphasizes the importance of production for understanding scribal practice: "Robinson's effort at defining the booklet then leans too much on the notion of *textual self-sufficiency*, and

second criterion) may take linguistic evidence into account, the purpose of paleographic study in the context of booklets is to account for the deployment of language in terms of its material features, rather than to unearth registers of significance for its semantic meaning.[33] Of course, one can hardly engage in paleography without looking at words, and the best paleographers develop an intimate sense of how semantic content can be garbled and restored in the process of textual transmission.[34] Nevertheless, for the fundamental consideration of how individual graphs (or "letters") are formed and what the formation of individual graphs may indicate about the agent who imposed them, it is not their content but the evidence pertaining to their mechanical deployment that comes to the fore ("the movements of the pen," as M. B. Parkes called it).[35]

Codicological units, including booklets, may be considered separately in terms of production or in terms of reception.[36] They can be distinguished within larger bound collections, both as evidence of the exigencies of manuscript production and as evidence of the conveniences of textual collection. The surviving forms booklets take – as produced ("production units") and used ("usage units") – can point to ways in which their texts could be understood by multiple, sometimes overlapping, medieval and postmedieval audiences. Later contributors to booklets and their collections frequently departed from the purposes their original makers had in mind. Later contributors to collections of material texts might associate and modify textual contents in ways wholly unintended by their original producers, so creating layers of textual affiliation not immediately evident in any examination of textual content undertaken without reference to evidence from material production. Indeed, in the framework I propose, it is especially important to establish material methods for uncovering layered and complex engagements with material texts by distinct agents over time. Too frequently, literary critics group texts within a single manuscript collection according to topic or theme without consulting

---

not enough on the notion of separately conceived production" (Ralph Hanna, "Booklets in Medieval Manuscripts: Further Considerations," *Studies in Bibliography* 39 [1986]: 100–111, at 107, emphasis mine; reprinted in "Booklets in Medieval Manuscripts," 29). Robinson's point is that texts can be identified by means of material analysis without recourse to their contents.

[33] A position ably defended in Derolez, *Gothic Manuscript Books*, 1–10.

[34] See, for example, Daniel Wakelin, "Not Diane: The Risk of Error in Chaucerian Classicism," *Exemplaria* 29.4 (2017): 331–48.

[35] Paleography focuses "on the movements of the pen in the process of handwriting to distinguish those characteristics that enable us to identify the handwriting of individual scribes" (M. B. Parkes, *Their Hands before Our Eyes: A Closer Look at Scribes: The Lyell Lectures Delivered in the University of Oxford, 1999* [Burlington, VT: Ashgate, 2008], xi.)

[36] See Hanna, "Booklets in Medieval Manuscripts" and Kwakkel, "Towards a Terminology."

material evidence for how medieval agents associated those same texts in production and in use. Even where a booklet, as such, cannot be identified, the codicological tools developed within the context of booklet theory can provide a material foundation for a replicable association of material texts conducted without direct consideration of their literary contents.

Not all book historians will readily agree to a paradigm that so neatly separates codicological considerations from textual considerations. For example, in the influential essay already cited, Hanna proposes three further criteria to be added to Robinson's original list of ten, of which two take into account semantic evidence as well as material evidence. He emphasizes "the desirability of rapprochement between the descriptive and analytical bibliography of the manuscript book," since "one cannot be properly concerned only with the texts contained in a codex or only with the physical composition of the vehicle for communicating texts."[37] As in the present study, for Hanna meaning emerges from the treatment of texts and books simultaneously: to describe one without the other is to overlook crucial evidence in the construction of cultural significance. Unlike the present study, Hanna asserts a central role for textual criticism – an examination of lexical content – in bibliographic analysis. In his discussion of booklets, Hanna argues for the importance of tracing textual likeness between different manuscripts in order to gain any understanding of how a specific manuscript was produced, in what contexts, and for what possible purposes. My approach and Hanna's, however, share a fundamental conviction that books and texts were produced within shifting fields of access and ability, as determined by the agents who made surviving copies and the agents who read them.

Hanna's description of the relationship between descriptive and analytical bibliography, made in a book-historical context, has weighty implications for literary study. Simply put: description implies literary criticism because description constitutes an interpretive act. In order to describe an object, physical or conceptual, material or immaterial, one must select and prioritize what features of that object are most important, and according to what criteria for measure. In order to describe the transmission of a textual object as a thing deployed from a specific source, one must select and prioritize some of its features over others (e.g., lexemes, orthography, dialect, use of headings, preparation for decoration, aids for reading, annotation, etc.). In order to describe the production of a book-object, one must similarly designate which material features are most significant (support, script, collation, ink, ruling procedure, layout, etc.) Such work is, of necessity, interpretive. Measurement entails flattening.

---

[37] Hanna, "Booklets in Medieval Manuscripts," 34.

If we might identify any comparable "rapprochement between" strictly book-historical and strictly literary-critical study, crucial questions remain. By what methods, and according to what assumptions, might critical conversation be conducted between books and their texts? How can the work of description, the work of analysis, and the work of criticism be brought together in a manuscript context? And what might the making of a single book reveal about how its makers and readers – its producers and its users – thought about its contents?

Such questions are not new, but they remain pressing. Since at least the declaration of the "New Philology" in 1990, medieval scholarship has not only acknowledged the importance of relationships between texts, books, and readers but increasingly placed those relationships at the center of literary interpretation. In Stephen G. Nichols's formulation, "philological practices that have treated the manuscript from the perspective of text and language alone have seriously neglected the important supplements that were part and parcel of medieval text production."[38] By treating manuscript books as repositories of texts alone, scholars overlook "the multiple forms of representation on the manuscript page."[39] While acknowledging the importance of literary study and book history, the New Philology brought to light multiplying ways in which a medieval book could be conceived at the confluence of many further representational strategies and cultural expectations. This broad interest in how the production of books – as material objects and as texts – might relate to the production of readers was not limited to the medieval period: similar trends arose at approximately the same critical moment in early modern studies, for example.[40] In terms of production, compilation, and reception, a single book might be interrogated for historical and literary interpretive possibilities, and for familiar and unfamiliar texts and textual paradigms, according to any number of competing features. "Materialist philology thus goes beyond traditional textual criticism," Nichols and Wenzel would add, in another publication, so that "far from being a transparent or neutral vehicle, the codex can have a typological identity that affects the way

---

[38] Stephen G. Nichols, "Introduction: Philology in a Manuscript Culture," *Speculum* 65.1 (1990): 7–8.

[39] Nichols, "Philology in a Manuscript Culture," 8.

[40] David McKitterick, *Print, Manuscript and the Search for Order, 1450–1830* (Cambridge: Cambridge University Press, 2003); D. F. McKenzie, *Bibliography and the Sociology of Texts* (Cambridge: Cambridge University Press, 1999); Adrian Johns, *The Nature of the Book: Print and Knowledge in the Making* (Chicago, IL: University of Chicago Press, 1998); Roger Chartier, *The Order of Books: Readers, Authors, and Libraries in Europe between the Fourteenth and Eighteenth Centuries* (Stanford, CA: Stanford University Press, 1994).

we read and understand the texts it presents."[41] Though few medievalists today declare themselves "new philologists," most would agree that we cannot study medieval texts without reference to the material circumstances surrounding the production of their books.

More recently, critics – many loosely affiliated with the "New Formalism" – have proposed a return to focused analysis of manuscript texts by way of the forms of their books. For example, Arthur Bahr and Alexandra Gillespie argue that "in much book history, the 'material book' has come to mean the book in your hand rather than the one in your head, the one with physical as opposed to ideal form," adding that an insistence on positivism in the study of books and their texts "risks turning the materialism of book history into its own kind of idealism."[42] Editing a special issue of the *Chaucer Review* dedicated to questions of manuscript aesthetics and form, Bahr and Gillespie wrote on behalf of many of the essays they collected, and many essays beyond, when they observed that book history and literary criticism have been severed unnecessarily in much scholarly practice. Hybrid approaches contribute to a "case for the material text *against* the literary text."[43] In order to theorize sufficiently the relation between medieval books as physical objects and medieval books as textual objects, Bahr and Gillespie propose two guiding principles. First, that "the forms of manuscripts can be read alongside, or as an intrinsic aspect of, the forms of literary texts"; and second, that "the aesthetic qualities and the sensual properties of manuscripts are *not* coextensive with nor finally constitutive of the meanings of the literary works that they bear."[44] With Bahr and Gillespie, *The Making and Meaning of a Medieval Manuscript* asks not only how the meanings of books and the meaning of texts are related, but also how their related meanings are disguised, obscured, or disrupted by their complex features and arrangements.

Material form and textual significance are inextricable. The medieval book demands attention as a material thing and as a textual thing in dozens of perspectives apiece, each mutually reinforcing and interconnected. Scholars and critics nevertheless have declined to establish guidelines for individual practitioners in methodological terms. For Bahr and Gillespie, "the 'aesthetic turn' is less an imperative than a resource" and for Nichols, it is a strength

---

[41] Nichols and Wenzel, *The Whole Book*, 2.

[42] Arthur Bahr and Alexandra Gillespie, "Medieval English Manuscripts: Form, Aesthetics, and the Literary Text," *Chaucer Review* 47.4 (2013): 351. See also Eleanor Johnson, *Practicing Literary Theory in the Middle Ages: Ethics and the Mixed Form in Chaucer, Gower, Usk, and Hoccleve* (Chicago, IL: University of Chicago Press, 2013); and Christopher Cannon, "Form," in *Middle English*, ed. Paul Strohm (Oxford: Oxford University Press, 2007), 177–90.

[43] Bahr and Gillespie, "Medieval English Manuscripts," 351; emphasis original.

[44] Bahr and Gillespie, "Medieval English Manuscripts," 354.

that "contributors do not represent a particular school or tendency" but instead "speak with remarkable individuality, circumspection, and freshness."[45] In literary study more broadly, it is nearly taken for granted that "New Formalism" constitutes "a movement," not "a theory or method," and so cannot afford to designate procedural approaches to any topic.[46] For these chief among many reasons, medievalists currently lack any replicable or generalizable answer to the root methodological question of how, precisely, books and texts might be related in critical practice. How – according to what procedures and commitments – do you read a medieval book?

This study provides one answer to two lingering questions about the breadth of possible ways to engage with books and texts. As pertains to form and aesthetics, I ask, with Bahr and Gillespie: "What is the relationship between the study of medieval books and the study of medieval literature?"[47] As pertains to the vast class of manuscripts that contain more than one text, I also ask, with Margaret Connolly: "How might a coherent methodology be developed to deal with multi-text volumes whose contents are intrinsically multidisciplinary and interdisciplinary?"[48]

These questions have been discussed at length, in theory. In practice, however, routes between physical evidence and textual evidence for individual manuscript objects remain obscure; and the most admirable scholarship often appears to be the least imitable.[49] If scholars agree that medieval books demand attention as witnesses to medieval texts, there is nevertheless little consensus about what common hermeneutic procedures or critical commitments might guide literary approaches to specific manuscript books. The absence of any replicable procedures for scholars to follow, modify, or critique has transformed theoretical strengths of the New Philology and the New Formalism into a common methodological weakness. Scholars have weighed in brilliantly on the relationship between the study of medieval books and the study of medieval literature; but we have not, for the most part, developed generalizable methods for connecting evidence from books with evidence from their texts.

Attention to method can help remedy a related phenomenon of exclusivity present in published scholarship, which tends to privilege a select few manuscripts that have become familiar to most researchers. Since the turn of the twenty-first century, dozens of essays, articles, and book chapters have discussed the mixed forms of named manuscripts in England (*the* Vernon, *the* Thornton, *the* Harley), manuscripts associated with Chaucer and the

---

[45] Bahr and Gillespie, "Medieval English Manuscripts," 354; Nichols, "Manuscript Culture," 9.
[46] Marjorie Levinson, "What Is New Formalism?," *PMLA* 122.2 (2007), 558.
[47] Bahr and Gillespie, "Medieval English Manuscripts," 346.
[48] Connolly and Radulescu, *Insular Books*, 8.
[49] E.g., Bahr, *Fragments and Assemblages*; Brantley, *Reading in the Wilderness*.

Chaucerians (*the* Fairfax; Cambridge, Trinity College MS R.3.20; Cambridge, CUL MS Gg.4.27; BodL. MS Arch. Selden B.24), along with manuscripts recording alliterative verse (Cotton Nero A.10, *the* Pearl-manuscript), romance (*the* Auchinleck), or exemplary verse (Bodleian Ashmole 61). Even a manuscript as bewildering as MS Bodley 851 ("*the* Map manuscript"?), has been treated by literary scholars almost exclusively in terms of its copy of *Piers Plowman* – despite the fact that the majority of its texts by number are lesser-known Anglo-Latin productions, and the greatest percentage of its pages by volume are taken up with Walter Map's *De nugis curialium*.[50]

Indeed, for every manuscript I might name that the average scholar of medieval books would have any hope of recognizing by shelfmark, title, or contents, there are dozens if not hundreds more comparable manuscripts that lie wholly neglected. Most commonly, the manuscripts discussed in scholarship are pre-selected by virtue of familiarity; and materially informed criticism on these manuscripts depends heavily upon alliances with contemporary methodologies not directly tied to book-historical study. Of course, it is only through continuous scholarly labor – codicological, editorial, and critical – that such manuscripts have achieved privileged status in the first place. On the other hand, celebrity of text leads most commonly to celebrity of manuscript: prized manuscripts are prized because they contain prized texts. Accordingly, widespread focus on delving further into what we already know, rather than exploring what we do not know how to describe at all, is not the result of a lack of theorization. It is the result of an emphasis on casting a discursive net that encompasses a familiar and inviting cross-section of texts (usually according to their association with a major author or genre; or else their topical relevance to critical concerns of the moment) rather than a massive and confounding cross-section of books.

The Codicological Unconscious

The Making and Meaning of a Medieval Manuscript proposes a generalizable book-historical method for examining mixed-content manuscripts in order to discover literary-critical perspectives on the texts those manuscripts contain. As I argue in Chapter 1, the interpretations presented in each chapter thus fall under the broad umbrella of analytical bibliography. In this introduction, my theoretical argument is that careful description of the material evidence for how individual medieval manuscripts were produced can provide a codicological foundation for understanding arrays of significance for the texts they contain. The physical act of scribal labor grounds the intellectual act of literary

---

[50] The outstanding exception being Joshua Byron Smith, *Walter Map and the Matter of Britain* (Philadelphia, PA: University of Pennsylvania Press, 2017).

interpretation, and so informs what Matthew Fisher has dubbed "scribal authorship."[51] It is not necessary, in the method I propose, for the material book and the textual book to share formal features or descriptive aspects.[52] Nor does the method assume that grouping texts according to evidence from production will result in textual affiliations that appear coherent or revealing at first view. The methodological procedure I describe does not *impose* coherence from the standpoint of modern criticism, as in Pearsall's warning against turning "an apparent miscellany into a continuing thematic meta-narrative" in order to discover "unifying controlling intelligences working so subtly that their strategies have hitherto escaped notice."[53]

Rather than asking how individual manuscripts might fit into prevailing critical understandings of medieval literary texts, I ask how individual manuscripts themselves preserve and generate knowledge about the construction of literature. I propose one mode of approaching the medieval book that might reliably disrupt "the methodological categories by which our scholarship operates."[54] If there are two overarching ways to read a medieval book (the book-historical and the literary-critical), then the majority of hybrid approaches can be understood to integrate those two ways in terms readily available to modern scholarship, such that medieval books function in some way like the texts they contain. The method I propose has the advantage of maintaining a clear distinction between book-historical and literary-critical evidence while providing a clear interpretive route that begins in the examination of a book as object and ends in the examination of literary texts. If some affinity between the two ways to read a medieval book is lost, some clarity concerning the flexible relationships available between two kinds of evidence is gained. We need not read every book as a text in order to better understand the composition of medieval texts through the construction of their books.

Theoretically underpinning the procedure I describe is careful attention to what I term the *codicological unconscious*. The codicological unconscious describes a mode of attending to the medieval book that allows scholars to consider interactions between medieval texts according to how those texts were constructed – and as they are now preserved – within the context of the production of their extant medieval manuscripts. This critical mode, as I propose it, is neither exclusive of considerations of agency nor dependent

---

[51] Matthew Fisher, *Scribal Authorship and the Writing of History in Medieval England* (Columbus, OH: Ohio State University Press, 2012).

[52] See Wakelin's invaluable reminder "that material form is not deterministically linked to literary function" (*Immaterial Texts*, 171).

[53] Pearsall, "The Whole Book," 18, 17.

[54] Elizaveta Strakhov, "Opening Pandora's Box: Charles d'Orléans's Reception and the Work of Critical Bibliography," *The Papers of the Bibliographical Society of America* 116.4 (2022), 535.

upon the recovery of authorial, scribal, or readerly intention. The purpose of the codicological unconscious is to index the material evidence for historical agency in manuscript production without attempting to recover any single individual experience of producing, or consuming, manuscripts. Attention to strategies of material and textual composition yields access to alternative cultural attitudes, imaginative expressions, and ideological configurations made evident by medieval books. The codicological unconscious in this way posits a mode of engaging codicological evidence in cultural analysis without direct recourse to social history.

The fundamental contribution of *The Making and Meaning of a Medieval Manuscript* to the fields of book history and literary criticism is the proposal of one portable method for future use in a wide array of manuscript contexts. I offer my method as one among many: as an approach to be adopted, improved, and critiqued in turn by book historians, literary critics, and researchers in the material cultures of the Middle Ages and further afield. Crucially, however, I do not claim *exclusivity*. The generation of one critical and analytic method need not preclude others, nor need the interpretations I develop throughout this study exclude alternative conclusions in terms of book, text, or method.

In the framing I propose, the codicological unconscious depends upon the conditions for the production of a material book, itself composed of texts and works, without necessarily interrogating the experience, expectations, or intentions of that book's makers. For students of Middle English, Paul Strohm influentially described the "textual unconscious" as that which addresses "what a text leaves unsaid – not just what it means to say, but what it cannot know, or especially, what it knows but will not or cannot say."[55] So too, attention to the codicological unconscious addresses what is unsaid, or not-said, by a manuscript book – what its historical makers and readers could not bring themselves to know or say. "Coining Strohm," Arthur Bahr has used the term "codicological unconscious," almost in passing, to describe a confluence of material and textual evidence. For Bahr, booklet 3 of the Auchinleck manuscript "uncannily evokes the structure of the manuscript as a whole in ways that elude demonstrable intention but nevertheless shed light on important literary and cultural relations among its texts."[56] Similarly, Sarah

---

[55] Paul Strohm, *Theory and the Premodern Text* (Minneapolis, MN: University of Minnesota Press, 2000), 166. Strohm's formulation owes much to Pierre Macherey's claim that we can "account for this latent knowledge" that conditions the production of a work "by recourse to *the unconscious of the work* (not of the author)" (Pierre Macherey, *A Theory of Literary Production*, trans. Geoffrey Wall [New York: Routledge, 2006]). The influence of Frederic Jameson, *The Political Unconscious: Narrative as a Socially Symbolic Act* (Ithaca, NY: Cornell University Press, 1982) looms throughout Strohm's work and will be felt in this study as well.

[56] Bahr, *Fragments and Assemblages*, 111, 17.

Kay has used the term, briefly, to argue that the inescapable physicality of the manuscript book provides perspective on how medieval scribes and readers may have been able to perceive the world differently – if only momentarily, fleetingly, and unwillingly; and even if such an alternative perception may have run contrary to deeply ingrained and dearly held prejudices.[57] These studies underscore the value of literary analysis conducted in absence of any single, interpretive influence from a supposed author, scribe, or compiler.

Attention to the codicological unconscious can draw attention to the subtle and often tangential relationship between conscious agency and literary meaning. It can uncover possibilities latent within individual manuscripts that were available to but not regularly assessed or examined by medieval readers. It need not, however, seek to discover any direct metaphorical resonance between material and textual evidence.[58] In making this distinction, I diverge in my theorization from the implications of prior scholarship. Bahr argues, for example, that "the Auchinleck manuscript as it stands today is structurally akin to one of the medieval romances for which it is so famous."[59] Kay asks "what it might mean for a medieval writer or reader to fix his attention on a page that faces him like a reflection of his own bodily surface, marked as his might be with pores, veins, scuffs, or scars"?[60] In the method I propose, the book need not bear a similitude to what it contains, nor need it create a similitude in those who engage with it. Although the construction of a book might reveal much about the meanings inherent in its texts, material construction and literary meaning need not share qualitative features in common.

We can distinguish the dynamic relation under consideration from the more static awareness that Martha Dana Rust has called "codicological consciousness," which she describes as constituted by "a reader's cognitive realization of the interplay among diverse semiotic systems that is only *in potentia* on the physical page."[61] I am not arguing that scribes and readers of medieval miscellanies such as Bodley 851 at any point consciously re-evaluated

---

[57] "I do not claim that these are conscious, welcome, or lasting effects. They may be so ephemeral as barely to register; they may make one wince or cringe; if they were to be consciously noticed they would likely be disavowed" (Sarah Kay, *Animal Skins and the Reading Self* [Chicago, IL: University of Chicago Press, 2017], 17).

[58] Here, the use of "unconscious" I propose most obviously reveals its debts to Marxian theory: "The true target of the Althusserian critique would seem to me not the practice of mediation but something else, which presents superficial similarities to it but is in reality a very different kind of concept, namely the structural notion of *homology* (or isomorphism, or structural parallelism)" (Jameson, *Political Unconscious*, 43).

[59] Bahr, *Fragments and Assemblages*, 106.

[60] Kay, *Animal Skins*, 3.

[61] Martha Dana Rust, *Imaginary Worlds in Medieval Books: Exploring the Manuscript Matrix* (Basingstoke: Palgrave Macmillan, 2007), 9. Compare Nichols, "Philology in a Manuscript Culture."

their deeply held and culturally conditioned convictions according to what may often amount to the accidents of contiguity in manuscript books. Rather, I argue that by way of close attention to the codicological unconscious, we can attend to what the physical state of a manuscript book obscures and, once interrogated, reveals about how its collected texts go about meaning in conversation with one another.

Such attention depends, fundamentally, upon prior scholarly work in book history and literary criticism. Indeed, the work of defamiliarizing mixed-content manuscripts and their texts cannot help but rely upon what scholarship has already taught us to find familiar. The necessary first step for addressing any codicological unconscious is a thorough book-historical description of how a given material book came to contain its textual contents. Accordingly, the trajectory of *The Making and Meaning of a Medieval Manuscript* follows a path from the known into the unknown, from what scholarship has uncovered to what critics have not yet observed.

The argumentative structure of *The Making and Meaning of a Medieval Manuscript* follows the material production of Bodley 851. The chapters of this study are connected sequentially, not by any single topic or theme but by the recovered activities of scribal contributors to its principal object of study. Accordingly, *The Making and Meaning of a Medieval Manuscript* begins with a thorough review of how Bodley 851 came to be (Chapter 1), in order to query in subsequent interpretive chapters how its texts might also come to mean as objects in conversation with one another (Chapters 2, 3, and 4). The interpretive chapters take up independent textual and conceptual material serially, and so propose discrete arguments about their core texts, even as they follow the logic of production for Bodley 851 rehearsed in Chapter 1.

As Chapter 1, I provide an account of the chronological production of Bodley 851 over time, what I have termed analytical codicology, or the "re-composing" of Bodley 851. The book-historical work I undertake in Chapter 1 would not be possible without the prior, more familiar work of descriptive bibliography and textual criticism already conducted by able scholars. In order to reconstruct how a manuscript was made, we must first produce a clear overview of its scope and contents. Description of the one kind (the overview) enables description of the other kind (the re-composition). Similarly, the literary critical accounts I provide in the following three chapters depend upon careful pieces of topical scholarship – according to author, genre, topic, theme, place, and pattern – that my own analysis nevertheless does not seek to replicate on their own terms. In order to show how individual manuscript books might revise our understanding of historical and cultural expectations concerning medieval texts, we must have some understanding in place to begin with. In this way, attention to the codicological unconscious need not supplant prior work in literary history. Rather, attention to the codicological unconscious nuances, rather than corrects, our understanding of literary interpretation otherwise.

Following the manuscript description undertaken in Chapter 1, each chapter of *The Making and Meaning of a Medieval Manuscript* attends to a different formation of the codicological unconscious within Bodley 851. In each chapter, I move from material evidence for textual affiliation into literary analysis of materially affiliated texts. Because each interpretive chapter uncovers one expression of the codicological unconscious within the manuscript under consideration, each interpretive chapter also provides a different perspective on method and intepretation within manuscript study more broadly.

Chapter 2 begins with the earliest fragment preserved within Bodley 851, which contains exactly two texts written in a scribal hand – that of Scribe B – nowhere else present in this manuscript. These two texts, Walter of Wimborne's *Ave virgo mater christi* and the anonymous *De coniuge non ducenda*, are almost wholly dissimilar, whether considered in terms of form, content, origin, or audience. I interpret these two texts as expressing opposing interests in insatiability, as the word describes exemplary enactments of feminine desire. Between these two poems, the modern reader can catch a glimpse of how even so overdetermined a concept as medieval misogamy might have been conceived differently, if only fleetingly, by the scribes who compiled poems such as these and readers who encountered them. Analysis of the codicological unconscious of a single fragment in this way turns on the evidence of scribal agency. It does not, however, undertake to recreate the total experience or personal motives of any single historical agent. We cannot dip our quills in the same ink twice.[62] To read the *Ave virgo* and the *De coniuge* together nevertheless provides fresh perspective on familiar topics and pressing social tropes. Attention to the codicological unconscious uncovers the confused and contradictory byways of thought that conditioned the act of reading for a late-medieval English audience and allows us to glimpse some perspective on the world strikingly different from dominant traditions we know so well.

In close examination of Walter Map's *De nugis curialium*, Chapter 3 asks how comparative approaches to a compiled book can inform comparative approaches to a compiled text. Because the only copy of Map's only surviving textual production (including the *Dissuasio*, which circulated separately) is contained within Bodley 851, the literary work and the individual manuscript book cannot be neatly disentangled. Fundamentally, modern confusion about the *De nugis* arises from its appearance in Bodley 851 as a text segmented into clearly demarcated distinctions and chapters. Chapter 3 engages Map's

---

[62] A pun: according to Plato, in *Cratylus* 402A, "likening existing things to the stream of a river he [Heraclitus] says that you would not step twice into the same river" (G.S. Kirk *et al.*, *The Presocratic Philosophers: A Critical History with a Selection of Texts*, 2nd edition [Cambridge: Cambridge University Press, 2007], 195.

text in terms of scribal modifications to its organization, attending to the layout of the inked text imposed by Scribe A and the implications of the rubricated text imposed by Scribe X. Through the scribal agents who read and preserved the *De nugis* in Bodley 851, I read for possibilities of productive interpretation within a text too often deemed too "untidy" for close analysis. In order to understand the significance of a difficult interpretive crux in one specific literary sequence (*De nugis* 2.11–2.13), I also examine major features of Map's authorial style. On the whole, Map's oblique narrative style combines together with the material confusion evident in the preservation of his text to present a bewildering array of discontinuities and fragmentations. What textual scholars and literary critics identify as ambiguity, at best, and irreparable chaos, at worst, arises jointly – and, often, indistinguishably – from original authorship and from the exigencies of manuscript transmission. I argue that attention to the codicological unconscious uncovers an analytic strategy for discerning literary sequences within a muddled textual compilation – for understanding what both the lexical text and the manuscript book together leave unsaid. Evidence from the contiguity of the manuscript book grounds a fresh perspective on how the *De nugis* engages with pressing questions of social capital, fictionality, and textual interpretation.

Finally, Chapter 4 asks how the arrangement of texts within Bodley 851 might reveal unexpected late-medieval perspectives on the authorship of its only Middle English text, the infamous sigil Z of *Piers Plowman*. On the basis of authorial ascriptions within Bodley 851, and in consideration of Walter Map's growing (if spurious) reputation in late-medieval England as author of a great mass of Latin satires and French romances, Chapter 4 demonstrates how the various labors undertaken by Scribe X might signal a false but fascinating belief, on his part, that Map was the unnamed author of *Piers Plowman*. What is important about the Z-text, for any examination of the codicological unconscious of Bodley 851, is not who originally wrote it or what that original composer thought he was doing with some prior version of *Piers Plowman*, but how this specific text of *Piers Plowman* can be understood within the larger field of material texts alongside which it was compiled in its manuscript context. An examination of the codicological unconscious of Bodley 851 sheds new light on how an early copy of *Piers Plowman* was received by its late-medieval audience.

Two extended case studies ground Chapter 4, both of which read *Piers Plowman* alongside texts aligned with Map through the production of Bodley 851: the *Apocalypsis goliae episcopi*, an anonymous anti-ecclesiastic satire ascribed to Map in Bodley 851; and the *De coniuge non ducenda* (discussed at greater length in Chapter 2), commonly ascribed to Map from the fourteenth century onward, together with Map's genuine misogamous epistle, the *Dissuasio Valerii ad Rufinum*. Although neither reading provides direct access to the experience of Scribe X, as maker and reader of Bodley

851, both case studies understand the material fashioning of Bodley 851 to inform a complex and suggestive interrelation of its texts. In each case, an examination of the manuscript conditions surrounding the text of *Piers Plowman* yields insight into the construction and reception of the fourteenth century's most baffling poem.

The chapters of this book do not by any means exhaust the affordances of the codicological unconscious in Bodley 851, much less its methodological value for examining further manuscripts, the known and (more importantly) the long-neglected. For example, the material arrangement of scribal hands plays a large role in *The Making and Meaning of a Medieval Manuscript*. Chapters 2 and 3 each foreground evidence from continuity, and Chapters 3 and 4 foreground evidence from apparent discontinuity, in the scribal production of closely related material. Paleography thus provides an accessible and in many ways familiar perspective on the physical ordering of texts across manuscript pages. The study of scribal hands, however, is certainly not the only avenue for understanding how the material features of medieval mixed-content books ground critical perspectives on the contents they mix.

By way of the codicological unconscious, students of the medieval book might begin to reclaim through careful description what Derrida memorably called "the power of *consignation*," the authority to gather together signs. Yet we need not feverishly pre-suppose a "system or synchrony in which all the elements articulate the unity of an ideal configuration."[63] By tethering literary analysis to material evidence – indeed, by proceeding from material description to literary significance without collapsing material evidence and lexical evidence together – we can productively reframe our conception of what is public and what is private in the making of a manuscript book. By attending to method, we can understand manuscripts, as fragmentary collections and as material records, to reflect how texts came to be experienced by historical agents whose experiences are themselves irretrievable.

---

[63] Jacques Derrida, "Archive Fever: A Freudian Impression," *Diacritics* 25.2 (1995): 10; emphasis original.

1

Recomposing Bodley 851

Method is inextricable from meaning. How we go about describing a given manuscript object delimits how we can go about describing the literary relationships between its component texts. Indeed, the process by which an assortment of disparate manuscript elements becomes a collection of texts affords multiple, sometimes contradictory perspectives on possible literary relationships among those texts. Manuscripts circulated "as objects within the cultural world, where people interact[ed] with them in meaningful, readable, ways" and modified them according to variable, competing cultural interests.[1] Manuscript scholars, however, do not use a single well-defined term for the act of describing the production and modification of a handwritten codex over time. In this chapter, through "recomposing" BodL. MS Bodley 851, I aim to make evident some of the multiple and overlapping relations between texts materially embedded within its pages, according to the material processes by which they came to be included alongside one another. I ask, in brief, how did such a codex come to be, in which Walter Map meets *Piers Plowman*? For whom might this meeting have been evident? How might it have signified? Under what conditions and assumptions were the material texts of Bodley 851 collected together? To what literary effects?

Traditionally, the task of reconstructing a book's production would be understood to fall within the remit of bibliographical analysis (or "analytical bibliography"). According to G. Thomas Tanselle, "Bibliographical analysis [as distinct from bibliographical description]... concentrates on using physical details to learn something about the manufacturing processes that produced a given book and its text, the historical influences underlying its physical appearance, and the responses that its design engendered."[2] Because the task of analytical bibliography necessarily entails a review of appearance and contents, "the two branches of bibliography overlap at many points."[3] The

---

[1] Michael Johnston and Michael Van Dussen, *The Medieval Manuscript Book: Cultural Approaches* (Cambridge: Cambridge University Press, 2015), 2.

[2] G. Thomas Tanselle, *Bibliographical Analysis: A Historical Introduction* (Cambridge: Cambridge University Press, 2009), 3.

[3] Michael F. Suarez and H. R. Woudhuysen, eds., *The Oxford Companion to the Book*, vol. 1 (Oxford: Oxford University Press, 2010), 525.

degree of overlap can be witnessed in Philip Gaskell's influential, if unwieldy, delineation of "an analytically descriptive bibliography" that "serves as a means of identifying other copies of the books it deals with and of evaluating their status."[4] In view of bibliographic research intended to produce an edited text, the "evaluation of status" depends essentially upon the identification of error.[5] Yet, as Michael Suarez has persuasively argued, "the animating question of bibliography" can be understood in conceptual, rather than text-critical, terms: not "*What is the ideal text[?]*" but "*How did this book come to be the way it is?*"[6] If it is true that scholars should "avoid practising bibliography for bibliography's sake," it is also true that bibliographic work underpins a great deal of work apart from textual criticism alone.[7] "The bounds of analytical bibliography are impossible to define" because careful attention to material production – and not merely textual production – necessarily plays a fundamental role in the construction of literary understanding in an open-ended array of critical situations.[8]

When discussing method, authoritative sources in bibliographical study tend to focus on application to the history of the printed book. It is therefore worth emphasizing that in codicology – "the study of all of the physical aspects of the manuscript book" – analytical bibliography and descriptive bibliography flow for a long time together in a single stream.[9] For the scholar of the handwritten book, methods in analytical bibliography need not be predicated upon an assessment of error (whether authorial or scribal), nor need the apparatus of analytical description – what Ralph Hanna calls "a sequence of analytical gestures at books" – necessarily be undertaken in service of textual criticism.[10] Rather, the material manuscript book itself informs and alters the significance

---

[4] Philip Gaskell, *A New Introduction to Bibliography* (New Castle, DE: Oak Knoll Press, 1995), 321.

[5] See Gaskell, *New Introduction*, 313–22; which makes primary references to Bowers and Greg.

[6] Michael F. Suarez, "Hard Cases: Confronting Bibliographical Difficulty in Eighteenth-Century Texts," *The Papers of the Bibliographical Society of America* 111.1 (2017), 3; emphasis original.

[7] Gaskell, *New Introduction*, 322.

[8] Roy Stokes, *The Function of Bibliography*, 2nd ed. (Aldershot: Gower, 1982), 7.

[9] Albert Derolez, *The Palaeography of Gothic Manuscript Books: From the Twelfth to the Early Sixteenth Century* (Cambridge: Cambridge University Press, 2003), 10.

[10] Ralph Hanna, *Introducing English Medieval Book History: Manuscripts, Their Producers and Their Readers* (Liverpool: Liverpool University Press, 2013), xiii. See Hanna's extended discussion, in the same volume, "Medieval Authors and Texts: The Middle English 'Benjamin'," 30–58.

of its contents.[11] On the one hand, the surviving condition of a manuscript in the archive today can be distinguished from the multiple processes of production and preservation that resulted in that condition.[12] On the other, the textual contents of a given manuscript can be distinguished from their relationship with further copies of the same texts in other contexts. In analytical bibliography and descriptive bibliography alike, individual instantiations can be examined on their own terms *and* within their broader textual contexts. Throughout *The Making and Meaning of a Medieval Manuscript*, it is the individual manuscript book, not some further array of textually affiliated manuscripts, which provides the primary context for understanding its textual contents.

By attending to the material construction of an individual manuscript for the purpose of further literary interpretation, this chapter undertakes what might therefore be called, as a book-historical method, "analytical codicology" – what I will term, in its literary-critical aspect, "recomposition." The purpose of the following analysis is to "recompose" how a single manuscript came to be. It is important to recognize that the surviving features of MS Bodley 851 may serve to occlude, rather than reveal, illuminating stages of its production over time. The assorted collection of folded parchment – scraped, sutured, punctured, scored, and bound – for which we now have a stable referent (the shelfmark: BodL. MS Bodley 851) did not always exist in its current material and textual arrangement, nor could most of its historical contributors have foreseen the precise arrangement of texts and contexts it now presents to the modern viewer. Rather, the agents who undertook to inscribe its component texts into its component material parts did so piecemeal and in stages, at times demonstrating little interest in collaborating with prior or subsequent contributors, and at other times responding directly to the labors they inherited or anticipated. By tracing the order of transcription and compilation according to the manuscript's physical evidence, I attend to how its material components may have appeared to its multiple scribal contributors as they undertook their labor in disparate stages. I examine the textual contents now preserved within Bodley 851 as individual components added by identifiable and distinct (and yet anonymous) agents to

---

[11] As in the "New Philology" and the "New Formalism"; see Introduction, pp. 19–21. The seminal study in print history remains D. F. McKenzie, *Bibliography and the Sociology of Texts* (Cambridge: Cambridge University Press, 1999).

[12] This is not true *only* of manuscript study: see Jeffrey Todd Knight, *Bound to Read: Compilations, Collections, and the Making of Renaissance Literature* (Philadelphia, PA: University of Pennsylvania Press, 2013). Moreover, manuscripts were commonly modified by users, even after reaching published states: Hannah Ryley, *Re-Using Manuscripts in Late Medieval England: Repairing, Recycling, Sharing* (York: York Medieval Press, 2022).

some pre-existing assortment of textual materials that had not yet become the whole we perceive today.

This is not "bibliography for bibliography's sake." The bibliographical purpose of recomposing Bodley 851 is to lay a foundation for further literary interpretation of the manuscript's texts according to the internal chronology of its production. Recomposition uncovers material facts necessary for understanding textual significance in a historical lens without necessarily pinning any act of scribal labor to a given historical year, specific historical personage, or any specific agential motive. To understand the mixed contents of this single manuscript in material relation to one another and in relation to the sum of the manuscript's parts is to begin to understand the terms of their possible relations as materially situated objects of literary interpretation. Accordingly, the scope of this chapter is material, and the remainder of *The Making and Meaning of a Medieval Manuscript* following this chapter conducts literary inquiry according to the material description deployed here.

To raise the methodological problem of what it means to describe the production of a single multi-text manuscript over time is to raise yet another longstanding terminological problem in categorizing multi-text manuscripts within codicological study. Any descriptive language that scholars might apply to a single manuscript must alter the kinds of critical methods available for analyzing its component parts. To classify a medieval manuscript – indeed, to classify any sufficiently robust archive – is to delimit an array of available interpretations for understanding that manuscript as a material object and as a repository for literary texts. While it may be illuminating to refer to Bodley 851 in its present state as an "anthology" (as did A. G. Rigg in his foundational descriptive bibliography of the manuscript) or a "miscellany" (as do Ralph Hanna and Kathryn Kerby-Fulton in debating the date and origin of some of its components), neither term fully accounts for the significance of the manuscript's past states in the hands of its disparate historical makers.[13]

---

[13] The essential description of Bodley 851 remains A. G. Rigg, "Medieval Latin Poetic Anthologies (II)," *Mediaeval Studies* 40 (1978): 387–407. Still relevant is the short description provided in Falconer Madan and H. H. E. Craster, eds., *A Summary Catalogue of Western Manuscripts in the Bodleian Library at Oxford* vol. 2.1 (Oxford: Clarendon Press, 1922), 574–576. The following studies are central to my understanding of the manuscript: Ralph Hanna, "MS Bodley 851 and the Dissemination of *Piers Plowman*," in *Pursuing History: Middle English Manuscripts and Their Texts* (Stanford, CA: Stanford University Press, 1996), 195–202; Kathryn Kerby-Fulton, "Confronting the Scribe-Poet Binary," in *New Directions in Medieval Manuscript Studies and Reading Practices: Essays in Honor of Derek Pearsall*, eds. Kathryn Kerby-Fulton, John J. Thompson, and Sarah Baechle (Notre Dame, IN: University of Notre Dame Press, 2014), 489–515; and Kathryn Kerby-Fulton, "Oxford," in *Europe: A Literary History, 1348–1418*, ed. David Wallace (Oxford: Oxford University Press, 2016), 208–26.

The term "compilation" is perhaps most adequate, as a material indicator, connoting both an action and its result. As we will see below, at least one of the material parts that now compose Bodley 851 may once have belonged to some prior compilation or may have been considered a compilation in its own right prior to the addition of further material. In order to describe the compilation of multiple material and textual parts, each potentially a compilation on its own, I will adopt the term "collection" – with the caveat that no perfect descriptive terminology yet exists which would distinguish a wholly medieval collection like Bodley 851 from those composite manuscripts so often fashioned by later collectors, such as Sir Robert Cotton, Matthew Parker, and John Bale.[14]

As recomposition eludes precise disciplinary taxonomy and as Bodley 851 eludes precise codicological classification, so too does one specific feature of Bodley 851 also continue to elude precise descriptive language: the illustrated claim to ownership located on fol. 6v (pl. 1). Rigg refers to this page as a "bookplate," borrowing the conventions of print history; following function, Hanna terms it an "ex libris" (a term replicated in the description provided by the Digital Bodleian); and Kerby-Fulton combines both approaches, calling it an "ex libris 'bookplate'" – and using "ex libris" as her preferred shorthand term.[15] As Kerby-Fulton has demonstrated, however the image occupying the top one-third of fol. 6v exceeds typical instances of either proposed category

---

[14] For taxonomic discussions, see Alexandra Gillespie, "Are The Canterbury Tales a Book?," *Exemplaria* 30.1 (2018): 66–83; Johann Peter Gumbert, "Codicological Units: Towards a Terminology for the Stratigraphy of the Non-Homogeneous Codex," *Segno e Testo: International Journal of Manuscripts and Text Transmission* 2 (2004): 17–42; and Julia Boffey and John J. Thompson, "Anthologies and Miscellanies: production and choice of texts," in *Book Production and Publishing in Britain, 1375–1475*, eds. Jeremy Griffiths and Derek Pearsall (Cambridge: Cambridge University Press, 1989), 279–316. For consideration of how post-medieval collectors and archivists can alter textual significance through material practices, see Zachary Hines, "'The Best Book of Romance': the Gawain Manuscript and Composite Miscellaneity," *HLQ* 85.4 (2022): 579–601.

[15] Rigg, "Poetic Anthologies (II)," 390; Hanna, "Dissemination," 196; Kerby-Fulton, "Scribe-Poet Binary," 496. High-quality digital scans of fol. 6v are available, along with the rest of the manuscript, at the Digital Bodleian: https://digital.bodleian.ox.ac.uk/objects/0cecbb9e-b126-4360-b514-eb949f851b43 (last accessed 9 July 2023). NB: The "Origin Note" derived from the Bodleian's *Medieval Manuscripts in Oxford Libraries*, was updated after I began circulating early forms of this project. The treatment of evidence from rubrication ("which does not seem to be correct") in the "Note" remains unsubstantiated by cited sources. I discuss the evidence for Rigg's position in detail, below.

in its execution (compare, e.g., Rate's fish in Ashmole 61).[16] The folio nevertheless conforms in language and function to a common class of notes of ownership in late-medieval English books.[17] It might be best described as a "decorative, figural ownership mark."[18] Such terminology is, however, liable to become burdensome in repetition. For my description below, therefore, I will follow common practice in terming the decorative, figural ownership mark an *ex libris* (so italicized), with the understanding that this specimen is unusual among late-medieval books more generally and exceptional in its performance of the function implied by the term.

As with the individual chapters of this book, the major sections of this chapter are organized around paleographic evidence for scribal activity within the manuscript.[19] I will emphasize, however, that paleography is not the only residue of scribal agency available for recomposition. Paleographic evidence for disparate acts of scribal production serves as one prompt among many to consider also how the deployment of rubrication, dialect, orthography, lineation, content, page design, and annotation, among other indicators, might alter the possibilities for how a manuscript's texts can be read together. In my descriptions of Bodley 851, I have relied primarily upon Clemens and Graham, *Introduction to Manuscript Studies* and Kerby-Fulton, Hilmo, and Olson, *Opening Up Middle English Manuscripts*.[20] In other settings, terms for the same manuscript features may vary. For aid in observing the intersection of paleographic evidence with other types of material evidence – particularly

---

[16] Kerby-Fulton, "Scribe-Poet Binary," 495–8. For Rate and his signatures, see the introduction to George Shuffelton, *Codex Ashmole 61: A Compilation of Popular Middle English Verse* (Kalamazoo, MI: Medieval Institute Publications, 2008). See also Myra Seaman, *Objects of Affection: The Book and the Household in Late Medieval England* (Manchester: Manchester University Press, 2021).

[17] Daniel Wakelin, "'Thys Ys My Boke': Imagining the Owner in the Book," in *Spaces for Reading in Later Medieval England*, ed. Mary C. Flannery and Carrie Griffin (New York: Palgrave Macmillan, 2016), 20–1.

[18] For this phrasing, I am indebted to the collected wisdom of Ian Cornelius, Elizabeth Hebbard, and Sarah Noonan at the "Peripheral Manuscripts" project.

[19] My assessment of scribal hands concurs substantially with Rigg's authoritative study: "Poetic Anthologies (II)." Where I have found it necessary to alter or elaborate upon Rigg's assessment in any way, I have relied upon M. B. Parkes, *English Cursive Book Hands, 1250–1500* (Oxford: Clarendon Press, 1969) and *Their Hands before Our Eyes* (Burlington, VT: Ashgate, 2008), supplemented with Derolez, *The Palaeography of Gothic Manuscript Books*. To aid the reader in observing paleographic details, I have provided images from the manuscript as reference (pls. 1–14, pp. 70–83). For further inspection, the reader may also consult high-resolution digital images of the whole manuscript made available by the Bodleian Library.

[20] *IMS*; *OUMEM*. For brevity, Derolez, *Gothic Manuscript Books* is often instructive.

the imposition of decorative schemes and the arrangement of texts within or across quires – I have provided an overview of the account described below (Table 2) to supplement the more traditional overview of texts.

Throughout this chapter, as throughout this book, I focus my attention on the portions of Bodley 851 that were collected and unified by its early scribes, culminating in the work of Scribe X. Discussion of the manuscript's reception and possible alterations later in the fifteenth century (including binding), in the sixteenth century (including some marginal annotations), and in the seventeenth century (including arrival at Bodley's Library) must await another occasion. Above all it should be recalled that Bodley 851 is an immensely complex book, since as Parkes affirms, "the physical as well as the provenance evidence is open to different interpretations."[21] Precisely because description is inextricable from interpretation, future descriptions will undoubtedly yield further interpretive possibilities.

Throughout this chapter, I place special emphasis on the three agents whose contributions ground the analytic arguments of the chapters to follow (Scribe B, Scribe A, and Scribe X). Of these three key agents, Scribe X is of particular importance, since it was under his direction that a smattering of disparate material components was first gathered together as a coherent collection.

Material Overview

BodL. MS Bodley 851 consists of 209 leaves containing at least twenty texts inscribed by at least eight scribes in seventeen quires (of 12, 10, 8, and 6) over the course of several years – likely several decades, possibly more than a century – sometime roughly between the middle of the fourteenth century and the middle of the fifteenth century. A. G. Rigg's descriptive account of Bodley 851 divides Bodley 851 into three major parts (Parts I, II, and III), to which frontmatter and backmatter were added, likely late in the fifteenth century.[22] The question of when the *ex libris* was added remains contentious. Part I runs from fol. 7r to fol. 77v and contains the sole extant witness of Walter Map's *De nugis curialium*, followed by a smattering of shorter texts. Part II runs from fol. 78r to fol. 123v and contains a wide array of Latin verse, by both known and anonymous authors. Part III runs from fol. 124r to fol. 208v

---

[21] Quoted in Kerby-Fulton, "Confronting," 495.

[22] All citations of Rigg's description are given from the revised version of "Medieval Latin Poetic Anthologies (II)" as printed in Charlotte Brewer and A. G. Rigg, *Piers Plowman: A Facsimile of the Z-Text in Bodleian Library, Oxford, MS Bodley 851* (Cambridge: D. S. Brewer, 1994). This is a distinct publication from their edition of the same text preserved in Bodley 851: William Langland, *Piers Plowman: The Z Version*, eds. Charlotte Brewer and A. G. Rigg (Toronto: Pontifical Institute of Mediaeval Studies, 1983).

and attests only an unusual rendition of *Piers Plowman* sometimes called the Z-text, which scholars of that poem frequently consider in terms of its unique first section (Part III(a), fol. 124r to 139r), its brief A-text continuation (Part III(b), fol. 139r to fol. 140v), and its much longer C-text continuation (Part III(c), fol. 141r to fol. 208v). The texts now present in Bodley 851 have been arranged according to at least three distinct schemes for decoration and rubrication, two of which appear in more than one major part of the manuscript. The volume may have been bound as early as the middle of the fifteenth century. The only alteration to its late-medieval binding that Rigg notes is that the spine has been repaired.

Texts

The order of the texts as they appear in the manuscript today, should one desire to read it from front to back, is evident in Table 1 (pp. 6–7). Throughout this chapter, I will refer to individual texts by their ordinated numbers – e.g., *The Fall of Carthage* as (2) or the Bridlington *Prophecy* as (12a) – especially when considering the material composition and compilation of a text largely exclusive of its contents. Note that (9) comprises three distinct compositions in sequence and that (12a) and (12b) appear separately in other manuscripts. In various publications on *Piers Plowman*, the "Z-text" can be used to refer to all of (21) or only (21a). Throughout this book, when I refer to the "Z-text" I mean (21a), the scribal redaction that is uniquely preserved in Bodley 851, and not (21b) or (21c), A-text and C-text continuations.

Scribes

Little is known about the scribes who contributed to Bodley 851, apart from the texts they left behind. Some were very likely associated with the Benedictine monastery at Ramsey, or else with its house at Gloucester College in Oxford, given the *ex libris* ascribing ownership to John Wells (on which and whom, more below). Adopting Rigg's system, I will refer to the contributors to Bodley 851 as Scribes A, B, C, S, Q, X, Y, and Dodsthorpe.

Technically, these should be referred to as "hands" rather than "scribes": "A *script* is the model which the scribe has in his mind's eye when he writes, whereas a *hand* is what he actually puts down on the page."[23] Human designers (scribes) with a single model (script) in mind might nevertheless produce remarkably different versions of that model in actuality (hand); moreover, a single designer (scribe) might be competent in several models (scripts) which take a drastically different appearances (hands) in different contexts. Accordingly, paleography remains an inexact science – in large part because

---

[23] Parkes, *English Cursive Book Hands*, xxvi.

any account of human agency must remain inexact.[24] The agents I call Scribes B and C could well have been the same person, setting down competing scripts with different materials at different points in time, such that differences in appearance of text arise from factors other than differences in copyist. Nevertheless, it seems likely to me, as it has seemed to prior scholars of Bodley 851, that the hands designated above largely correspond to separate individual human agents. Unless otherwise noted, throughout this chapter "Hand B" simply means "the hand of Scribe B," where "Scribe B" refers to a historical human agent and where "Hand B" refers to features of his handwriting.

Rigg posits that the scribes of Bodley 851 contributed material in the following order: B, C, A, X and S, Q (possibly Q^1 and Q^2), Dodsthorpe and Y. Dodsthorpe appears to have been the manuscript's final compiler, or else the manuscript's final compiler added no further textual material once Dodsthorpe's work was complete. Dodsthorpe and Y, working at approximately the same moment, but not in collaboration, contributed material to the flyleaves and added several items where blank page-space had otherwise remained present in the manuscript, as (4) and (5). They did not, however, add any further quires to pre-existing collections of quires that constitute Parts I, II, and III, as Scribes A, X, and Q had done. Some further marginalia may be the responsibility of an early modern reader as late as the seventeenth century, judging by the thin, looping secretary pen-strokes found most commonly in the margins of (1), (12a), and (14).

In recomposing Bodley 851, I will revise some aspects of the relationship between Scribes B, A, and X, since any degree of collaboration between some or all of these three scribes, in particular, would compress the timeline for the manuscript's production and clarify connections between its component texts. Scribes B, A, and X take center stage in this study, because they present to us a stable way of reading literary components within the complex material and textual construct that is Bodley 851. These three scribes also ground the interpretive arguments made sequentially in each following chapters: Chapter 2 revolves around Scribe B, Chapter 3 around Scribe A and Scribe X together, and Chapter 4 around Scribe X.

Decoration and Rubrication

Three competing decorative schemes recur unevenly throughout Parts I–III(a) of Bodley 851. For clarity of presentation, in this chapter I enumerate these schemes. I do not therefore imply they were added to the manuscript in the order of their enumeration. I will consider the timing of their imposition more

---

[24] See, for example, Lawrence Warner, "Scribes, Misattributed: Hoccleve and Pinkhurst," *SAC* 37 (2015): 55–100; and Sonja Drimmer, "Connoisseurship, Art History, and the Paleographical Impasse in Middle English Studies," *Speculum* 97.2 (2022): 415–68.

exactly as part of my discussion of Scribe X, below, since at least two schemes were imposed while he had control of the manuscript's component parts:

- Scheme #1 is the most limited decorative scheme. It consists of alternating marginal paraph marks in red and blue (pls. 5–8). This first scheme corresponds to that used for the table of contents that appears at the close of (1) in Part I, along with (6)–(8) in Part II. Rigg notes that "guide marks are still visible."[25]
- Scheme #2 consists of initial letters for individual lines touched in red ink (pls. 6–9). This decorative practice was common from the thirteenth century, when many of the texts of Part II were originally composed or most widely transmitted.[26]
- Scheme #3 consists of initials of varying sizes at the beginnings of texts and subsections, of the type *OUMEMS* terms "Lombard capitals" and Derolez "flourished initials" or "plain initials" (pls. 2–4, 6, 8–9, 11, 13–14). Rigg terms them "inset display initials."[27] These are in both red and blue, but more commonly in blue; and most blue initials have received red penwork, while no red initials have received any penwork whatsoever. Since not all initials are flourished (e.g., pls. 8–9), and since not all are rubricated (i.e., in red), I will use "penwork initial" as a general term and "flourished initial" when appropriate. Note the two puzzle initials, at the beginning of (1) and (21a) (pls. 2, 12); and the initial **S** containing inset decorative features, at the beginning of (7) and (14) (pls. 6, 9).

For most of the texts in Parts I–III(a), rubricated titles have been provided. As I demonstrate below, these were imposed by Scribe X in between his first stint of work on the manuscript and his second stint of work.

Provenance

At least one part of the manuscript was owned during the fourteenth century by John Wells, a monk of Ramsey, *prior studentium* at Gloucester College, Oxford, and somewhat famous anti-Wycliffite.[28] Wells's name forms the central element of the *ex libris* that is now appended to Part I (fol. 6v, pl. 1), facing the incipit to Walter Map's *De nugis curialium* (fol. 7r, pl. 2). Identification of a "monachus Rameseye" has been added to the elaborate scrollwork of the *ex libris* in red ink.

---

[25] Brewer and Rigg, *Facsimile*, 24.

[26] *IMS*, 25. See, for example, the images presented throughout Susanna Fein, ed., *Interpreting MS Digby 86: A Trilingual Book from Thirteenth-Century Worcestershire* (York: York Medieval Press, 2019).

[27] Brewer and Rigg, *Facsimile*, 24.

[28] A. B. Emden, *A Biographical Register of the University of Oxford to A. D. 1500*, vol. 3 (Oxford: Clarendon Press, 1957), 2008.

Charlotte Brewer and A. G. Rigg claimed that John Wells was, in fact, Scribe X, and so should be considered not only the owner of the Z-text of *Piers Plowman* but responsible for transcribing that text as (21a). While their claim for the authorial priority of the Z-text in the textual tradition of *Piers Plowman* has been widely debated on further metrical and editorial grounds, their claim for the identity of Scribe X and John Wells has not enjoyed wide acceptance among book historians or paleographers.[29] Rejecting claims advanced by Brewer and Rigg, Ralph Hanna located the production of Part III entirely in the fifteenth century and set forth the alternative suggestion that Wells may have been Scribe A, rather than Scribe X.

Whether or not Wells, personally, had any interest in *Piers Plowman* or wrote in this manuscript now containing his *ex libris*, his ownership allows us to associate some materials present in Bodley 851 with the Benedictine Monastery at Ramsey and with the Benedictines at Oxford. The association with Ramsey may explain aspects of the Middle English dialect used in its copy of *Piers Plowman*; and the book's Benedictine affiliation may explain how various scribes acquired access to its widely varied component texts. In her analysis of the *ex libris*, Kathryn Kerby-Fulton has argued for significant London connections as well. Overall, the composition and decoration of the manuscript suggests either multiple and rapid shifts in ownership or a great deal of travel for its various material parts, if not for John Wells, then for other owners now anonymous.[30]

Dates

Attempts to settle on a possible latest date of production for various parts of Bodley 851 have had vexing ramifications for literary scholars. The key figure has been John Wells, who died in 1388. It seems reasonable to infer that the *ex libris* attesting his ownership was added to some subset of its current collection of texts before the time of his death. Yet the straightforward question of whether the Z-text of *Piers Plowman* predated Wells's *ex libris* in the production of Bodley 851 sparked one of the fiercer debates in Middle

---

[29] See especially A. V. C. Schmidt, "The Authenticity of the Z Text of *Piers Plowman*: A Metrical Examination," *Medium Aevum* 53.2 (1984): 295; Hoyt N. Duggan, "The Authenticity of the Z Text of '*Piers Plowman*': Further Notes on Metrical Evidence," *Medium Ævum* 56.1 (1987): 25–45; and George Kane, "The 'Z Version' of *Piers Plowman*," *Speculum* 60.4 (1985): 910–30.

[30] For consideration of the East Anglian textual affiliations of the Z-text and the proposition that Wells may have been Scribe A, see Hanna, "MS Bodley 851"; and for discussion of the manuscript's affiliations with both London and Oxford, see Kerby-Fulton, "Confronting" and "Oxford."

English textual scholarship at the close of the twentieth century.[31] If Wells himself owned and possibly transcribed this text of *Piers Plowman* (as Rigg and Brewer argue), much of the textual tradition surrounding that poem would need to be reconsidered. If, however, Wells owned only Part I of Bodley 851, or only Parts I and II of Bodley 851 – or, for that matter, no part at all – then little is clarified about the production of the Z-text, at least in chronological terms. I will address the timing of the addition of the *ex libris* in my discussion of Scribe X later in this chapter. For now, I emphasize that conclusions about the timing of the addition of the *ex libris* alter nothing in the literary analysis that occupies the chapters to follow.

Because Bodley 851 contains multiple distinct parts, often interwoven among single quires and decorative schemas, it can be difficult to assign a single date or range of dates for any part of its production. Paleographic features on display in Bodley 851 could technically range from the close of the thirteenth century to the middle of the fifteenth. While Rigg, Hanna, and Kerby-Fulton have each posited a fairly late point of completion for (6) and (7) – usually in the final quarter of the fourteenth century – there is no strictly paleographic evidence that would prevent competing hypotheses for a much earlier moment of production (c. 1300), a slightly earlier moment of production (c. 1350), or a somewhat later moment of production (c. 1425) for much of the manuscript. Judging by scribal hands alone, it is possible to imagine Scribe B and Scribe X working a century apart – or mere weeks apart. Since the earliest examples of the use of Anglicana script in books come from the final quarter of the thirteenth century, c. 1300 remains a bold – indeed, untenably bold – hypothesis; similarly, producing Hand B in the 1420s would already have amounted to an act of intentional anachronism. These extreme dates are not likely, especially given the manuscript's contents; but neither are they impossible from a material vantage. Expert eyes have never, to my knowledge, posited a date of writing earlier than the third quarter of the fourteenth century or later than the first quarter of the fifteenth century.

Most of the individual texts preserved within Bodley 851 were copied much later in time than their original points of authorial composition. Indeed, the vast majority of texts preserved in Parts I and II were originally composed in the twelfth and thirteenth centuries – much earlier than is possible for any material component of Bodley 851. Accordingly, their appearance in Bodley 851 reveals little about its date of composition.

Texts datable closer to the most likely timeframe for the manuscript's composition hardly narrow its possible range. For example, the *Battle of Crécy*,

---

[31] Apart from scholarship already cited, for two opposing summaries of the controversy, see Charlotte Brewer, *Editing Piers Plowman: The Evolution of the Text* (Cambridge: Cambridge University Press, 1996); and Ralph Hanna, "Studies in the Manuscripts of *Piers Plowman*," *YLS* 7 (1993): 1–25.

1346 (16) could not have been added to the manuscript before the actual battle it describes occurred in 1346, suggesting a firm *terminus post quem* in that year. But we know that this poem was added by at least the fourth scribe to contribute to the manuscript's production, Scribe X; and in fact, as I demonstrate below, we can surmise that Scribe X added (16) late in his own extended labors on Bodley 851. Two other manuscripts contain a separate version of the poem – Cotton Titus A.20 and Rawlinson B.214, both discussed by Rigg in his "Poetic Anthologies" sequence – but neither serves to narrow a possible date of transcription in Bodley 851, since Titus A.20 was compiled "at a large monastery, probably in the London area, 1367–1400" and since Rawlinson B.214 was written "sometime after 1469… possibly copied directly from Tx [Titus A.20]."[32] Moreover, it is not difficult to imagine ongoing interest in poems describing English superiority in the Hundred Years' War, given the ongoing nature of the political conflict itself.[33] In the context of Bodley 851, on account of this poem, we can say only that Scribe X completed his work in Part II sometime between the middle of the fourteenth century and the middle of the fifteenth century, such that Scribes B, C, and A completed their work sometime before Scribe X began his. If it is true that this range is technically delimiting, it is also true that it is not very informative.

Recomposition

Dating is messy work. Yet the calendrical measurement of time need not interfere totally with the process of describing how a manuscript came into being over time. In order to track the process by which a complex medieval collection such as Bodley 851 was produced, I will work infrequently with absolute dates, either in terms of the original composition of its texts or in terms of the timeline for their addition to this manuscript's material parts. My immediate concern is the internal chronology of how this object was made.

Scribe B

The earliest surviving material unit of Bodley 851, now quire ix[12], is found near the center of the bound codex. It begins with the sixth line of a six-line stanza of a long devotional poem in regular sequence praising the Virgin Mary (6). (6) is followed immediately by an unfinished copy of a misogamous

---

[32] A. G. Rigg, "Propaganda of the Hundred Years War: Poems on the Battles of Crecy and Durham (1346): A Critical Edition," *Traditio* 54 (1999): 170.

[33] For a recent engagement, albeit one that does not engage at length with specific Anglo-Latin poems witnessed in Bodley 851, see Daniel Davies and R. D. Perry, eds., *Literatures of the Hundred Years War* (Manchester: Manchester University Press, 2024).

dream-vision conducted in goliardic verse (7). These two texts, (6) and (7), are the earliest two items present in Bodley 851, and they are the only two texts written in the hand of the manuscript's earliest scribe, Scribe B.

Scribe B writes a hand modeled on the Anglicana Formata script characteristic of the second half of the fourteenth century (pls. 6–7). Both poems copied by Scribe B are now incomplete, the first lacking some number of initial stanzas (probably 88 of them) and the second lacking some number of final stanzas (almost certainly three of them). Scribe B's two poems have been rubricated in a common pattern, using alternating red and blue paraph markers for consecutive stanzas. Scribe B also indented the first stanza of (7) in anticipation of a four-line initial: there now stands a penwork initial **S** in blue ink with red penwork (pl. 6). As I demonstrate below, neither rubricated markers nor decorated initial letter were present at the conclusion of Scribe B's labor: they would be added during Scribe X's first stint.

I follow A. G. Rigg, who edited both texts that Scribe B copied, in referring to (6) as the *Ave virgo mater christi* of Walter of Wimborne and (7) as the anonymous *De coniuge non ducenda*. As numbered in Rigg's edition, which adopts Oxford, Corpus Christi College MS 232 (CCC 232) as its copy text, (6) begins with the sixth and final line of the eighty-eighth stanza, preserving in full only stanzas 89–164 – just under half of the total poem. The first eighty-seven and five-sixths stanzas, along with any materials which might have accompanied them, have not been found. Where (6) concludes at the bottom of fol. 80rb, (7) begins at the top of fol. 80va, with no text or significant gap intervening.

We can infer that at least one quire that once sat at the head of quire ix has been lost, containing at least the first part of (6) along with some quantity of further material. Rigg refers to the lost quire as quire *ix, but it is worth making the qualification that *ix could have consisted of any number of quires or leaves. We can only guess at the conditions under which the missing quire(s) *ix came to be separated from quire ix of Bodley 851, just as we can only guess at its (or their) contents. Based on his examination of CCC 232, where (6) is followed by Wimborne's *De mundi vanitate*, Rigg posited that the same poem might have preceded (6) in Bodley 851. Given that neither Bodley 851 nor CCC 232 is a copy of the other, however, as well as the reversal of order necessary to form this supposition, we might better err on the side of more general uncertainty.[34] The textual contents of those preceding pages must

---

[34] Uncharacteristically, Rigg's accounts of the order of these poems contradict one another: in his description of Bodley 851, he notes that in CCC 232, the *Ave virgo* "is preceded by the *De mundi vanitate*" (Brewer and Rigg, *Facsimile*, 34), but in his edition of Wimborne's poetry, has it "preceding *De mundi vanitate*" (A. G. Rigg, *The Poems of Walter of Wimborne* [Toronto: Pontifical Institute of Mediaeval Studies, 1978], 144). Thomson confirms the second case: that in CCC 232, the *Ave virgo* comes

remain unknown (barring their actual discovery), and it would be difficult to overestimate the possible variety of material they might have contained.

Almost certainly, (6) and (7) once existed within a larger grouping of poems that may also have been transcribed by Scribe B. Furthermore, given the amount of page-space Scribe B left blank (more than nine full folios in quire ix!) along with the incomplete ending to (7), we can infer that Scribe B expected some further quantity of text to be added to his own work – which is to say, he likely thought of himself as contributing to a textual compilation that he did not complete. (6) and (7) formed only the most recent entries within a larger collection, the beginnings of which are now lost. Whether Scribe B envisaged a particular set of texts for the remainder of his incipient compilation, and whether the texts now present in Bodley 851 correspond in any way to his vision, remains a mystery.

Scribe C

Of the early contributors to Bodley 851, Scribe C undertook to transcribe the least amount of material. His presence is most important as an indicator of separation between Scribe B and Scribe A.

Scribe C began his transcription of Michael of Cornwall's bombastic *First Invective* against Henry of Avranches (9) at the top of the second column following the incomplete copy of (7) left by Scribe B (fol. 81vb, pl. 7). There, Hands B and C appear side-by-side, along with the hand of Scribe X. The hand of Scribe C is immediately distinguishable from that of Scribe B in overall aspect. Despite stark differences in appearance, Hand C is also modeled on Anglicana Formata (pls. 7–8). That Scribe C intended for the title to (9a) to appear more formal than the text is evident from the larger size and even more squared-off shape of the letter forms and the proliferation of capital letters (fol. 81vb, lines 1–3; pl. 7). Scribe C makes regular use of Latin abbreviations and frequently places a *punctus* at the required location in the penthemimeral hexameter of (9a).

Scribe C completed his transcription of the *First Invective* and contributed no further material to the manuscript. Scribe C did not copy the *Second* and *Third Invectives* Cornwall penned against Avranches, as found in several other English manuscripts.[35] As such, it is more accurate to refer to his contribution

---

first, then the *De mundi vanitate* (Rodney M. Thomson, *A Descriptive Catalogue of the Medieval Manuscripts of Corpus Christi College, Oxford* [Cambridge: D. S. Brewer, 2011], 116–17).

[35] See Thomas C. Sawyer and Paul Vinhage, "Michael of Cornwall's *First Invective* Against Henry of Avranches," *JMLat* 33 (2023): 17–55; and Alfons Hilka, "Eine Mittellateinische DichterFehde: Versus Michaelis Cornubiensis Contra Henricum Abrincensem," *Mittelalterliche Handschriften* (Leipzig: Karl W. Hiersemann, 1926), 123–54.

as (9a) the *First Invective* of Michael of Cornwall; since the *Second* and *Third Invectives*, (9b) and (9c), would be added by another scribe (Scribe A).

Quire ix contains, therefore, multiple production units. Where the texts copied by Scribe B were unlined and somewhat erratic in presentation, the remainder of quire ix is carefully pricked for ruling at 48 lines of text to a column (for 96 lines to a page and 192 to a folio). Scribe C follows the ruled lines carefully. While ruling itself is not visible for many folios, punctures from the act of ruling are evident in the margins throughout the remainder of gathering ix[12] (fols. 82ra–89; e.g., pl. 8). The clearest folio for viewing ruling is fol. 88r. Fol. 81vb is not itself ruled, but its lineation matches that of the page facing (82r), confirming that Scribe B's text must already have been written before Scribe C acquired the quire. Possibly, the untouched folios of the quires were pricked at once; though I am not aware of another example of scribes adopting this procedure for a quire already partially inked with text.[36] With a three line incipit, at 48 lines to a column, had Scribe C also transcribed (9b) and (9c), his work would have concluded at the bottom of fol. 88rb (accounting for the three-line incipit, 1276 lines of text, as in the Hilka edition, and 2–3 lines for each subsection heading). This transcription of the *First Invective*, then, was carefully plotted by Scribe C to occupy a predetermined amount of space on each page, such that the text he began would be complete with a single folio left blank at the end of the gathering. Possibly, this blank page was intended to protect an unbound booklet. The final folio in quire ix[12] (fol. 89) does show some signs of wear, especially in its outer-bottom corner, that we might associate equally with disuse or heavy use.

Scribe C did not rubricate his title, which was later underlined in red (pl. 7). He allowed a blank space at the front of lines 17–18 of the poem (or lines 20–21 on the page), which at first glance appears to be meant for a decorated initial of some kind, being two lines tall and indented by the width of three or four graphs. It appears to have been taken this way by a later rubricator, who touched the first letter of each line in red, down to this indent and no further. More likely, however, Scribe C – or the scribe responsible for his copy text – was perplexed by the poem's obscure reference to "Crisogoni."[37] The double virgule in the inner margin may mark the omission, but it may also have been imposed by a later scribe, perhaps the same who was responsible for marking the beginning of (8) and (9) with a marginal indicator (having the appearance of "cc"; pl. 7, top of column *b*; cp. pl. 12). At any event, Scribe C did not

---

[36] *IMS*, 15–16; Daniel Wakelin, *Immaterial Texts in Late Medieval England: Making English Literary Manuscripts, 1400–1500* (Cambridge: Cambridge University Press, 2022), 74–81.

[37] Wakelin notes that "Scribes commonly left such gaps for words which they cannot understand" ("Writing the Words," 53). For an explanation of the reference to Chrysogonus, see Sawyer and Vinhage, "*First Invective*," 51n5.

indent any of his lines in expectation of further decorative lettering, as we will see was the case for Scribe A. No decoration was present in the manuscript when he completed his copying. Paraphs were later added to (9a) in alternating red and blue, according to a scheme matching that imposed on (6) and (7) – and, remarkably, (8), not present at time of Scribe C's transcription – but not matching any of the texts from (9b) onward. Whether the lost gathering (*ix) was present when Scribe C undertook his brief contribution to Bodley 851 remains unknown.

It is difficult to make a reasonable supposition concerning the working relation between Scribe C and Scribe B. On one hand, we might suppose that Scribe C had some awareness, if not of Scribe B's project, then of the poem he was transcribing (7), and allowed the remainder of column 81va for its completion accordingly. On the other hand, Scribe C made no attempt to complete the unfinished poem himself, nor did he attempt to imitate the aspect of Hand B or its (absent) *ordinatio*. The premature explicit to (7) may be in his hand. He certainly plotted out the layout of his poem with more care than did Scribe B. It is clear Scribe C conceived of his contribution to what is now quire ix of Bodley 851 as distinct enough from the text already present to warrant leaving what, in the late fourteenth century, was a significant amount of usable space on the page. Though he had ruled through the end of the quire, Scribe C left the second half of quire ix blank (fols. 83vb–89v). While it is likely that Scribe C believed the remainder of quire ix would be filled with (9b-c), we must pass on any speculation concerning his vision for further contents of the compilation otherwise, as we did in the case of Scribe B. Whether quire *ix was present yet remains a mystery.

Scribe A

By far the greatest portion of inked text now found in Bodley 851 was copied by Scribe A, whose overarching contributions to the disparate parts that now compose the manuscript would be excelled only by the labor of Scribe X. In this section, I describe the texts Scribe A contributed and the evidence for the relation of Parts I and II as material components at the time of his contributions. I will also describe how Scribe A anticipated decorative schemes that he himself did not impose.

In Part II, which has occupied our attention thus far, Scribe A added the final two *Invectives* of Michael of Cornwall, (9b) and (9c), to the copy Scribe C had begun (9a). Scribe A completed his work on (9c) at fol. 89ra. He contributed five further complete texts, (10) to (14), filling out quire ix and appending three further quires (x-xi^{12} + xii^{10}), with the text of (10) following immediately after (9c) at the bottom of fol. 89ra. Scribe A left the majority of quire xii blank, from the fifth line of fol. 115vb to the bottom of fol. 123vb – eight out of ten total folios, plus the better part of the column where he finished (14). As with

Scribes B and C, we cannot be sure whether or what further text he might have expected to be added in that space.

In Part I (quires iii$^{12(-2)}$ + iv-viii^{12}), Scribe A copied the full text of Walter Map's *De nugis curialium* (1), including a table of contents for Map's text at its close (pls. 2–4). He also copied a short moralizing story (2) immediately after the table of contents for (1). Scribe A wrote out the chapter titles for the table of contents that follows the text of (1), with a blank line allowed for breaks between distinctions (pl. 5). In Part I, he left blank the final four folios of quire viii (fols. 74–77), having completed his transcription of (2) at the bottom of fol. 73rb.

Scribe A, too, writes a hand modeled on Anglicana Formata script, and the formation of individual graphs of Hand A correspond generally to the individual graphs of Hand C. Their resemblance is close enough in duct, albeit not in aspect, that it must be considered whether (9a) and (9b)–(14) were undertaken by a single scribe whose skill, writing utensil (especially regarding the cut of the nib), or attitude toward his project somehow shifted between stints of the same poem.

In Part II, Hand A (pls. 8–9) has a more squared-off aspect than Hand C, evident on the page where they meet (fol. 83v; pl. 8), and so assumes a slightly more formal appearance by comparison. Hand A also makes use of more cursive features than does Hand C, especially in the linking of its minim strokes but also noticeable where the nib curved below the line (e.g., *infers* and *furtum*, fol. 83vb, line 2; pl. 8). Furthermore, Hand A is also larger than Hand C, taking up more space vertically and horizontally, and so filling 41 rather than 48 lines to a column throughout Part II. Hand A emphasized majuscule letters at the beginnings of lines with more flourishes. Hand A is slightly more rounded in Part I but remains recognizable throughout Bodley 851 (pls. 2–5). If any single graph differentiates the two, it is final **s**, which in Hand C is usually closed and which in Hand A occasionally remains open so as not to form a top chamber. I will treat Hand C and Hand A as products of distinct scribes more on practical grounds than according to any strict paleographic evidence: it seems unlikely that the same agent would in turn follow (Scribe C) and then totally disregard (Scribe A) prior ruling; and as I discuss in detail below, the approaches to preparing for rubrication and decoration differ immensely between the sections copied in Hand A and Hand C.

As currently preserved, all of the texts copied by Scribe A now display at least one of the three decorative schemes that appear within Bodley 851. These texts – (1), (2), (9b–c), (10–11), (12a), (12b), (13), and (14) – are among the only items within Bodley 851 that appear to have been finished according to their original design.[38] Scribe A was not himself responsible for decorating

---

[38] Besides all of Scribe A's texts, (8), (18), and (21a) by Scribe X also were decorated as intended, according two different schemes; on which, more below.

according to the first or third schemes. He may have imposed the second scheme himself (more below). He nevertheless made space for rubricated headings and subheadings where appropriate.

Decoration would not be imposed until after Scribe X had begun his work on the manuscript. Scribe A nevertheless anticipated the third scheme (the use of decorated initials) and possibly the first (the use of alternating paraphs). Accordingly, I provide a description of their applications to his inked texts in this section, as they currently appear. Recall throughout, however, that the actual work of decoration would be completed either by Scribe X or under his supervision, after the work of Scribe A was complete.

The full text of (9) presents each of the three competing decorative schemes that all recur unevenly throughout Parts I–III(a) of Bodley 851. No paraph marks (scheme #1) appear in column *b* of fol. 81v, where (9a) begins, though several are evident in column *a*, containing the final stanzas of (7) and the entirety of (8). Beginning on fol. 82ra in (9a), these marks appear at many but not all locations where Sawyer and Vinhage's text indicates breaks (e.g., "Cum te collaudes" at line 84 in Sawyer and Vinhage's text and "Inproperas nobis" at line 96, but not "Post mortem si nos" at line 90, in between). Double virgules can still be seen beneath the paraph marks now present, and the rubricator appears not to have skipped any double virgules apart from those already noted (fol. 81vb, at the omission of "Crisogoni"; pl. 7) These alternating paraphs continue through to the end of (9a) on fol. 83va (pl. 8) and do not appear at all in (9b) or (9c). The initial letters of the first column of (9a) have been touched in red (scheme #2), down to the space Scribe C omitted for "Chrysogonus" (pl. 7). The same pattern of touching in red resumes at the top of fol. 83ra – still in (9a) – and continues uninterrupted until the final line of fol. 84vb, one column short of the end of (9b) (pl. 8). No initials are so touched on fol. 85r, where (9b) ends at the bottom of column *a* and (9c) begins at the top of column *b*. The first thirteen initials from the top of fol. 86ra are so touched, but not the rest of the folio; and both columns of fol. 87r are so touched, but none of the verso, nor any of the rest of the poem to follow. I have not discerned any predictable scheme that would account for this practice.

For the second of Cornwall's *Invectives* (9b), Scribe A allowed space for a rubricated title, a penwork initial of two lines in height, and occasional penwork initials that would fit into their corresponding lines (scheme #3), sometimes causing a slightly larger space between lines than usual. As with the placement of paraphs in (9a), the placement of these initials in (9b) does not uniformly correspond to the capitalized divisions present in Hilka's edition of the poem, but the distribution is similar. Many guide-letters are still visible, but at least one rubricated majuscule was first given outlined shape in the same brown ink used for the text ("O" in "O iudex iuste," fol. 84va). For the third of Cornwall's "flytings" (9c), Scribe A allowed room for only a title and one initial of two lines in height (fol. 85rb). He left no further space for initials in the text, even where present in Hilka's edition.

The abrupt inclusion of scheme #3 in (9b) suggests strongly that Scribe A and Scribe C were not working in tandem; if nothing else it confirms that, if they were working together (however unsuccessfully), they did not share a common plan for lineation or decoration when lines for the *Debate* were ruled and when Scribe C began to write. It should be emphasized, however, that a single decorative plan does not govern all of the text Scribe C copied as (9a), either, which lacks paraph marks in its first column (fol. 81vb; pl. 7). In (9b) and (9c), all colored capitals now visible are in alternating red and blue.

The dominant decorative scheme throughout texts copied by Scribe A is scheme #3. Scribe A left space for initials consistently throughout his work on Part II. At the beginning of (10–11), (12a), and (12b), he left space for an initial of two lines in height, which have each been decorated in blue lettering with red penwork (with no alternating red lettering whatsoever). For (12a) but not (12b) and for (10) but not the putatively separate text of (11), he left space between separate texts for the inclusion of a title. For (13), he left eight full lines blank at the top of fol. 94vb, presumably to allow room for the title which now occupies that space, and left indented space for an initial of three lines in height. The density of penwork initials within the text of (13), a dramatic poem with multiple speakers, is the highest for any text preserved within Bodley 851, as an initial seems to have been included at every change in speaker (pl. 9, column a). Sixty-six such one-line penwork initials in alternating red and blue appear on the seven pages containing the text of (13).

Finally, for (14) in Part II, Scribe A left six lines blank at the top of fol. 97vb, now filled with a rubricated title as with (13), and allowed indented space for an initial of three lines in height (pl. 9). He also left a break of three lines between the text of the poem and its *moralitas* (fol. 114ra). Throughout the text, he allowed space for further initials according to the conventional subsections for the poem, along with the occasional indentation continuous with the text, where no subsection break occurs. Scribe A occasionally failed to provide space for an initial letter that the rubricator expected, as in the subsection titled "Burnellus maledicit rustico" (fol. 102va), where the first line of the subsection is in the usual brown ink for the inked text. Scribe A also wrote out one subsection title in brown, which the later rubricator dutifully cancelled and rewrote in red ("Reditus Burnelli," fol. 102vb). Guide letters for rubricated initials are not visible, confirming that the rubricator had access to a text sufficiently like Scribe A's copy text for the purpose of determining them. The text of the *Speculum stultorum* preserved within Bodley 851 represents an early form of the poem only preserved in two other manuscripts out of more than fifty surviving copies (BodL. Bodley 761 and London, Lambeth Palace

Library, 357).[39] Overall, given the lack of guide-letters, the relative lack of errors in leaving space for subsection titles, and the subsection title in brown, it is likely that that Scribe A and the rubricator were working from a common copy. This situation suggests, but cannot confirm absolutely, a relatively short span of time between copying and rubricating – and so between the work of Scribe A in Part II and the first stint of Scribe X. Although the third scheme is most consistently applied, the second scheme (red-touched letters) can be found applied sporadically throughout the texts Scribe A copied in Part II of Bodley 851 and occasionally in (1) in Part I. It is also present in the first two columns of (7), copied by Scribe B (but nowhere else in Scribe B's texts). As a general overview of its use in Part II, we might observe that it is not used at all in (10–11), only on versos in (12a) with the exception of fol. 94r, only in the final column of (13) (to match the first section of (14)?), and in some sections of (14) that appear in quire x, generally on rectos but not versos, but not in quire xi or xii.[40]

In Part I, Scribe A copied the only extant complete text of Walter Map's *De nugis curialium* (1) and the significantly shorter *Fall of Carthage* (2) (fols. 7ra–74va), the majority of Part I. Throughout the text of the *De nugis curialium*, Scribe A attempted to leave space for interleaved running chapter titles. He did not usually provide a full line break for those titles. This was a constant source of confusion for the later rubricating scribe, Scribe X. The majority of chapter titles run into one or both margins of their columns, and in extreme cases Scribe X entered his text vertically, as at the title to *De nugis* 1.28 appears in red text running vertically in the inner margin ("Item recapitula*cio* carthusiencium," fol. 22r; pl. 3). There are occasional lines left fully blank for chapter titles (as at *De nugis* 2.10, fol. 26ra), but only in those cases where the final line of the preceding chapter happened to end evenly right-adjusted within its column. Otherwise, Scribe A seems to have expected the first word of each individual chapter to be aligned left in its column, and he usually shortened the first line of a given chapter in expectation of a title that would fit into the final line of the preceding chapter and the space left blank in the first line of the chapter at hand (pls. 3–4). Accordingly, the text usually appears in this format:

---

[39] My thanks to Jill Mann, who graciously shared her research on the textual significance of Bodley 851 in preparation for her new edition of the *Speculum stultorum*: Jill Mann, *Nigel of Longchamp, Speculum Stultorum* (Oxford: Oxford University Press, 2023). The publication timeline for the present book has, unfortunately, allowed for only small opportunity to engage with her work in full.

[40] More precisely, the following folios display initial rubricated highlighting: 80va-b in (7), 81vb, 83r, and 83va in (9a); 83va-84v in (9b); 87v in (9c); none in (10-11); 90v, 91v, 92v, 93v-94r in (12); 97va in (13); and 97vb-98r, 99r, 100r, 101r in (14).

> perierunt terra autem sub pedibus iltuti mansit
> et saluatus est haec de cadoco brenin. **De apari**
> Aliud non miraculum **cionibus fantasticis.xi.**
> sed portentum nobis Walenses refe
> runt Wastinum Wastiniauc secus
> stagnum brekeinauc quod in circuitu duo
> miliaria tenet mansisse aiunt et vidis
> (fol. 26rb.6–12; rubricated text in bold)

The text running "perierunt… brenin" concludes *De nugis* 2.10 and the rest of the text not in bolded red font here forms the beginning of *De nugis* 2.11 ("Aliud non miraculum sed portentum… aiunt et vidis…"). The title to *De nugis* 2.11 appears broken in half by the initial words of the chapter it introduces, and at the completion of Scribe A's labor would have appeared as follows:

> perierunt terra autem sub pedibus iltuti mansit
> et saluatus est haec de cadoco brenin.
> liud non miraculum
> sed portentum nobis Walenses refe
> runt Wastinum Wastiniauc secus
> stagnum brekeinauc quod in circuitu duo
> miliaria tenet mansisse aiunt et vidis

The chapter title itself is not an afterthought, however. It is clear that Scribe A expected a title to be included, or else he would not have broken the first line so early (at "miraculum"). We must understand the scheme to be intentional.[41] Moreover, Scribe A was also responsible for copying out chapter titles in the table of contents that concludes the *De nugis* (fols. 72vb–73va), meaning he was aware not only of their existence but also of their contents and their lengths. This confirms the persuasive argument made by Joshua Byron Smith that the chapter titles to (1) precede the copy present in Bodley 851 but postdate Map's original text.[42]

Still, Scribe A consistently underestimated the amount of space the titles required. His practice for leaving space becomes more generous over the course of the text, so that on fol. 71ra, for example, two full blank lines intervene between the close of *De nugis* 5.6 and the beginning of *De nugis* 5.7

---

[41] It is not quite the case that "sometimes scribe A began a new chapter, wrote a few words, and then realized he had forgotten to leave space for the chapter heading, so he immediately stopped and skipped to the next line" (Joshua Byron Smith, *Walter Map and the Matter of Britain* [Philadelphia, PA: University of Pennsylvania Press, 2017], 67).

[42] Smith, *WMMB*, 65–8.

(pl. 4). Even here, where space has been left most generously, Scribe A breaks off the first line of the chapter well before reaching the end of the column. Although the rubricating scribe might have fit his title in the space provided, he has duly allotted the chapter number (vii) to the first line of body text, so interrupting body text with rubricated text as in the example above. Generally, Scribe A only allowed a full page break, with a blank line remaining between two lines of text, between distinctions of the *De nugis*; e.g., where *De nugis* 1 ends and *De nugis* 2 begins (fol. 24ra).

Throughout (1), Scribe A left space at the beginning of each chapter for a multi-line initial, usually two lines in height but sometimes three lines, as in the example given above, or less frequently one line (e.g., *De nugis* 2.13 at fol. 27va; pl. 13, row 2, column 1). He left space for occasional one-line initials within the text of individual chapters as well, though it is not immediately clear according to what plan.[43] In general, penwork initials at the beginnings of chapters are in blue with decorative red penwork, following the third decorative scheme described above as it is applied to the majority of (14). Within chapters, however, penwork *litterae notabiliores* alternate between red and blue. The same style of initial, in blue with red penwork, begins the text of (2). Very sporadically, letters touched in red (the second scheme described above) can be found throughout (1), most commonly but not always at the first letter of a new sentence or at a proper noun.[44] I have not discovered any overarching principle for their imposition. Scribe A also left space for an eight-line initial and a four-line title at the beginning of (1).

In the table of contents for (1), the rubricator copied chapter numbers from the main text.[45] Alternating paraph marks in red and blue – the first scheme discussed above – have been provided for each chapter title in the table of contents. These intervene, on the page, between the rubricated chapter numbers and the titles themselves.

As first noted above, we can only be certain Scribe A anticipated the use of the third scheme as it now appears in the texts he copied. The actual imposition of those initials and the inconsistent deployment of floriated penwork (for blue but not red initials), specifically, occurred after Scribe A ceased his work. Since Scribe A left indented spaces and guide letters rather than virgules or marginal indicators, as did Scribe B and C, we might safely infer that he did

---

[43] Smith observes that "scribe A often uses *litterae notabiliores*… to mark out different sections of the text, even within the same chapter, especially if the chapter is long; he usually does so quite sensibly" (*WMBB*, 68). What constitutes a "sensible" section, however, appears to remain a matter of taste.

[44] Letters are highlighted at the following locations: fols. 31r, 35r–38r, 39v, 57v–58v, 61r, 64v, 71v.

[45] With one exception: at *De nugis* 1.18, on fol. 14ra, the rubricator writes "•**18** •" rather than "•**xviii** •" as in the table of contents on fol. 73ra.

not anticipate the use of the first scheme (alternating red and blue paraphs). Since these were used for the text of (8), not present when Scribe A undertook his labor, we can also date their use later than Scribe A's copying. Only the second scheme (touching occasional letters in red) could have been imposed by Scribe A himself. No letters in any of the texts copied by Scribe X or other later scribes have been touched in red.

While we can be certain that Scribe A anticipated a common decorative scheme for his contributions to Parts I and II, it is not necessarily the case that Scribe A copied Part I and Part II in their current order or that he considered their distinct material parts to be part of the same project. "Like a great many late-medieval manuscripts," Hanna explains, "Bodley 851 does not reflect a single act of production but a series of separate assays, probably widely separate in time; the conjuncture of parts is, in some measure, 'accidental' when viewed in relation to the production of any individual piece, in that such conjuncture may never have been intended by the copyist of any single section."[46] We can qualify Hanna's description with the observation that the conjuncture of at least (9b)–(14) was intentional, on Scribe A's part, as was the conjuncture of at least (6)–(7) on Scribe B's. We might further narrow the length of time that Hanna's statement implies between the work of Scribe C and Scribe A in Part II (given that Scribe A completes Scribe C's project, but not Scribe B's), as well as Scribe A's work in Part II and Scribe A's work in Part I (bounded maximally by Scribe A's lifetime). Access to a common exemplar for (14) and possibly (1) is also suggestive of a short interval between Scribe A and Scribe X. Nevertheless, we cannot be certain that Scribe A left the manuscript in its current order, or that he conceived of what are now Parts I and II as two parts of a whole.

The physical state of Part I suggests that it remained unbound for some substantial period of time after Scribe A had completed his transcriptions of (1) and (2). It was not uncommon for gatherings of parchment to remain unbound for relatively long periods of time, and – whether left to collect dust in a chest, in a cabinet, or on a shelf; or whether circulated among some uncountable multitude of borrowing copyists – the outer pages of unbound booklets could become worn and, eventually, deteriorate.[47] Such signs of wear, therefore, are instructive for our understanding of a manuscript's compilation over time. The last page of gathering viii[12] (fol. 77v) – where the *De nugis* ends, now preserved in the middle of the codex – shows many of the signs of wear that would result from being left unbound. The first page of gathering iii[12] (fol. 7r), where the *De nugis* begins, however, shows fewer such signs of wear (pl. 2). Well over half of a millennium has passed, and its ink still stands out on

---

[46] Hanna, "Dissemination," 196.
[47] For a broad overview of signs of manuscript wear, see *IMS*, 57; for a discussion of wear in this particular manuscript, see Kerby-Fulton, "Confronting" and "Oxford."

the page clearly in brown and red and blue. Still, a few blots and blemishes can be found on the parchment, which may indicate that it stood exposed at some time. Similar blots are not evident elsewhere in the manuscript.

Other defects are easily located throughout the manuscript, however, even in the middle of gatherings. With the possible exception of fol. 89 – the final folio of quire ix mentioned above, which Scribe C may have considered unusable – such internal defects are more likely a result of the use of low-quality parchment than parchment badly handled (e.g., in Part II, the mid-quire tearing present at fols. 104 and 113; or the rough quality of the parchment at fols. 114–115).[48]

All of this suggests that what is now the first page of Part I likely sat exposed for a limited period of time and was ultimately placed underneath some other gathering of parchment (such that fol. 7r remains unworn) but that no parchment sat underneath the bundle that would become Part I (such that fol. 77v is quite worn). As with fol. 89, all such wear may have occurred well before any inscription took place.

Some similar observations can be made of Part II. The first page of gathering ix[12] (fol. 78r), where we now find Scribe B's inscription, shows no signs of wear whatsoever; and the final verso of that gathering shows wear only at the edges, which indicates some use but not constant exposure. The final verso of gathering xii[10] (fol. 123v), however, does show signs of wear and remains blank in the manuscript's final state.

Based on the condition of the gatherings within Bodley 851, it seems more likely that what Scribe A left behind was not a single stack of parchment in the form of a book, but two stacks of unbound parchment containing distinct textual entries – not an "it" but a "them." Most likely, Scribe A took possession of two or more unbound gatherings of parchment – quire(s) *ix and ix – where Scribe B had completed his work on (6) and (7) and Scribe C had begun the inscription of (9). There, Scribe A completed (9) and added another quire in twelves (x[12]), so that he could copy (10)-(13). He then began work on (14), which required two further gatherings (xi[12] and xii[10]) of parchment, making it the longest verse entry in either part, and the second longest entry, after (1), in Part I or II. From his disregard for visible ruling and the regularity with which texts end mid-column and mid-quire, it is clear that Scribe A had little interest or little skill in plotting out the full use of the material quires he added. Such signs point to personal use, or use within a non-professional community; a description which the Benedictine monks at Ramsey (or Gloucester College, Oxford) fit well enough. As I noted above, the wear on fol. 123v (the final

---

[48] Bodley 851 does not follow the typical case, in professional or semi-professional productions, that "there are more leaves with holes toward the end of a manuscript than earlier on" (*IMS*, 12).

page of xii[10]) indicates this total collection of parchment may have been left aside for some time, or travelled significantly, or both.

At some point in relation to his work on gatherings ix-xii, which now constitute Part II of Bodley 851, Scribe A completed his transcription of (1) and (2) in Part I. These two groups of parchment must have been stored such that the first page of gathering iii[12] (fol. 7r) received some limited exposure and the first page of gathering ix[12] (fol. 78r) received no exposure whatsoever. At the bottom of two piles, what are now fols. 77v and 123v. may have been shuffled around regularly, accounting for their worn condition. We can safely imagine fol. 78r secure in the midst of two stacks of parchment, protected from the rough dangers of the table, bench, or lectern. Indeed, we know there was at least one gathering, now missing, preventing it from being exposed to the world's myriad disturbances. The evidence for fol. 7r is less secure. Most likely what came to safeguard fol. 7r – at some indeterminate time later, but not substantially later than the inked text was copied by Scribe A – is what sits atop that folio now: the *ex libris*. I return to this hypothesis concerning the *ex libris* after discussing the contributions of Scribe X.

Scribe X

Scribe X made some alteration to every major part of Bodley 851. Although he was not responsible for the eventual binding of its constituent material pieces, it was under his oversight and direction that the disparate textual materials preserved in Parts I, II, and III could be said to form a single *collection* for the first time. Scribe X's labor proceeded in five overarching stages:

- First, in some order, Scribe X wrote (8) and (18) in Part II, and (21a) as Part III.
- Second, he imposed or caused to be imposed the third decorative scheme as described above (penwork initials).
- Third, Scribe X wrote out all rubricated titles, subtitles, chapter headings, page headers, *incipits*, and *explicits* in Parts I, II, and III, adopting a slightly more formal variant of the same script he used for writing main texts.
- Fourth, he imposed or caused to be imposed the first decorative scheme described above (alternating paraphs).
- Fifth, but possibly at some significant remove from his prior work, in a second stint of scribal activity Scribe X wrote out (3), (15), (16), and (19) in a slightly more compact version of his usual hand, filling space he had previously left blank in the manuscript.

At some point in undertaking his labor, Scribe X also corrected the text of (1) in several locations. He may also have corrected the text of (14). Whether he wrote the rubricated inscription for the *ex libris* at fol. 6v during the third stage remains a contentious question. In this section, I discuss all five of stages of Scribe X's labor, with particular emphasis on the first four, after which the collection could be said to have a definite structure and form.

As a copyist, Scribe X's work was limited but formative. For his first stint as copyist, in Part II he copied (8) in the space Scribes B, C, and A left between (7) and (9). Then, after allowing five full blank pages to follow (14), he copied (18) at the end of gathering xii (fols. 116r–118r), such that six blank pages followed (18) to close out the quire (fols. 121r–123v). Finally, Scribe X also copied (21a) as Part III. Each of these texts would receive some decoration in either the first or third scheme described above. For his second stint as copyist, in Part I he copied (3) in the space Scribe A left following (2), allowing six blank pages to close out the quire, and in Part II he copied (15), (16), (17), and (19), allowing six blank pages to close out the quire. These texts lack any rubrication or decoration whatsoever. Accordingly, we can ascertain that Scribe X copied these later items in a second stint (the fifth stage), after all decorative work on the manuscript had been completed. It is impossible to determine the precise span of time that elapsed between the final imposition of decoration and the transcription of texts in the second stint.

Scribe X writes his main texts in a neat and flowing hand, modeled primarily on Anglicana Formata, that shows definite influence of Secretary in its overall aspect but adopts few strictly Secretary features (pls. 7, 10–12). Because the texts of his first stint – (8), (18) and (21) – are much neater in appearance than the texts of his second stint – (3), (15)–(17), and (19) – displaying wider spacing between lines and anticipating some form of decoration, there is an argument to be made for terming the later texts hands modeled on Anglicana (or *anglicana libraria*) rather than Anglicana Formata, or for suggesting a pragmatic hybrid between the two. Both "Hand S" and Hand X, as deployed in the later texts, follow the same script, although the brief stint of "Hand S" displays significantly thicker ascenders and descenders. Throughout Scribe X's writings, **w** follows the "113-shaped" Anglicana form – found frequently in Middle English, as "wente wyde in this world wondres to here" in (21a) (fol. 124r; pl. 12) and less frequently in Anglo-Latin, as "Wastinu*s* Wastiniauc" (fol. 26rb; pl. 13, row 1, column 3), "Edwardo" (fol. 90rb), or "Edward*us*" (fol. 117ra; pl. 10). Scribe X uses abbreviations regularly in his Latin texts but sparingly in his copy of *Piers Plowman* (21a).

It is necessary to dispel some confusion present in Rigg's description of the relationship between "Scribe X" and "Hand S" that appear in texts of the second stint. Rigg arranges his description of scribal contributors to Bodley 851 such that each scribe receives one short paragraph, one or two sentences long.[49] His paragraph on Scribe X, however, contains mention also of "hand *S*" that does not receive its own paragraph description:

---

[49] E.g.: "*B* wrote fols 78ra-81va (and presumably the missing quire *ix), Nos. 6–7 at the beginning of Part II. Anglicana Formata; 47 lines per column" (Brewer and Rigg, *Facsimile*, 25).

X wrote No. 3 on fols. 74ra–74va (49 lines per column), No. 8 on fol. 81va and No. 18 on fols. 118va–120vb (48 lines per column); in collaboration with *S* he wrote Nos. 15–17 on fols. 116ra–118rb (here *X* writes 50 lines per column, *S* 54). *X* also wrote Part III(a), fols. 124r–139r, using a darker ink (50 lines per page). He was responsible for the rubric headings in Parts I and II and in the bookplate on fol. 6v. He wrote a small neat Anglicana Formata script, with some broken strokes; hand *S* is an even smaller version of the same script.[50]

I have noted the technical distinction usually made between a "scribe" and a "hand," where the first describes a human agent and the second describes the features of his writing. Rigg's description seems to suggest that "hand S" was imposed by a distinct scribal agent, separate from the person I have been calling "Scribe X," such that they can work "in collaboration."

Three clarifications suggest otherwise. First, Rigg slightly exaggerates the role Hand S plays in this section of the manuscript. Hand S is nowhere present in the text of (15): he contributes 71 lines to (16), a poem of just over 250 lines, and he writes all three lines of (17). This sums to 74 lines in Hand S out of approximately 500 total lines copied during the fifth stage of Scribe X's labor. Second, there are exactly two columns (out of ten) in the relevant section (fols. 116ra–118ra) that run to 54 lines (fol. 17ra–b). Two columns of (16) contain 52 lines (fol. 117va–b), and another two columns contain (or are set to contain) 53 lines. All of these are written fully in Hand X. Third, while there are some clear differences in appearance between Hand X and Hand S, they share the vast majority of notable features. Set side-by-side on fol. 117r, Hand S and Hand X are easily distinguished in their aspect, and especially by their ascenders and descenders, which appear in much thicker strokes in Hand S than in Hand X (pl. 10). Nevertheless, we can understand Hand S to have been modeled on the same script as Hand X, if not on Hand X itself. Moreover, because we know that (15)–(17) were added late in the production of Bodley 851, the different aspect of Hand S may be an artifact of developments in Scribe X's writing style over time. Alternatively, they may have emerged from a pressing need to fit a set amount of textual material into a set amount of space on the page (between (14) and (18)). For these reasons, I consider Hand S a variant hand of Scribe X.

In his rubrication (stage three), most elements of Scribe X's hand remain consistent, despite the more formal appearance in those instances than in the inked texts he copied (pls. 1–5, 8–9, 11, 13). Some differences are noteworthy, however. The form of **a**, while still two-chambered, takes on a slightly more slanted back; and for both **a** and the "Tironian" **et**, a decorative cross-bar is often added or emphasized, such that **a** extends a tick to the right of its back. Perhaps the single most-changed graph in the rubricated headings is **d**, for

---

[50] Brewer and Rigg, *Facsimile*, 25.

which the ascender curls up and away from the bottom chamber as in the Textura graph, rather than back toward it as in the Anglicana graph, which is defined by its counter-clockwise loops.[51] The occasional **d** is formed after the usual fashion, as in the first (but not the second) **d** in "Edwardo" (fol. 90rb). But **d** of the formal type can be found occasionally in Scribe X's body text, especially in (21a), as in "schrodus" or "wondres" (but not "wyde" or "world") (pl. 12; lines 2 and 4).[52] Of some note is his habit of extending the final stroke of "6-shaped" **s**. At the ends of lines, rather than curving back toward the bottom chamber to form a closed (or nearly closed) upper chamber, the upper stroke of final **s** continues in an extended horizontal squiggle, having the appearance of a tail (see the **s** at the end of "passus" in most images in pl. 14; the final **s** in "regis" in pl. 2; in "cantuariensis" in pl. 8; and in "Apocalipsis" in pl. 11).[53] The graph appears to have been formed in the opposite direction as most modern writers today form their **s**: the stroke begins at the bottom of the **s**, then curls up and around to meet itself in a counterclockwise stroke (as in **o**), then curls in a clockwise stroke away to form the upper curve, along with Scribe X's characteristic tail-squiggle. A more elaborate **s** of the secretary type can often be found at the beginnings of words.

Rubrics in the formal version of Hand X have been added to the following items: (1), (2), (9b), (9c), (10–11), (12a), (13), (14), (18), (21a). I will emphasize that the subsection breaks for distinct passūs in (21a), the Z-text of *Piers Plowman*, correspond to the same hand as is used throughout Parts I and II of the manuscript: see, e.g., "passus secundus" on fol. 126v, which displays the same formal **d** and long-tailed **s** (pl. 14, row 1). I will also emphasize that the rubricated chapter headings to the *De nugis curialium* (1), anticipated by Scribe A, were added in the formal, rubricating hand of Scribe X.

In focusing attention on paleographic elements, I have passed over from the first to the third major stage of Scribe X's work on Bodley 851, as described above. That is, I have passed from the features of the hand used in the first stage of his production – the addition of (8), (18), and (21a) – to the features of the hand used in the third stage of his production – the addition of rubricated titles and subtitles – without consideration of the decorative schemes that

---

[51] Derolez remarks upon the influence of Textualis on loopless **d** in Anglicana "from the end of the fourteenth century onwards" (*Gothic Manuscript Books*, 137; and cp. 87); but note common use by university scribes of the base form, as in Parkes, *English Cursive Book Hands*, pl. 16(ii), here accentuated by a clockwise flourish at the top of the ascender.

[52] The first 18 lines of (21a) are slightly more widely spaced, vertically and horizontally, than the rest of the text and have the greatest density of quasi-formal features such as the Textura **d**.

[53] A similar formation, with a slightly less exaggerated tail, appears in another odd copy of *Piers*, the *Ilchester* MS; see *OUMEM*, p. 69 (fig. 14).

were applied to Parts I and II in between (the second stage). This order is by no means a given. It was most common for text to be imposed before rubrication and decoration in medieval manuscripts. In some manuscripts, space for decoration was provided but no decoration was ever imposed. Unlike the provision of illuminated figures, which almost always took place after all other elements were completed, there was no standard practice for the order of imposing rubricated text and penwork initials in the production of manuscripts.[54]

In Bodley 851, rubricated titles and subtitles throughout Parts I, II, and III(a) were added after both initial letters and penwork had been imposed. Clear evidence can be found at the beginning of (9b) on fol. 83va (pl. 8); the title and incipit for (13) on fol. 94vb; and the title and incipit for (18) on fol. 118va (pl. 11). In each of these cases, the rubricated titles follow the contours of the penwork initials seamlessly, without running into the margin. An especially helpful instance for understanding the production of Bodley 851 occurs at the beginning of (1) on fol. 7ra (pl. 2). There, the top bar for the puzzle initial **I** (a letter eight lines in height, imposed in blue and red) intersects with the first letter of the body text (a majuscule **N** in Hand A) while the bottom bar covers over parts of the descenders in line 8 and ascenders in line 9. It was clearly imposed after the inked text had been written. The rubricated text, in turn, uses the red penwork line surrounding the initial **I** as its baseline, such that the descenders for **f** and long **r** cut down into the blue of the initial. The rubricated text was clearly imposed after the initial **I** had been imposed. The same relationship, albeit without a rubricated title, governs the puzzle initial **I** at the beginning of (21a), where Scribe X allowed a tapering indent of 16 lines, and where the **I** can be seen intersecting with the first letter of the body text (pl. 12).

For the texts that received penwork decoration and initial block letters, the style of the letters imposed remains constant throughout. Again of special interest is the similarity of red-and-blue penwork pattern filling the initial **I** for (1) and (21a) (pls. 2, 12); and of further interest is the deployment of initial **S**, which at the beginning of a text is given a three-dot pattern in its fill (pls. 6, 9).

I have also gathered a collection of images to highlight a feature of the penwork decoration less visible in the other images, but present in the decorative scheme throughout Bodley 851 (pls. 13–14; but cp. pls. 2, 4). For these decorated initials, the loops of the penwork around the letter bubble outward and curl around themselves – forming a shape that is nearly face-like,

---

[54] For descriptions of the process of decorating, see *IMS*, 20–2. From Alexandra Gillespie and Daniel Wakelin, eds., *The Production of Books in England 1350–1500* (Cambridge: Cambridge University Press, 2011), see also Stephen Partridge, "Designing the Page," 79–103 and Martha Driver and Michael Orr, "Decorating and Illustrating the Page," 104–28.

looking left with protruding nose or chin and resembling, in my view, a Picasso-esque line-drawing of a pouting old man. In conversation, one colleague termed it "frog-like." This shape appears frequently, though not uniformly, throughout the manuscript – including nearly all floriated initials for (21a), the Z-text of *Piers Plowman* – and may be taken as indicative of the penwork rubricator's style.

There is little room to doubt that the same agent was responsible for all such decorated initial letters in Bodley 851. Whether the decorator was Scribe X himself cannot be ascertained, much less whether he was John Wells of Ramsey. Nevertheless, it is evident that Scribe X was the last contributor of body text prior to decoration – in the form of at least (18) and (21a), and likely (8) – and also that he was responsible for the imposition of rubricated text once decoration had been imposed. He was also responsible for a later group of texts that would never receive any decoration whatsoever.[55] We can therefore associate all penwork decoration with Scribe X's stint as copyist, even if Scribe X did not undertake the work of imposing initial letters himself. As described, penwork initials can be found in the following texts: (1), (2), (7), (9b–c), (10–11), (12a–b), (13), (14), (18), and (21a).

Whereas initial letters were added to the manuscript prior to the addition of any rubricated text, alternating red and blue paraphs were added to the table of contents for (1) and to (6)–(8) after rubricated headings had been imposed. On fol. 7ra, for example, in the incipit to (1), Scribe X (or his agent) left a generous amount of horizontal space (that is, space on the same line) between his inscription of the work's title and his inscription of "Cap*itulum* pr*imum*," where a blue paraph mark has now been inserted (pl. 2). Similarly, in the table of contents to (1) (fols. 72vb–73ra), Scribe X left horizontal space between his rubricated chapter numbers and the titles already provided by Scribe A, as in:

 i· ¶Prologus
 ii ¶Epilogus
(fol. 73rb; pl. 5, rubricated text in bold)

For higher numbered chapters requiring more characters in Roman numerals, however, paraphs can be seen covering over the raised punctus following. A clear example of this can be seen in

 xxvii ¶De quoda*m* prodigio·

---

[55] If the original composition of any of (3), (15)–(17), or (19) could be securely dated after 1388, this alone would confirm that Scribe X was writing on behalf of John Wells but was not himself John Wells. Dating all post-decoration texts in Hand X prior to 1388, however, does not confirm that Scribe X was John Wells.

which before the imposition of paraphs would have read

> **xxvii** • De quoda*m* p*r*odigio•
> (fol. 73rb; pl. 5, rubricated text in bold, paraph underlined to signify blue ink)

The imposition of these paraphs onto (6)–(8) is otherwise unremarkable: whoever did the work mechanically followed the double-virgule markings left behind by each respective scribe (B, X, and C), with the exception of Scribe C's omission of "Chrysogonus" in the first column of (9a). Overall, it is not clear to me according to what pattern or principle various Roman numerals or chapter titles were bracketed between, or followed by, raised points, in the table of contents to (1).

Apart from providing chapter headings in the body of the text and chapter numbers in the table of contents, along with arranging for (if not imposing himself) the inclusion of decorated features, Scribe X also made corrections throughout the text of (1), although not consistently or evenly in every section. Kerby-Fulton has proposed that he made some corrections to (14) as well.[56] The ink he used now stands out darkly, nearly black in comparison with the ink used by Scribe A, though it is impossible to know whether it would have appeared so at the time of writing (pls. 3–4). Indeed, it is unclear exactly when Scribe X undertook his corrections, in relation to his other work on the manuscript, or in what relation to Scribe A. Nevertheless, the corrections made to (1) indicate that Scribe X was at least passingly familiar with the contents of a text he was not directly responsible for copying.

We can gain from his corrections two important pieces of information. First, Scribe X was a reader of Walter Map – so gaining membership in a group of historical agents both elusive and difficult to quantify. Second, when Scribe X acquired (1), either the exemplar Scribe A had used for his transcription (now lost) or some other copy of the text (hitherto unheard of), was available for consultation. He made numerous corrections to the text of (1), which may suggest that he was in possession of a copy.[57] Moreover, this situation matches that proposed above, for shared access between Scribes A and X to a single copy of (14) (itself a representative of a minority recension).[58] Because I discuss the implications of Scribe X's ascription of (18), as well as (1), to Walter Map at length in Chapter 4 of the present monograph, I will leave

---

[56] Kerby-Fulton, "Confronting," 495.

[57] E.g.: "insident" in "insident floribus et mellis" (fol. 8rb), "immitere corrosisq*ue* pe*r*ire" in "de*n*tes p*r*op*r*ios in se fecit immitere corrosisq*ue* pe*r*ire manib*us*" (fol. 8va), or the "e*n*t" of "uitent" in "timeant et uitent ut ille fieri" (fol. 8va), all in *De nugis* 1.10. In these as in most cases, the prior reading has been scraped away to make way for the correction.

[58] See Mann ed. *Speculum Stultorum*, lxiii–cxxv, esp. lxxxiii–lxxxv.

further consideration of this affiliation aside. It is enough, for now, to observe that one scribe responsible for furthering Map's pseudonymous reputation had some significant familiarity with his actual writings.

The Ex Libris (fol. 6v)

The paleographic features I have already described, along with Scribe X's activity as writer, decorator, rubricator, and corrector, serve to substantiate the hypothesis – first proposed by Rigg, later supported by Brewer and (to a degree) Kerby-Fulton – that Scribe X was responsible for the rubricated inscription on the Wells *ex libris* at fol. 6v (pl. 1).[59] Many of the individual graphs represented on the *ex libris* are unremarkable, and it should be emphasized that such a small sample size must remain inconclusive for paleographic inquiry. That said, it is possible to make some tentative observations in favor of an identity between the rubricating hand of Parts I–III(a) and of the rubricating hand of the *ex libris*.

Of special note is the use of formal **d**, discussed above, otherwise not found outside of Hand X in Bodley 851. Further similarities emerge between the formation of the majuscule **R** in "Rameseye" (*ex libris*, fol. 6v) and majuscule **R** in chapter titles in (1), as in "Rege" (fol. 10vb), "Rasone" (fol. 41rb; pl. 13, row 2, column 3), "Rollone" (fol. 42va), and "Recapi*tu*lacio" (fol. 71ra; pl. 4). The majuscule **I** of the *ex libris* in "Iste" and "Iohanni," too, are identical to that used in "Incipit" for various distinctions in (1), as at fols. 24ra 34ra, and 59ra, where *De nugis* 2, 3, and 5 each begin. (At the incipit to *De nugis* 4 on fol. 43, the **I** is missing its crossbar but is formed according to the same motion.) One might further compare forms of majuscule **m** between the *ex libris* ("monacho") and various titles in Parts I and II, especially "magister" in description of Walter Map (fols. 7ra, 118va; pls. 2, 11). Finally, as Kerby-Fulton has noted, the form of *y* in "Rameseye" shows the influence of Middle English, which is to say, in the context of Bodley 851, *Piers Plowman*.[60]

That we can ascribe all rubrics throughout the remainder of the manuscript to a single agent (Scribe X), on the one hand, and that the forms used in that agent's formal hand in Parts I and II correspond to the forms used in rubricated ink within the scroll of the *ex libris*, on the other, suggest strongly that Scribe X was responsible for providing the rubric within the scroll of the *ex libris*.

Some may object that the evidence is too scant to support such a conclusion. Of course, it remains possible that the rubric for the *ex libris* was been imposed by some agent entirely apart from those scribal agents already discussed – say, a "Scribe Z" – who may have worked in close proximity with the artist of the *ex libris*, or with Scribe A, or with Scribe X, or with none of these at all. It is, in fact, always possible to posit two or more scribes employing the same

---

[59] See nn15–18 on pp. 34–5 above.
[60] Kerby-Fulton, "Confronting," 495.

script in two almost identical hands: nothing in paleographic study prevents us from hypothesizing successful imitation between human agents. For the same reason, nothing prevents paleographers in any setting from hypothesizing five scribes, or ten, or fifty, either, where the work of one or two might suffice. The simplest solution, however, and that tacitly assumed by all paleographic work apart from the hotly contested, is to posit a single scribe in response to a single hand in a single manuscript context, even if that hand shows slight variation in its deployment according to size, placement, formality, quality of parchment, and so on.

Accordingly, because the hand used for the *ex libris* corresponds in every distinguishing feature to that used for the rubricated titles elsewhere in Bodley 851, and because it does not correspond substantially to any other hand present in the manuscript, I consider it most likely that Scribe X – rather than some further, unknown, anonymous agent (our "Scribe Z") – was responsible for that writing on the scrollwork, just as he was responsible for all rubrics in Parts I, II, and III(a). While the question cannot be settled conclusively, any further consideration of the *ex libris to* Bodley 851 must take into account the broader contexts of the manuscript's production in accounting for the features of its scripts. It can no longer be "categorically stated that there is no paleographic basis whatever for the proposition that the same hand wrote the *Iste liber constat* assertion and the text on fols. 124r–139r."[61]

Adopting this hypothesis does not necessarily imply that Scribe X himself was the historical person, John Wells. (Nor, for that matter, does the hypothesis preclude such an identification.) The hypothesis does, however, link the *ex libris* concretely to Parts I, II, and III(a) of Bodley 851, and so suggest some connection between the manuscript's total contents up to the point of rubrication and the historical person of John Wells (or else some other Brother John, monk of Ramsey, surname Wells). On the problem of claims to ownership, Kathryn Kerby-Fulton writes:

> The quality of the drawing is astonishing: the brilliant shaded scrollwork of the name "wellis" thematically linking Saint Christopher's oar and the lion are highly sophisticated for England at this date. Lucy Sandler informs me that she knows of no East Anglian or Oxford artist who could have produced comparable chain-and-scrollwork sophistication before 1388 and suggests therefore that London is the likeliest point of origin. The Wells bookplate itself has never been examined before in aid of 851's provenance, partly since it was added to the manuscript at an indeterminate point in relation to the addition of Z. But we know it was added *before* Wells's death in 1388 given the present tense verb of ownership ("constat"), and likely done by a London artist.[62]

---

[61] Kane, "The 'Z-version,'" 911.
[62] Kerby-Fulton, "Confronting," 498.

Why would a scribe write that a book displaying a remarkably well-crafted *ex libris* "belongs" to someone (rather than "belonged" to someone) who is dead? It is, of course, possible that Scribe X had not yet been informed of Wells's death, or that he briefly botched up his Latin conjugations, writing a present tense verb when he meant to write in a past tense. That the book would be prepared for distribution or a broader library collection seems unlikely, given the absence of similar claims to ownership by Wells elsewhere in the manuscript record. While there is no reason to assume that the *ex libris* itself and the rubricated text on its scrollwork were added at the same approximate point in time, there is also no escaping the fact that the ascription rather obviously reads "WELLIS" and that the rubricated script in the scrollwork reads "constat... Johanni."

Whether or not Wells was personally responsible for the transcription of (21a) is impossible to determine. That the transcription declares his ownership of the parts of the manuscript preceding the inclusion of the *ex libris* is inarguable. If the *ex libris* contains rubricated text corresponding to some concrete collection of texts, then Wells's ownership, too, should be considered over that same collection of texts.

Therefore, the material evidence points to an association between the elaborate scrollwork, John Wells, and Parts I–III(a) of Bodley 851, which at that time would have included: (1) *De nugis curialium*, (2) the *Fall of Carthage*; (6) *Ave virgo mater christi*, (7) *De coniuge non ducenda*, (8) *Debate between heart and eye*, (9a-c) Michael of Cornwall's three *Invectives* (10–11) the anonymous "Pergama flere volo" and its companion the anonymous "Viribus arte minis danaum," (12a) the Bridlington *Prophecy*, (12b) "Cambri carnaruan," (13) *Babio*, (14) *Speculum stultorum* with epistle, (18) *Apocalypsis goliae episcopi*, and (21a) the Z-text of *Piers Plowman*. It is important to emphasize that the mixed contents of MS Bodley 851 could for the first time truly be considered a *collection* – in the sense of a group of texts intentionally bound together according to some governing purpose or plan – with the texts of Scribe X's second stint still absent from the manuscript.

Above, we observed that what Scribe A left behind was more likely a "them" than an "it" – two collections of parchment, the first almost entirely defined by the text of (1) and the second consisting of texts (6)–(14) without (8). These were copied but undecorated, clearly unfinished and not clearly associated with one another according to any material metric. With the imposition of rubricated organizing material, along with two parallel decorative schemes either in the hand of or under the direction of Scribe X, it becomes possible to refer to the group of inked, decorated, rubricated parchment comprising quires iii–xiv as a single collection. Although Parts I, II, and III(a) were not yet bound, they nevertheless shared features that would associate a concrete selection of texts with one another, as named above: (1), (2); (6)–(14), (18);

and (21a). It is this collection of texts that belonged to "Fratri Johanni de monacho Rameseye."

Unfortunately, it is impossible to determine whether quire(s) *ix, now missing, were missing by the time this collection of texts came into being. So, it is impossible to determine whether the collection, as Scribe X fashioned it, included the companion texts originally transcribed along with (6)–(7). It is nevertheless certain that with Scribe X we can for the first time confidently refer to a single textual collection, well before the various material parts of Bodley 851 were to be formally bound together.

Table 2. Analytic overview of BodL. MS Bodley 851. Arranged to reflect production of the manuscript over time. This table contains the same information as is listed in Fig. 1 (pp. 6–7), reordered according to the chronology of the manuscript's production (**Added No.**) rather than the manuscript's current arrangement.

Added No.	Title	Scribe	Rigg No.	Part
1	Ave virgo mater christi	B	6	II
2	De coniuge non ducenda	B	7	II
3	Michael of Cornwall, First Invective	C	9a	II
4	Michael of Cornwall, Second and Third Invectives	A	9b–c	II
5	Fall of Troy	A	10-11	II
6	Bridlington Prophecy	A	12a	II
7	Cambri carnaruan	A	12b	II
8	Babio	A	13	II
9	Speculum Stultorum	A	14	II
10	De nugis curialium	A	1	I
11	Fall of Carthage	A	2	I
Decoration imposed: scheme #2				
12	Debate between heart and eye	X	8	II
13	Apocalypsis goliae episcopi	X	18	II
14	Piers Plowman: Z-text	X	21(a)	III
Decoration imposed: scheme #1, scheme #3				
Rubrication imposed				
15	Epistola sathanae	X	3	I
16	Battle of Neville's Cross	X	15	II

17	Battle of Crécy	X	16	II
18	Untitled verse (three lines)	X	17	II
19	Untitled riddle	X	19	II
20	Convocacio sacerdotum	Dod	5	I
21	Geta	Dod	20	II
22	Execution of Archbishop Scrope	Y	4	I
23	Piers Plowman: A-text continuation	Q	21(b)	III
24	Piers Plowman: C-text continuation	Q	21(c)	III

When a Book Becomes a Book

The unity of Bodley 851, absent its binding, gestures towards a broader difficulty at the intersection of codicological study and literary analysis, namely: at what point in time is it possible to analyze a *codex* – or, at least, a *collection* – rather than some assortment of unrelated material quires bearing texts? In an antagonistic review article of Brewer and Rigg's text-edition of the Z-text in Bodley 851, George Kane noted that "MS Bodley 851 did not exist as an entity until the fifteenth century," by which he meant that the manuscript did not "exist as an entity" until it was bound, possibly by Dodsthorpe, in 1450 or later.[63] Accordingly, Kane considered any analysis of the text of *Piers Plowman* present within Bodley 851 prior to the fifteenth century "not a hypothesis in any strict sense, but an assemblage of arguments, linked by iterative assertion, in support of a poorly based and admittedly subjective literary opinion."[64] Of course, Kane's judgment as a textual critic carries substantial weight. Yet, his codicological assumption is characteristic of how editors might underestimate the evidence from manuscript production in tracing textual likeness. For Kane, to identify a date of binding is to identify the point in time at which it becomes possible to discuss the collection as a *book*, rather than as some assortment of disparate textual data. In the exemplary case of Bodley 851, however – as representative of many composite manuscripts – codicological analysis identifies a significantly earlier moment in the production of the manuscript when the assortment of parchment can accurately be termed a *collection*. This moment comes, for Bodley 851, not with binding but with the imposition of regular rubrication and decoration. In that moment, the collection could have contained *more* text than it does now, particularly within the absent quire *ix, but it could not have contained *less*. Accordingly, while the scope of *The Making and Meaning of a Medieval Manuscript* is not

---

[63] Kane, "The 'Z Version,'" 911.
[64] Kane, "The 'Z-version,'" 910–11.

comprehensive of all possible historical content, it is precise with respect to surviving material evidence. The method of recomposition offers perspective on surviving material evidence: it does not offer totalizing perspective on evidence that may have been lost.

Insofar as the compilation of the book is concerned, whatever the *ex libris* might signify, we must admit that Bodley 851 is fundamentally Scribe X's manuscript. Scribe X's broad investment in the quality of the whole of the manuscript serves to shore up a claim latent in Brewer and Rigg's much more ambitious argument about the identity of Scribe X: namely, that John Wells was the *owner* of Bodley 851, even if he was not its primary scribe. If Scribe X was not himself John Wells, he nevertheless played the most significant overarching role in compiling John Wells's book. We can safely locate all rubrication and decoration within the span of his activity. And we can plausibly attribute to him the final touches on the folio declaring ownership of his collection to John Wells. For Scribe X, whoever he was, either the manuscript looked much the way it does today, or he endeavored to make it so.

By the time Scribe Q, Dodsthorpe, and Scribe Y came to possess Bodley 851, it was in a mostly complete state, although its completeness did not stop them from adding further material where they saw fit. Scribe Q – perhaps Q^1 and Q^2 – contributed a long extension of *Piers Plowman* to Part III in a fifteenth-century secretary hand, appearing initially to follow a text from the A-tradition (21b) and eventually settling into a textually unremarkable copy in the C-tradition (21c). Between Dodsthorpe and Scribe Y, final material was added to the folios already present – first the *Convocatio sacerdotum* (5) and then the *Execution of Archbishop Scrope* (4) to Part I, as well as the *Geta* of Vitalis of Blois (20) to Part II. Dodsthorpe supplied an extra quire to the beginning of the manuscript, to which he added further textual material. He also added floral symbols in the margins of some texts (e.g., pl. 3). Sometime in the fifteenth century, a final compiler, perhaps Dodsthorpe himself, provided some extra end-leaves, crammed an astonishing amount of poetic material in a cramped hand to its flyleaves, and bound the manuscript in its current state.

What remains to be said by way of conclusion to this chapter is limited. Two arguments bear repeating, however. First, and most importantly, it must be understood that how we go about describing the material production of a given manuscript object delimits how we can go about describing the literary relationships between its component texts. A simple list of contents, as in a standard catalogue entry, hardly provides enough information for even the most astute researcher to trace material and historical connections available between disparate medieval texts in a given mixed-content manuscript. Moreover, such lists often obscure divisions of scribal labor between texts that appear self-evidently similar to us, according to modern generic conventions. So, where scholarship might be inclined to group the *Apocalypsis goliae* (18) with the *De coniuge non ducenda* (7) as goliardic texts, Scribe B instead grouped the

De coniuge (7) with Walter of Wimborne's devotional work, *Ave virgo mater christi* (6), while Scribe X drew a concrete connection (by way of authorial ascription) between the *Apocalypsis goliae* (18) and Walter Map's *De nugis curialium* (1). The work of descriptive codicology such as that begun by Rigg in the 1970s must be understood as foundational for any medieval literary study that accounts for scribal agency. Such work must also be supplemented, however, with analytic codicology – the recomposition of material production over time absent any necessary return to external or absolute chronologies.

Second, the date of binding need not be binding for assessment of manuscript compilations in literary criticism or textual criticism. The Z-text of *Piers Plowman* in Bodley 851 provides a memorable – because inherently contentious – example of how a coherent manuscript collection might be identified prior to any formal binding process. Many late-medieval and early modern manuscripts would benefit from further analysis according to a similar mode of approach. Our understanding of medieval compilations as disparate in origin and contents as MS Digby 166, Harley MS 978, and Cotton MS Titus A.20, early modern compilations such as Cambridge, Corpus Christi College MS 450 and Bodleian Library MS Lat. misc. c. 75, and medieval-and-early-modern composites such as the Bekynton anthology – all manuscripts that I mentioned as comparable to Bodley 851 in the introduction to this book – might benefit from closer attention to how their component parts came to be materially related. Such manuscripts are more than repositories of texts: they are material evidence for how texts came to be, and be read, by historical agents otherwise inaccessible to us.

The complexity involved in recomposing Bodley 851 makes it a difficult test case. On account of its difficulty, the same complexity makes this manuscript collection an especially interesting model for future study. Most essential to the method I have proposed is the uncovering of relation among material texts within the confines of a specific and unique codicological object as made evident by the idiosyncratic traces of a series of historical agents still observable upon that object. The object itself can in this way only be defined through close examination of scribal labor. Though historical scribes were not, in the formulation I propose, necessarily "authors" – nor even, in Bonaventure's oft-cited fourfold division, were many of them "compilers" – the effects of their actions can clarify interpretive possibilities present in, between, and among the material texts they inscribed.[65]

---

[65] For the classic discussion of Bonaventure's fourfold distinction, see Alastair Minnis, *Medieval Theory of Authorship: Scholastic Literary Attitudes in the Later Middle Ages*, 2nd ed. (Philadelphia, PA: University of Pennsylvania Press, 2010); for a stronger claim that most medieval scribes acted in an authorial capacity, see Matthew Fisher, *Scribal Authorship and the Writing of History in Medieval England* (Columbus, OH: Ohio State University Press, 2012); and for evidence of scribal attentiveness

Moreover, by blurring some familiar relationships between texts – particularly those already blurry categories we are accustomed to calling "genres" – according to their material contexts, we can see some less familiar relationships come into focus, in arrangements productive for our contemporary reconstruction of the medieval reading experience. Such relations can only be perceived as critically relevant according to their own local features. Small changes in perspective alter our material and critical perceptions of how a manuscript came into being and where literary resemblances between its contents lie.

---

to literary detail in the act of copying, see Daniel Wakelin, *Scribal Correction and Literary Craft: English Manuscripts 1375–1510*, 91 (Cambridge: Cambridge University Press, 2014). Of relevance is McKenzie, *Sociology of Texts*; but see also Peter L. Shillingsburg, "The Semiotics of Bibliography", in *Textuality and Knowledge: Essays* (University Park, PA: The Pennsylvania State University Press, 2017), 28–47, especially the acute observation that "The significance of the sociological confluence of events is vested in, and indexed by, the whole *material* text – the tangible product of the forces at work at the time – not by the lexical text alone" (40).

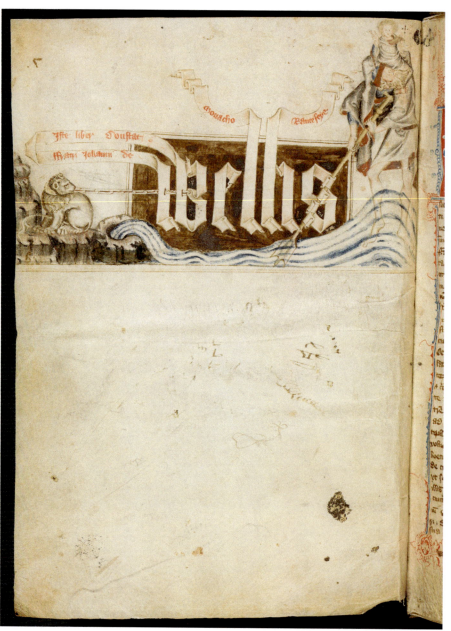

Plate 1   BodL. MS Bodley 851, fol. 6v. Showing *ex libris*. To the left, a lion and a font; to the right, St. Christopher bearing the Christ-child. Center, elaborate scrollwork reading "wellis," now bearing rubricated text.

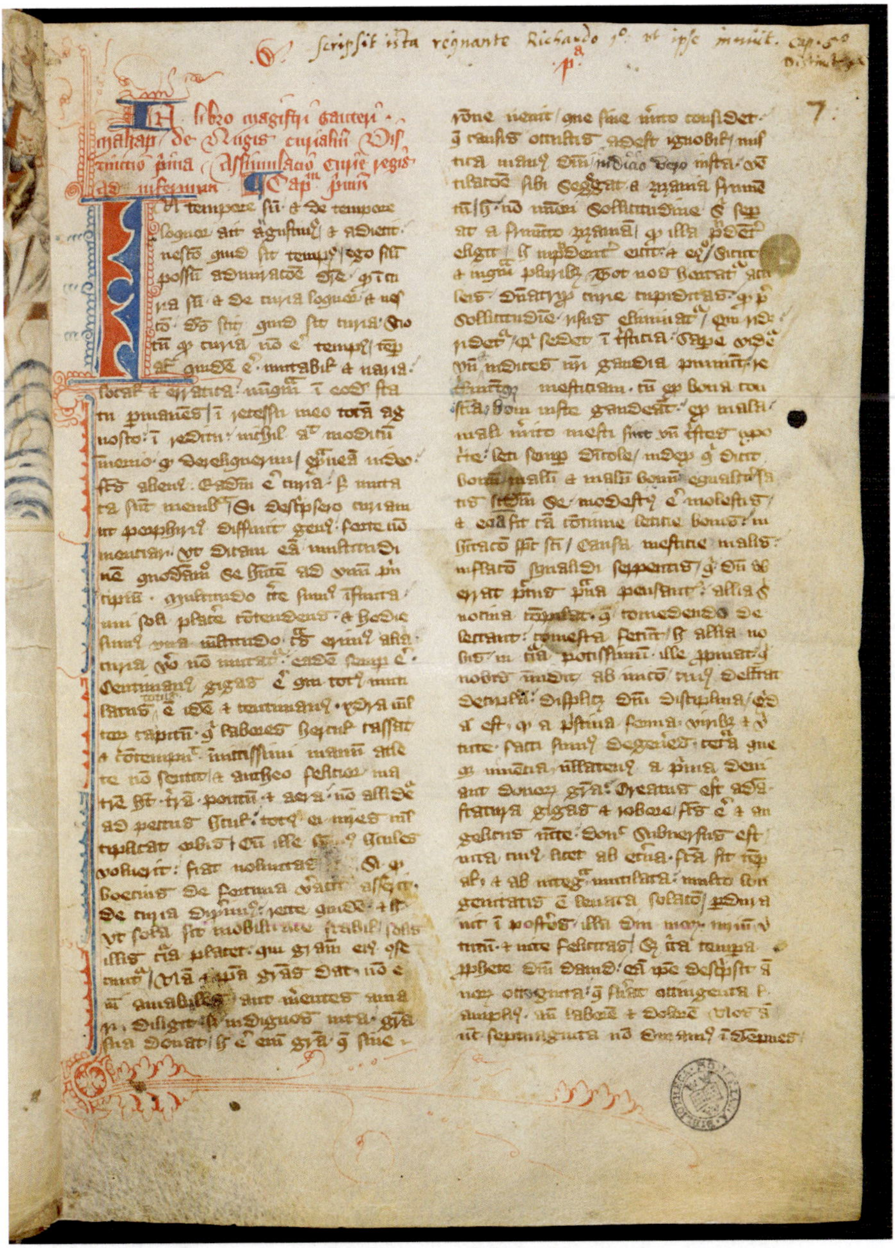

Plate 2   BodL. MS Bodley 851, fol. 7r. Showing (1) in Hand A and rubricated title in Hand X, with penwork puzzle initial **I** eight lines in height. Note blemishes on page, also visible on reverse (fol. 7v). Note penwork face in floriation for **I**, as in pl. 13.

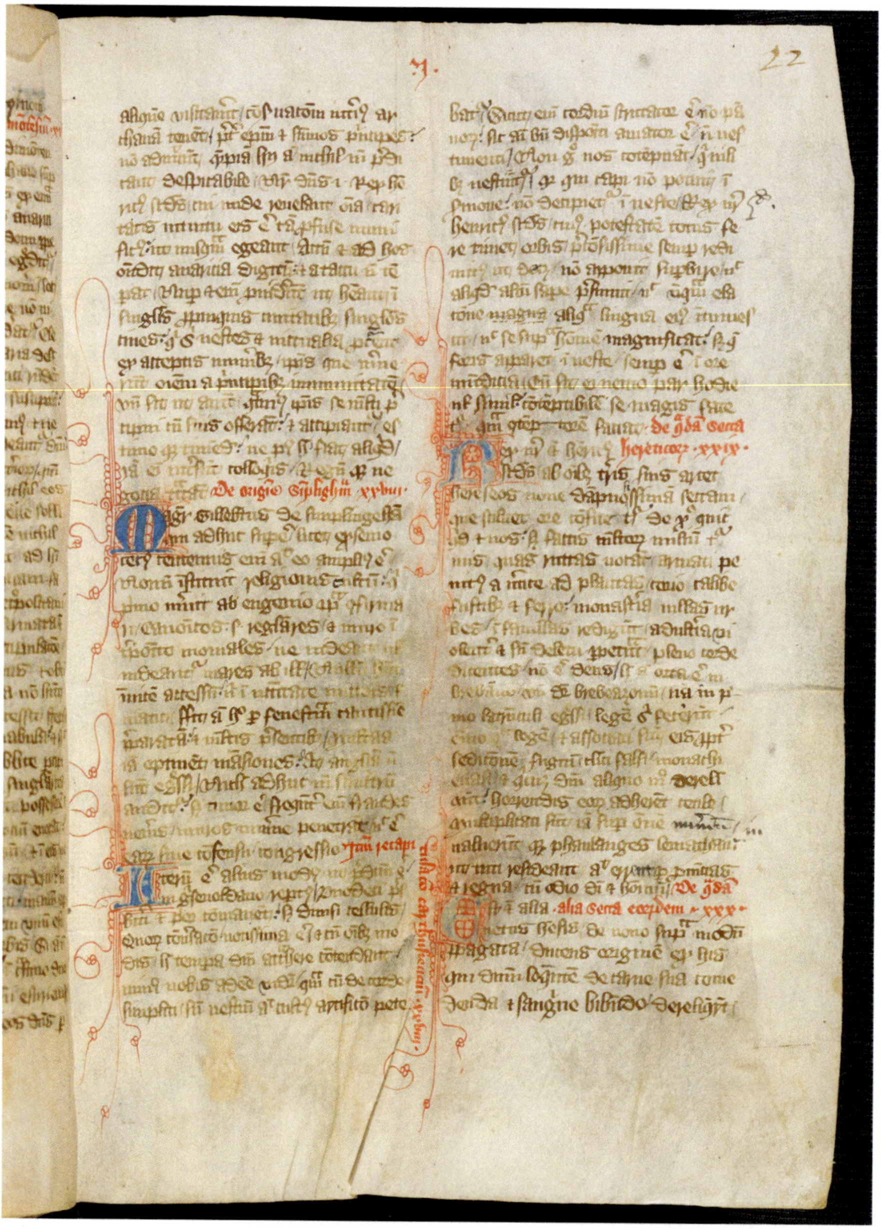

Plate 3   BodL. MS Bodley 851, fol. 22r. Showing (1) in Hand A and rubricated titles in Hand X, with penwork initials in blue and floriation in red. Note the regular deployment of chapter titles, with one noteworthy exception running vertically in center margin. Note also two layers of corrections in darker ink.

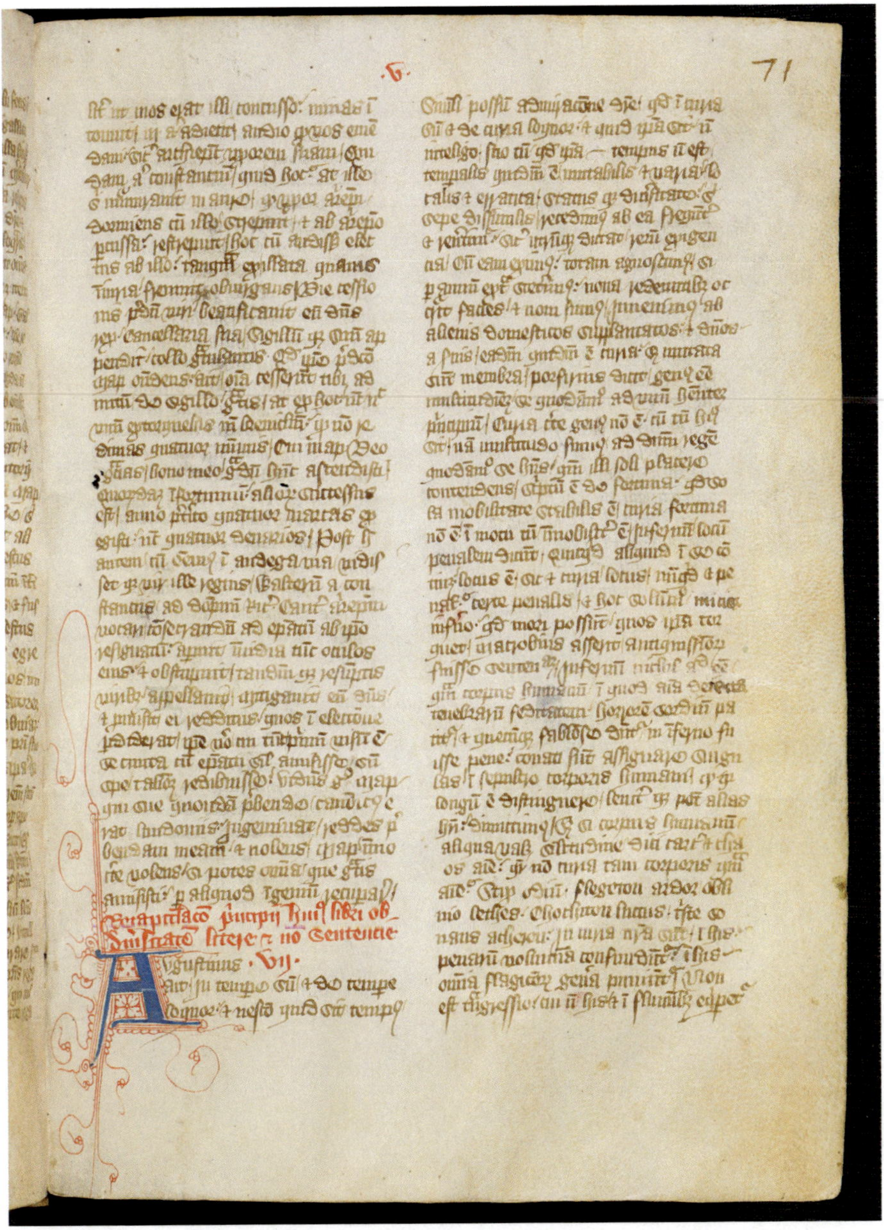

Plate 4   BodL. MS Bodley 851, fol. 71r. Showing (1) in Hand A and rubricated title in Hand X, with relatively few corrections, ample space set aside for title, and chapter number set intentionally into first line of inked text. Note penwork face in floriation for penwork initial **A**, as in pl. 13.

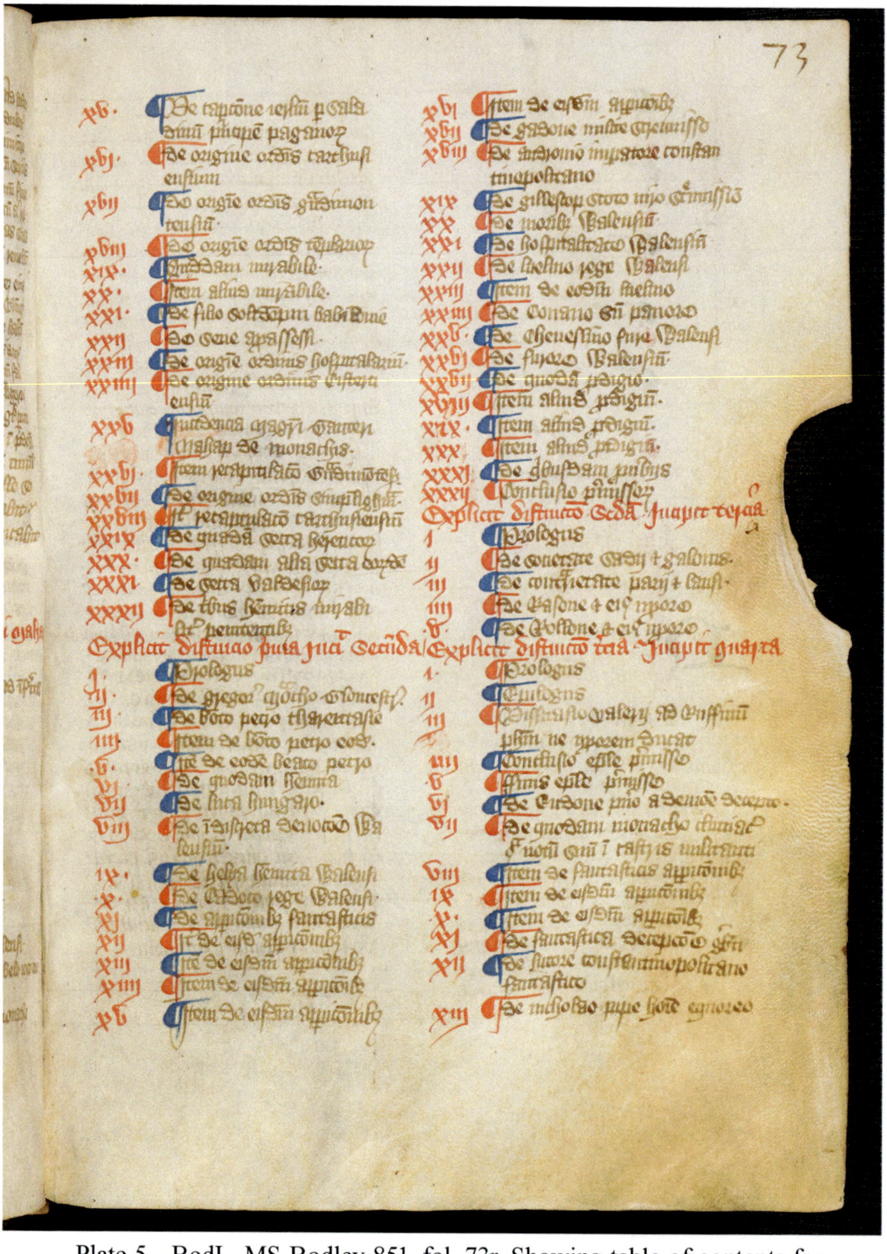

Plate 5 BodL. MS Bodley 851, fol. 73r. Showing table of contents for (1) in Hand A with rubrication in Hand X, with alternating red and blue paraphs. Note occasional erasure of rubricated numerals for longer titles.

Plate 6   BodL. MS Bodley 851, fol. 80v. Showing (7) in Hand B, with alternating red and blue paraphs, initial inked letters touched in red, and a penwork initial **S** of four lines in height.

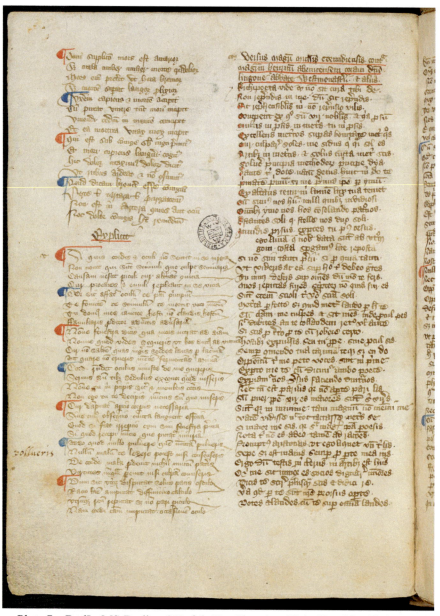

Plate 7 BodL. MS Bodley 851, fol. 81v. Showing (7) in Hand B, (8) in Hand X, and (9a) in Hand C, with alternating red and blue paraphs and some initial inked letters touched in red. Note rubricated underlining for the title to (9a).

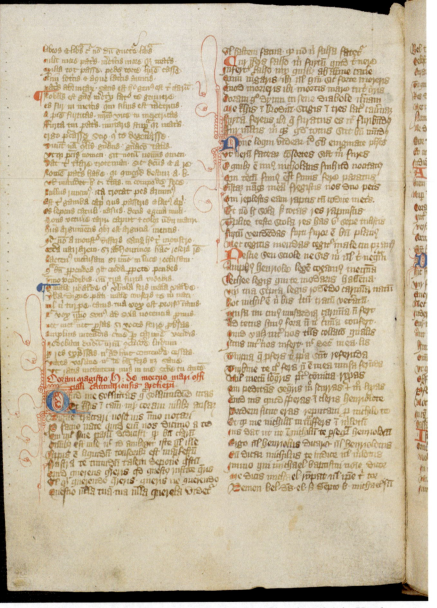

Plate 8 BodL. MS Bodley 851, fol. 83v. Showing (9a) in Hand C, (9b) in Hand A, and rubricated title in Hand X between; along with alternating paraphs and initial inked letters touched in red. Note the lack of penwork floriation for initials in red.

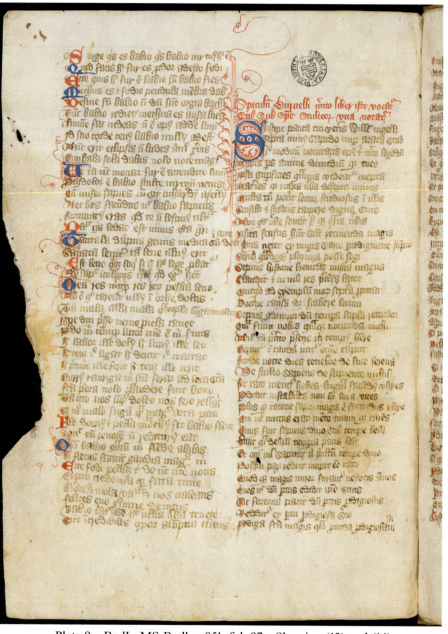

Plate 9   BodL. MS Bodley 851, fol. 97v. Showing (13) and (14) in Hand A and rubricated title in Hand X, with initial inked letters touched in red and alternating penwork initials.

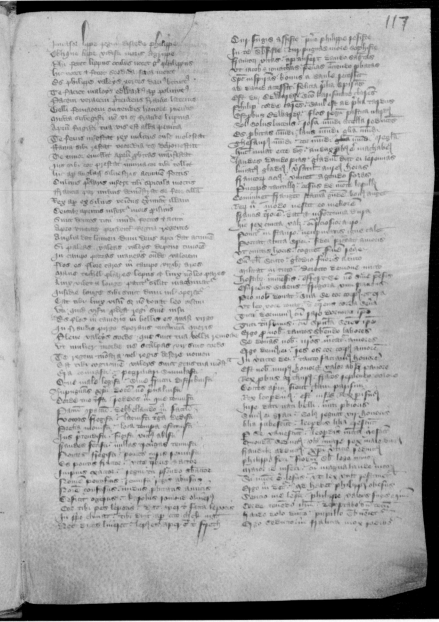

Plate 10 BodL. MS Bodley 851, fol. 117r. Showing (16) in Hands X and S. Note "Edwardus" in column 1, line 6, with **w** and both forms of **d** in the Latin text.

Plate 11 BodL. MS Bodley 851, fol. 118v. Showing (18) in Hand X with rubricated title in Hand X, with penwork initials alternating in red and blue, and penwork initial **A** four lines in height.

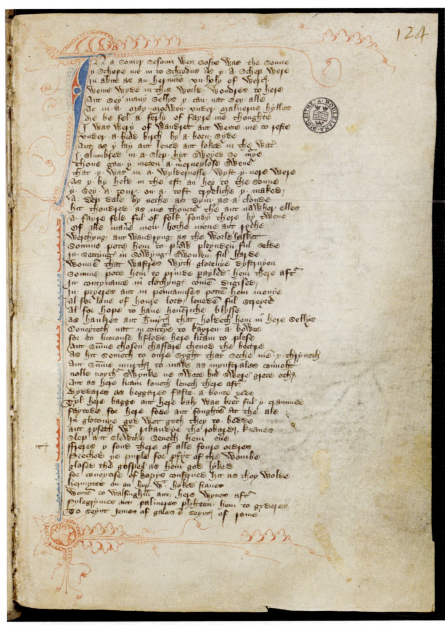

Plate 12 BodL. MS Bodley 851, fol. 124r. Showing (21a) in Hand X, with penwork puzzle initial **I** seventeen lines in height.

Plate 13   BodL. MS Bodley 851, fols. (row 1) 17vb (detail), 25vb (detail), 26rb (detail); (row 2) 27va (detail), 33vb (detail), 41rb (detail); (row 3) 44ra (detail), 55rb (detail), 59ra (detail); (row 4) 59vb (detail), 63ra (detail), 73va (detail); (row 5) 111vb (detail), 112ra (detail), 119rb (detail); (row 6) 119va (detail), 119vb (detail), and 120ra (detail). Showing penwork face-like or frog-like squiggle in floriation throughout Parts I and II.

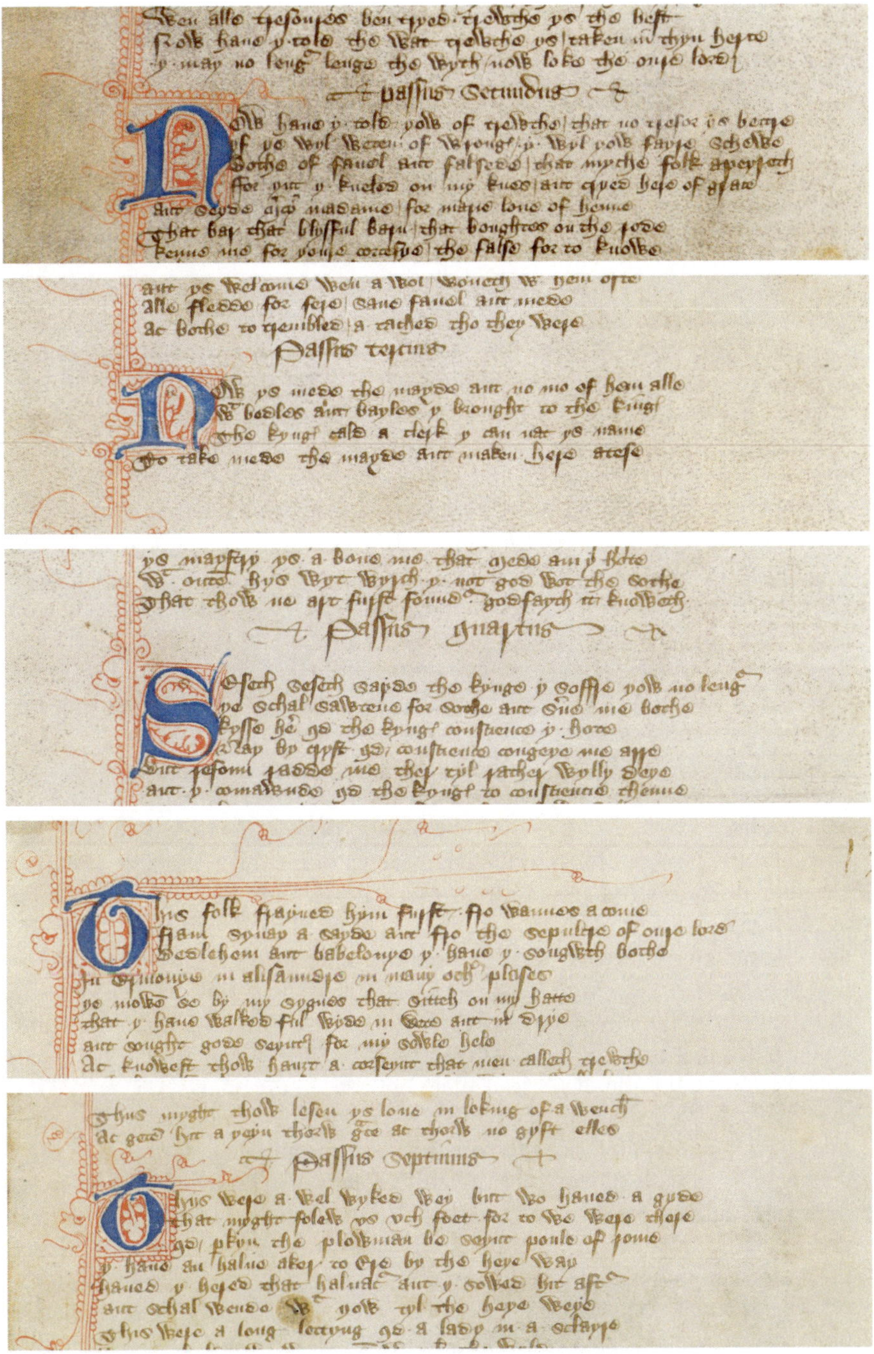

Plate 14 BodL. MS Bodley 851, fols. 126v (detail), 128v (detail),
130v (detail), 134r (detail), and 135r (detail). Showing penwork
face-like or frog-like squiggle in floriation for (21a).

2

Misogamist Fragments

Following the recomposition of Bodley 851 undertaken in Chapter 1, this chapter begins where Bodley 851 began, with the only two texts transcribed by Scribe B into the oldest remaining material portion of the manuscript (Part II, fols. 78r–81v). Scribe B copied what survives as a partial text of Walter of Wimborne's *Ave virgo mater christi* ("Hail virgin mother of Christ") and a scribal copy of the anonymous *De coniuge non ducenda* ("On the necessity of avoiding marriage"). I ask how the unique material affiliation between the *Ave virgo* and the *De coniuge* might reveal concomitant literary, historical, and cultural affiliations between these two poems. I argue that the convergence of the *Ave virgo* and the *De coniuge* in quire ix reveals a refracted perspective on misogamist discourse otherwise unavailable to modern scholarship oriented around familiar categories of genre, authorship, topic, and theme. I examine Scribe B's surviving texts in order to pose a straightforward but difficult question of interpretation: how might the modern literary critic go about reading these two poems – and only these two poems – together, comparatively, as interlocutors rather than in isolation?

    The *Ave virgo* and *De coniuge* together provide a single window into two familiar, but not often combined, currents of medieval thought, bringing together devotion and prejudice in one cultural complex at once easy to acknowledge and difficult to describe. In order to understand the swirling and contradictory impulses that characterize the earliest fragment of Bodley 851, it is necessary to understand the breadth and weight of misogynous and misogamist discourse, on the one hand, and the intensity of Marian devotion, on the other, that characterized reading practices in the thirteenth and fourteenth centuries in both Latin and vernacular contexts. In my analysis, I invoke the misogynist book described by Chaucer's Wife of Bath. The looming presence of the Wife of Bath's Prologue serves two purposes: first, as a text at once deeply imbued with and straightforwardly conscious of the negative valences of medieval discourse around women; and, second, as a text with a rich critical and theoretical history canonically representative of fourteenth-century literary production on the whole. The bulk of this chapter, however, engages with the two specific texts that Scribe B compiled, and it is on account of their relative obscurity in current scholarship that I provide an overview of their contents and comparative manuscript situations as well.

The method I have adopted does not pre-determine topical or thematic material for discussion: subsequent chapters need not address identical conceptual figures, even as they address the same material object. Instead, topical and thematic material for discussion in this chapter follows from the choice of manuscript made subject of examination. Accordingly, although my research method is not motivated by any specifically feminist research questions – concerning, for example representations of gendered agency or abstracted cultural identities – the conversation between medieval misogyny and Marian devotion appears at once familiar and surprising in the context of Bodley 851. For Scribe B's texts as interlocutors, spiritual practice and social pragmatics circulate together in a single, mutually dysfunctional, textual apparatus. What follows from a critical examination of these texts on their own terms is in many respects an account of ways in which the two poems fail to establish the kind of topical coherence modern scholarship sometimes takes for granted. If it is the case that medieval readers thought of Mary in categorically different terms than they did all living women, then it is also the case that the uncommon pairing of Marian and anti-matrimonial material in Bodley 851 remains opaque to perspectives already available in modern scholarship on Marian devotion and misogynist representations of women in late-medieval literature.

Only the specific material contingency of these two poems preserved together within the bindings of Bodley 851 might cause a modern reader to focus critical attention on the material contingencies of the women they imagine. The self-contradicting feminine ideal captured by the unique conjunction of the *Ave virgo* and the *De coniuge* is neither static nor familiar, though it may – in the end – be productively framed in terms of more familiar critical perspectives on medieval misogyny, misogamy, and anti-feminism. These two poems are not a "book of wicked wives" in miniature, nor do they participate evenly (though their debts are immediately recognizable) within a prominent form of late-medieval cultural discourse. Between these two poems, we might emphasize how contingent any representation of gendered agency might be, even in the most apparently overdetermined literary and historical contexts.

Misogyny, Misogamy, and the Medieval Book

What is in a book of wicked wives? The question and its best-known answer come from Geoffrey Chaucer's Wife of Bath, in her description of one such manuscript owned by her fifth husband, Jankyn, a clerk of Oxford. According to Alison, although the compilation contained various antifeminist materials "bounden in o volume," Jankyn called his book, "Valerie and Theofraste" (*Wife of Bath's Prologue* III 681, 671).[1] The shorthand title refers to two tracts

---

[1] Quotations from Chaucer's works are cited parenthetically from Geoffrey Chaucer, *The Riverside Chaucer*, ed. Larry Benson *et al.*, 3rd ed. (Boston, MA: Houghton Mifflin, 1987).

against marriage familiar to medieval European audiences: Walter Map's *Dissuasio Valerii ad Rufinum* (*Valerius Dissuades Rufus* [c. 1170]), for which Map adopted the pseudonym "Valerius"; and Theophrastus's *Aureolus liber de nuptiis* (*Golden Book on Marriage*; c. 300 BCE ?), which may in fact be a fabrication of Jerome's (393 CE).[2] The two texts share a rhetorical enthusiasm for scorning marriage; and Map's diatribe adopts a characteristically clerkly stance in its disdain for women as morally compromised, sexually voracious, and too-embodied.[3] As Eve "gave birth to disobedience," the *Dissuasio* proclaims, "disobedience will not cease to overcome women until the end of the world, so that they never tire of dragging out to its full consequences what they first drew from their mother."[4] Alongside these two most notable components, Jankyn's book also contained an impressive collection of further texts loosely united by their interest in how to represent medieval women, female bodies, and feminine desire. Alison names, with varying degrees of precision, Jerome's *Against Jovinian*, Tertullian, Chrysippus, Trotula, Héloïse, Ovid's *Ars amatoria*, and excerpts from Proverbs; and her prologue further suggests the book contained excerpts from Ecclesiasticus and selections from Valerius Maximus's *Memorable Doings and Sayings* (*Wife of Bath's Prologue* III 634–53, 666–81).

Scholars have long observed that the texts listed by Alison are "identifiable": they existed in medieval copy and can be examined in extant medieval manuscripts. For just as long, however, scholars have conceded that it is unlikely Chaucer had access, still less immediate and continuous access, to all of the texts his imagined Wife names for her imagined husband's imagined book.[5] For many references, Chaucer likely relied on compilations of extracts, or *florilegia*, such as the *Communiloquium* of John of Wales, that spoke to a

---

[2] Ralph Hanna and Traugott Lawler, *Jankyn's Book of Wikked Wyves*, vol. 1 (Athens, GA: University of Georgia Press, 1997).

[3] For concise reviews of antifeminist rhetoric in the later Middle Ages and into modernity, see Alcuin Blamires, *The Case for Women in Medieval Culture* (Oxford: Oxford University Press, 1997); and Holly A. Crocker, *The Matter of Virtue* (Philadelphia, PA: University of Pennsylvania Press, 2019). See also the essays collected in the Colloquium on "Historicizing Consent," eds. Carissa M. Harris and Fiona Somerset, in *SAC* (2022): 268–367.

[4] Hanna and Lawler, *Jankyn's Book*, 1:124–7. "Parentavit inobedientiam, que citra mundi terminum non absistet expugnare feminas ut sint semper indefesse trahere in consequentiam quod a matre sua traxerunt."

[5] Hanna and Lawler, *Jankyn's Book*, surpasses previous scholarship and has become the standard authoritative source on medieval antifeminist compilations. But see the work of Robert A. Pratt, to which Hanna and Lawler turn often, especially: "The Development of the Wife of Bath," in *Studies in Medieval Literature: In Honor of Professor Albert Croll Baugh*, ed. MacEdward Leach (Philadelphia, PA: University of Pennsylvania Press, 1961), 45–79; "Jankyn's Book of Wikked Wyves: Medieval

wide variety of topics and themes apart from the representation of wives and women.[6] While granting the existence of composite manuscripts of the kind Alison describes, book historians note that the sheer breadth of textual material named for Jankyn's book of wicked wives suggests exaggeration verging on parody. No surviving manuscript begins to accommodate the breadth of its constituent texts, and insofar these survive in medieval manuscripts, they do not routinely accompany one another.

If, as Alison famously declares, "experience... is right enough" (*Wife of Bath's Prologue* III 1) for her to understand the breadth and extremity of medieval prejudices against women, and especially against wives, it remains the case that her experience is also a literary fiction produced, in part, by an exaggerated textual compilation. Her experience, like Jankyn's staggeringly capacious collection of misogamous authorities, reveals much about how a medieval author and his audiences may have thought about women, wives, and marriage. The richness of Chaucer's *Wife of Bath's Prologue* and *Tale*, however, should not cause modern readers to assume that the fiction of Jankyn's book can provide unmediated access to the medieval experience of reading "Valerie and Theofraste." Nor does the fiction of Alison's experience provide unmediated access to the medieval experience of suffering from the effects of medieval misogyny. The historical value of both compilations – Jankyn's and Chaucer's – derives from their imaginative force, rather than from the transparency of their gendered representations.

Still, late-medieval readers recognized the breadth and relative uniformity of misogamous writing. In a letter addressed to Pierre Col, dated 2 October 1402, Christine de Pizan tells of a man accustomed to use *The Romance of the Rose* as a self-sufficient testament to the sinfulness of wives. "When his passion takes hold of him most violently," de Pizan writes,

> he goes to fetch his book, reads it before his wife, and then he strikes her and beats her up, saying: "Foul woman, just like the one he speaks of, truly you are playing the same kind of trick on me. That good and wise man Master Jean de Meun knew well what women are capable

---

Antimatrimonial Propaganda in the Universities," *Annuale Mediaevale* 3 (1962): 5–27; and "Saint Jerome in Jankyn's Book of Wikked Wyves," *Criticism* 5 (1963): 316–22.

[6] Robert A. Pratt, "Chaucer and the Hand That Fed Him," *Speculum* 41.4 (1966): 619–42. Pratt's analysis is not limited to the *Wife of Bath's Tale*. For the medieval use of compilations of extracts more generally, see Richard H. Rouse and Mary A. Rouse, *Preachers, Florilegia and Sermons: Studies on the Manipulus Florum of Thomas of Ireland* (Toronto: Pontifical Institute of Mediaeval Studies, 1979) and the relevant sequence in *Authentic Witnesses: Approaches to Medieval Texts and Manuscripts* (Notre Dame, IN: University of Notre Dame Press, 1991), 101–258. On John of Wales, see Jenny Swanson, *John of Wales: A Study of the Works and Ideas of a Thirteenth-Century Friar* (Cambridge: Cambridge University Press, 1989).

of doing!" And at each word that he finds applicable to him he strikes a blow or two with his foot or the palm of his hand.[7]

Although they disagree about the moral efficacy of such a book, both de Pizan and the domestic abuser she describes share the opinion that the *Rose* serves to vilify women generally and wives specifically.

Texts like Map's *Dissuasio*, Jerome's *Against Jovinian*, and the *Rose* had an enormous influence on late-medieval readers – such as de Pizan and Chaucer.[8] They gained immense and immediate pan-European popularity, spawning imitations, translations, commentaries, and countless conversations in multiplying social spheres. From these same texts, modern critics have learned the most basic features of medieval misogyny: what it was like, around the turn of the fourteenth century, to express prejudice against wives and women.

I treat medieval misogamy as a type of medieval misogyny. Most basically, misogyny refers to any "hatred or dislike of, or prejudice against women."[9] As psychoanalytic theorists have long argued, however, misogyny often corresponds to "a male fear of female sexuality" that is also "a projection of male fear of male sexuality."[10] Moreover misogyny need not be limited to individual feeling, as in the passions of de Pizan's domestic abuser. Kate Manne has described misogyny in structural terms, as "the system that operates within a patriarchal social order to police and enforce women's subordination and to uphold male dominance."[11] Misogamy, likewise, can take more or less overt and individuated forms, sometimes in competition but more frequently operating in tandem with one another. The case of Map's *Dissuasio*, as cited above, is indicative of the typical relation between misogyny and misogamy in medieval texts. Map claims to argue not against women in general but against

---

[7] David F. Hult, ed., *Debate of the Romance of the Rose* (Chicago, IL: University of Chicago Press, 2010), 182.

[8] Writing of a later context, Helen Swift observes that "generally speaking, each work [i.e., each literary defense of women] defines its position in relation to one of two threads of literary tradition: to the catalogue form stemming from Boccaccio's *De mulieribus claris*, and its French translations, or to the debate tradition which takes issue with the alleged literary misogynists Jean de Meun and Matheolus, and which thus participates in the reception history of the late medieval best seller *Le Roman de la rose*" (Helen J. Swift, *Gender, Writing, and Performance: Men Defending Women in Late Medieval France, 1440–1538* [Oxford: Oxford University Press, 2008], 6–7). See also Renate Blumenfeld-Kosinski, "Christine De Pizan and the Misogynistic Tradition," *Romanic Review* 81.3 (1990): 279–92.

[9] *OED*, s.v. "misogyny."

[10] Caroline Walker Bynum, *Holy Feast and Holy Fast: The Religious Significance of Food to Medieval Women* (Berkeley, CA: University of California Press, 1987), 15.

[11] Kate Manne, *Down Girl: The Logic of Misogyny* (Oxford: Oxford University Press, 2018), 33.

marriage specifically. His ostensibly misogamous argument, however, traffics constantly in misogynist assumptions, as in his reflection on Eve's disobedience, which trait he understands as defining all women, not wives alone. While it is possible to imagine a misogamous text that is not also misogynist, in practice misogamous texts almost always rely upon misogynist thought.

Accounting for the fervor and predictability of medieval rhetoric surrounding the description of wives and women, scholars often refer to misogamous and misogynist prejudices as corresponding to medieval "antifeminism." Instances of antifeminist prejudice can be found in nearly any genre, from sermon collections to fabliaux, from theological treatises to romance adventures, and in school texts, love poetry, allegory, drama, exegesis, and conduct literature alike. None of these genres is categorically misogamous – not all representative texts of these multiple and multiplying generic fields uniformly reproduce misogamous rhetoric – but each contains a significant sample of misogamous writing.[12] Given the astounding prevalence of prejudice against women and wives in medieval writing, it is important to acknowledge that a book of wicked wives "could conceivably have contained almost anything."[13]

Although medieval antifeminism can be found in nearly every instance of medieval writing, there are no widely recognized examples of extant manuscript collections thematically organized around misogamy. In the way that we possess thematic, formal, or generic compilations of lyric poetry (Harley 2253, Kildare), Middle English romance (Auchinleck, Thornton), Middle English alliterative verse (Cotton Nero A.10, Arundel 292), Middle English religious writing (Vernon, Simeon), troubadour poetry (Vat. Lat. 3207), or Latin songs (Cambridge Songs, Carmina Burana), we have uncovered no codicological evidence of medieval readers arranging texts as Chaucer imagined for his fictional Husband of Oxford. Mixed-content manuscripts are not "books of wicked wives" in the sense that Alison's account of Jankyn's

---

[12] For studies in a number of literary fields that discuss misogynist, misogamous, or "antifeminist" representations of women in generic terms, see, e.g.: R. Howard Bloch *Medieval Misogyny and the Invention of Western Romantic Love* (Chicago, IL: University of Chicago Press, 1991); Crocker, *Matter of Virtue*; Bynum, *Holy Feast*; Elaine Tuttle Hansen, *Chaucer and the Fictions of Gender* (Berkeley, CA: University of California Press, 1992); C. Stephen Jaeger, *Ennobling Love* (Philadelphia, PA: University of Pennsylvania Press, 1999); D. L. D'Avray, *Medieval Marriage Sermons* (Oxford: Oxford University Press, 2001); Barbara Newman, *God and the Goddesses* (Philadelphia, PA: University of Pennsylvania Press, 2005); Warren S. Smith, ed., *Satiric Advice on Women and Marriage* (Ann Arbor, MI: University of Michigan Press, 2010); Nicole Nolan Sidhu, *Indecent Exposure* (Philadelphia, PA: University of Pennsylvania Press, 2016); Emma Maggie Solberg, *Virgin Whore* (Ithaca, NY: Cornell University Press, 2018); and Glenn Burger, *Conduct Becoming* (Philadelphia, PA: University of Pennsylvania Press, 2018).

[13] Hanna and Lawler, *Jankyn's Book* 1:4.

book has conditioned us to imagine them. In their frequent juxtapositions of unlike texts, medieval collections rarely replicate familiar formulations of the dominant misogamous tradition.[14]

While single manuscript collections are not generally organized around misogyny, and while our most memorable misogynist collections are more fiction than fact, medieval antifeminism nevertheless emerges from a thoroughly bookish tradition. Accordingly, to begin to understand the reading experience of medieval antifeminism, we must set aside our interest in imagined books and fictional misogynists in favor of actual books compiled by and for historical readers. As in de Pizan's introduction to *The Book of the City of Ladies*, where she wonders why "so many different men – and learned men among them – have been and are so inclined to express both in speaking and in their treatises and writings so many wicked insults about women and their behavior," so Jankyn's book describes a kind of routine misogyny collected from a broad reading of disparate manuscript texts.[15] As Mary and Richard Rouse observe, "Every manuscript that survives was created not casually but deliberately, as a result of someone's decision that it should exist."[16] In examining manuscript evidence, we also must resist the temptation to compile imagined critical or theoretical manuscripts of our own from the sources we know best, into collections comparable in kind and organization to Jankyn's tome. While scholarly anthologies usefully frame the possible breadth of medieval antifeminist discourse, it is important to recognize that no single medieval reader ever had access to such an anthology.[17] Many medieval expressions of antifeminism were less dogma than a muddled array of individually held beliefs refracted at once unevenly and with remarkable consistency in manuscript texts. Mixed-content medieval manuscripts such as Bodley 851 provide illuminating, historically specific, material glimpses of how even so overdetermined a concept as medieval misogamy might have been conceived differently, if only fleetingly, by the scribes who prepared them and readers who encountered them.

---

[14] As Alastair Minnis observes in relation to religious opinion, so too in critical formulations of gendered prejudice we might be wary of the "sweeping and simplistic grand narratives" forced upon the late-medieval period, "with its alleged homogeneity being used as a point of contrast with later, supposedly more complicated, cultures" (*Fallible Authors* [Philadelphia, PA: University of Pennsylvania Press, 2008], 348).

[15] Christine de Pizan, *The Book of the City of Ladies*, trans. Earl Jeffrey Richards (New York: Persea Books, 1982), 3–4.

[16] Rouse and Rouse, *Authentic Witnesses*, 3.

[17] See, for example, as invaluable a scholarly resource as Alcuin Blamires, Karen Pratt, and C. William Marx, eds., *Woman Defamed and Woman Defended* (Oxford: Oxford University Press, 1992).

In reading the *Ave virgo* and *De coniuge* together, I will examine the two poems' opposing interests in *insatiability*, as the word describes exemplary enactments of feminine desire: positively, in the *Ave virgo*, by way of the Virgin's erotic union with the divine; and negatively, in the *De coniuge*, by way of the imagined wife's proclivity for sexual transgression. Rather than proposing a single overarching cultural system that might account for such disparate poems – as in Marina Warner's influential dictum that "there is no place in the conceptual architecture of Christian society for a single woman who is neither a virgin nor a whore" – I seek instead to discover what features these two poems share, although they are wholly unlike in terms of our most common measures, such as genre, theme, or style.[18]

By analyzing these poems together within their specific material context, I attend to the codicological unconscious of the earliest fragment of Bodley 851. My interpretation does not, I will emphasize, seek to discover any metaphorical resonance between material and textual evidence. Indeed, while the disjunctive perspectives on female embodiment and feminine desire evident between the *Ave virgo* and the *De coniuge* may well be described as "fragmentary" – as the two copies of these poems preserved within Bodley 851 are each fragmentary – I do not contend that the incompleteness evident in the material quire that preserves them must necessarily characterize any interpretation of their contents. Nor do I suggest, in my attention to the scribal juxtaposition of the *Ave virgo* and the *De coniuge*, that some large-scale alternative to "antifeminism" lurks behind the act of manuscript compilation, waiting to upset well-known medieval forms of misogamy. Rather, I show how the conceptual points of contact between these two poems uniquely preserved within Bodley 851 reveal baffling and contradictory impulses that informed medieval misogamy and complicate common structures of scholarly engagement with misogamist writing.

The Ninth Quire of Bodley 851

Quire ix of Bodley 851 is a bewildering codicological object, showing evidence of multiple production units and containing several competing textual and decorative schemes (see Chapter 1; pl. 6). Two facts concerning quire ix, however, are inescapable: first, that Scribe B did not contribute any other texts to any other part of Bodley 851; and second, that Scribe B's labor constitutes the earliest chronological contribution to any part of the manuscript. Although they are neither book nor booklet, strictly defined, the two poems Scribe B copied form a discrete codicological unit. It is not necessary to infer scribal intent – to ask why, precisely, Scribe B may have copied these two poems

---

[18] Marina Warner, *Alone of All Her Sex* (New York: Vintage Books, 1983), 235.

together contiguously, or what he may have copied previously – in order to associate them exclusively in the surviving manuscript record.

The simplicity of describing the material conditions of Scribe B's contribution to quire ix is matched by the simplicity of describing its textual contents. The textual fields represented in more capacious multi-text manuscripts often comprise dozens of texts modified by addition and excision over the course of decades or centuries – as in the Bekynton manuscript, the Vernon manuscript, the Auchinleck manuscript, the Harley manuscript, or the remainder of quire ix in Bodley 851. Accordingly, it can be difficult to distinguish, even in careful scholarly descriptions of manuscript compilations, the order or timing of the many constituent parts for books such as these.[19] The same situation holds true for most mixed-content manuscripts containing the *De coniuge*, many of them dating from the fifteenth century, such as BL Cotton MSS Vespasian E.12 and Titus A.20, both textually related to Bodley 851 and sharing a number of its texts.[20] Moreover, the lack of thematic uniformity between manuscript texts of uncertain origin and compilational procedure may lead the modern observer to select texts for interpretation according to categories used in modern research that may not have had any bearing on their medieval compilation. Because the earliest production unit of Bodley 851 is fragmentary, however, it affords sustained attention to all (that is, both) of its individual texts as preserved in one well-defined manuscript context. Analysis in this limited case can provide a starting point for analysis of more complex compilations that require the consideration of a greater number of texts. I take one such step forward in Chapter 4.

Furthermore, we have clear evidence of how later scribal agents responded to the texts Scribe B transcribed. Although some of Scribe B's labor has been lost, careful analysis of Scribe B's clearly delineated codicological fragment might therefore provide insights useful to studies of the contents later compiled alongside it. Understanding the *Ave virgo* and *De coniuge* together as a material fragment helps locate material afterlives in terms of the construction and deployment of antifeminist ideologies in fourteenth-century England, in an imagined community with ties to Wycliffite controversy, *Piers Plowman*, Walter Map, and Chaucer's Wife of Bath.

---

[19] For a magisterial example of codicological sleuthing, see Carter Revard, "Scribe and Provenance," in *Studies in the Harley Manuscript: The Scribes, Contents, and Social Contexts of British Library MS Harley 2253*, ed. Susanna Fein (Kalamazoo, MI: Medieval Institute, Western Michigan University, 2000), 21–109.

[20] See many of the manuscripts described in the sequence of articles published by A. G. Rigg titled "Medieval Poetic Anthologies", *Mediaeval Studies* I (1977): 281–330; II (1978): 387–407; III (1979): 468–505; IV (1981): 472–97. Rigg cheekily refers to Bodley 851, Cotton Vespasian E.12, and Cambridge, Trinity College O.9.38 as a goliardic "Oxford Group."

The *Ave virgo mater christi* and the *De coniuge non ducenda*

The first of Scribe B's poems, the *Ave virgo*, ought to begin "Ave virgo mater christi" (c. 1275; "Hail virgin mother of Christ"), as it does in two other surviving manuscript witnesses. In Bodley 851, approximately the first half of the poem has been lost, so that the poem as it survives in quire ix begins at the sixth line of the eighty-seventh stanza. Because any local variants that may have been preserved within those stanzas are now lost, I restrict my analysis in this chapter to the text of the *Ave virgo* still present within Bodley 851, from stanza eighty-eight onward. The *Ave virgo*, written in Anglo-Latin, takes the form of an encomium, stitching together in all three of its manuscript renditions an ardent series of praises to Mary in her capacity as virgin, as intercessor, and as mother of God. Long thought anonymous, or else composed by some other, more famous Walter, the poem was first attributed to Walter of Wimborne, eighth Franciscan lector at Cambridge (*fl.* 1261–1266), by A. G. Rigg, whose analysis places the text's origin at the Franciscan house in Norwich in the third quarter of the thirteenth century.[21] The *Ave virgo* ranges widely in its exploration of Mary's perfection among devotional images both familiar, as in the first stanza's "fenix virginum" ("the phoenix of virgins"), and unfamiliar, as in the 114th stanza's "celestis irudo" ("leech of the heavens," a metaphor I discuss in further detail below). The poem does not appear to follow any recognizable organizational schema or make use of a single source-text, although consecutive groups of stanzas often string together thematically coherent threads.[22]

The *Ave virgo* survives in only three manuscripts of widely disparate textual construction, and there is little evidence for substantial circulation of the poem otherwise. The poem is in this way representative of Wimborne's poetic production more generally. Wimborne was known as a poet, but he was not celebrated for any particular work by his peers or by later readers.[23] The only

---

[21] A. G. Rigg, "Walter of Wimborne, O.F.M.: An Anglo-Latin Poet of the Thirteenth Century," *Mediaeval Studies* 33 (1971): 371–8. See, too, the entry on Walter of Wimborne in the *ODNB*, also written by Rigg. For a discussion of Walter of Wimborne's place within Franciscan intellectual production in the thirteenth century, see David Townsend, "Robert Grosseteste and Walter of Wimborne," *Medium Aevum* 55.1 (1986): 113–17.

[22] I know of no modern compendium of Marian epithets otherwise constructed; but see the many tropes identified in Brian K. Reynolds, *Gateway to Heaven: Marian Doctrine and Devotion: Image and Typology in the Patristic and Medieval Periods* (Hyde Park, NY: New City Press, 2012).

[23] For overviews of Wimborne's place in Anglo-Latin literary production more generally, see the introduction to A. G. Rigg, *The Poems of Walter of Wimborne* (Toronto: Pontifical Institute of Mediaeval Studies, 1978), along with A. G. Rigg, *A History of Anglo-Latin Literature, 1066–1422* (Cambridge: Cambridge University

close textual witness to Bodley 851 is Oxford, Corpus Christi College MS 232 (CCC 232), which also preserves Wimborne's *De mundi vanitate* ("On the world's vanity") and *De mundi scelere* ("On the world's filth") in a booklet bound together with Robert Grosseteste's *Château d'amour* and a French version of the Life of Mary of Egypt. The manuscript mixes devotion with hagiography, didactics, and allegory. CCC 232 displays few of the themes most evident in the *De coniuge*, linking devotion to more obviously similar subjects for spiritual use, likely in Franciscan circles. BodL. MS Digby 19 preserves a later scribal edition of the *Ave virgo*, of uncertain relation to the textual tradition preserved in Bodley 851 and CCC 232. The Digby text is significantly shorter than the text preserved in CCC 232. There, all stanzas have been sorted – it is not known by whom or at what point in the poem's transmission – into four groups according to one of three introductory words ("Ave," "Salve," or "Gaude"), so that a series of stanzas beginning with *Salve* is followed by a series of stanzas beginning with *Gaude*, followed by a series of stanzas beginning with *Ave*, followed finally by a series of stanzas beginning with *Salve* once more. If a given stanza (as read in the Bodley 851 and CCC 232 texts) did not happen to begin with one of those words already, it was rewritten to accommodate this organizational schema. In Digby 19, the *Ave virgo* follows a full transcription of Aelred of Rievaulx's *De genealogia regum anglorum* ('On the genealogy of English kings") and is followed by a selection of Eusebius's life of Constantine, then by moral tales. Its contents do not coincide with those displayed by CCC 232, nor does either manuscript give much purchase on the *Ave virgo*'s conjunction with the *De coniuge* in Bodley 851.

The *De coniuge*, begins "Sit deo gloria" (c. 1200; "Glory be to God"), and the copy in Bodley 851 lacks the final three stanzas present in the majority of other witnesses. The *De coniuge* circulated widely across Europe in a variety of manuscript contexts, with significantly more textual changes than had the *Ave virgo*, frequently in miscellanies and anthologies that also contained further antifeminist and anti-ecclesiastic satires, revelatory visions, drinking songs, and moral tales. The poem is attested in more than fifty-five manuscripts still extant in libraries ranging from Cambridge to Florence, Madrid to Vienna, and at Prague, Paris, and Munich.[24] While the precise origins of the *De coniuge* are unclear, its earliest manuscripts can be dated roughly to the turn of the thirteenth century. The poem was recycled for use in a wide array of contexts:

Press, 1992); Beryl Smalley, *English Friars and Antiquity in the Early Fourteenth Century* (Oxford: Blackwell, 1960), 50–1; and F. J. E. Raby, *A History of Secular Latin Poetry in the Middle Ages*, 2 vols. (Oxford: Clarendon Press, 1934).

[24] A. G. Rigg, *Gawain on Marriage: The Textual Tradition of the De Coniuge Non Ducenda with Critical Edition and Translation* (Toronto: Pontifical Institute of Mediaeval Studies, 1986), 13–22.

while the copy discussed here names the dreamer as "Walter" (perhaps a nod to posited authorship?), other copies name him as Gawain, William, Gilbert, Golias, Michael, Colin, Calvin, or Robert.[25] We know of later translations into French and into Middle English, the former anonymously included in BL Harley MS 2253 and the latter composed by John Lydgate.[26] If ever there was a "hit" medieval poem, it was the *De coniuge*; and yet this poem is little interpreted in the modern academy.

Of particular importance to the poem's place within Bodley 851 are a group of English manuscripts sharing numerous texts and demonstrating reliance on a single textual tradition for most of those texts that A.G. Rigg refers to as the "Oxford Group," of which the present manuscript is an early member.[27] These manuscripts most frequently contain the *De coniuge* and the *Apocalypsis goliae episcopi* as well as an assortment of similar satirical Latin poems frequently called "goliardic"; they show an interest in the poems of other Walters, whether of Wimborne or Châtillon; and they combine invective materials (against church officials, more often than against wives) with ecclesiastic texts, devotional poems, and moral tales. Like Bodley 851, these manuscripts likely emerged from ecclesiastic or monastic contexts, though their contents often speak to secular concerns, rather than theological matters or the business of the church as a social or political institution.

In all of its manuscript copies, the *De coniuge* takes the form of a dream vision, wherein the dreamer is visited by three "angels" who attempt throughout the poem to convince the dreamer not to marry his betrothed, as he intends. These angelic authorities may, in fact, be intended to represent doctors of the Church better known to twelfth-century churchmen than modern scholars: they are traditionally identified as John Chrysostom, Peter of Corbeil, and Lawrence of Durham. The original authorship of the poem is unknown, though surviving manuscripts attribute it to various authors and authorial personas including

---

[25] Rigg, *Gawain on Marriage*, 4–6.

[26] Rigg provides an overview of adaptations in the Appendix to *Gawain on Marriage*, 101–04; and both translations are printed in Thomas Wright, *The Latin Poems Commonly Attributed to Walter Mapes* (London: Camden Society, 1841), 292–9. For Lydgate's incomplete translation of the poem, "The Pain and Sorrow of Evil Marriage," see also John Lydgate, *The Minor Poems of John Lydgate, Part II*, eds. Henry Noble MacCracken and Merriam Sherwood, EETS o.s. 192 (London: Oxford University Press, 1934), 456–60. For a discussion of the manuscript contexts for the anonymous French translation in Harley 2253, see Barbara Nolan, "Anthologizing Ribaldry" in *Studies in the Harley Manuscript*, ed. Fein, 289–327.

[27] The other manuscripts of the "Oxford Group" are BL Cotton MS Vespasian E.12 and Cambridge, Trinity College, MS O.9.38. Both are datable to the second half of the fifteenth century. They are closely related to BL Cotton MS Titus A.20; and four other manuscripts held in the Bodleian at Oxford: MSS Bodley 603, Digby 166, Rawl. B.214, and Rawl. G.109.

Golias, Primas, Walter Map, and – most amusingly – St. Bonaventure. As with the *Ave virgo*, the poem's copies display a wide array of metrically sufficient lections; and to a much higher degree than the *Ave virgo*, individual stanzas of the *De coniuge* are apt to be rearranged, misplaced, forgotten, or improvised in specific contexts. It could be taught to great effect as showcasing the scribal nature of most medieval textual transmission and the ribald nature of popular misogamist attitudes. Surviving manuscripts may represent a much more robust oral tradition.[28] We might understand the poem to provide an index of shared sentiment, however farcical, in the thirteenth through fifteenth centuries, among any so fortunate (or unfortunate) as to be able to repeat, however boisterously, and to parse, however weakly, its jangling Latin.

Medieval audiences appear to have taken some significant pleasure in the poem's adolescent mode. The *De coniuge* plays repeatedly on the perceived contextual sufferings of medieval husbands: many of its facile jokes rely on the assumption that you've heard this one before. Accordingly, the *De coniuge* does not follow the most common rhetorical attempts in medieval antifeminist literature to soften its anti-matrimonial language. As Rigg notes early in his introduction to the poem, the *De coniuge* contains no references that depend uniquely on Map, Jerome, or Theophrastus as medieval authorities, nor to Ovid or Juvenal as classical influences. It refuses to praise virginity as an alternative to sexual temptation using biblical, classical, or historical examples (the hallmark of writings following the rhetoric of Jerome's *Against Jovinian*), and it does not make any mention of virtuous women who endeavored to thwart temptation (as in many writings following Augustine). The absence of any mention of virginity, chastity, or fecundity is especially notable in the context of Bodley 851, where its companion poem (the *Ave virgo*) meditates constantly upon Mary's perfect, erotic, virginal fecundity. The invective of the *De coniuge* ignores entirely any discussion of the effects of aging on looks, the fading tendency of flashing affections, or the effects of gossip among cohorts of women gathered together. It bears little resemblance to the antifeminism of popular vernacular texts. It chooses starkness over subtlety and pursues with single-minded repetition the downfalls of marriage, no matter the apparent virtues of the bride.

As these overviews demonstrate, the *Ave virgo* and the *De coniuge* make an unlikely pair. They fail to establish the kind of thematic or generic coherence assumed by most modern critical endeavors, whether carried out in literary or historical terms. Taken in isolation, the *Ave virgo* and the *De coniuge* would not likely be read alongside one another as formal, aesthetic, thematic, or ideological companions – nor have they, in scholarship, on the few occasions when either text has been discussed at all. There has been

---

[28] Rigg, *Gawain on Marriage*, 53–7.

no sustained critical analysis of the *De coniuge*, although it is mentioned frequently in discussions of goliardic verse and of anti-marital rhetoric in late-medieval Europe.[29] Perhaps on account of the fervor of its misogamy, the *De coniuge* was commonly attributed to Walter Map from the fourteenth century onward.[30] Although the *Ave virgo* is occasionally mentioned in discussions of Franciscan writings in England and Anglo-Latin literary production (Beryl Smalley refers to Wimborne as a "scamp"), and although later devotional writings in praise of Mary display debts to Wimborne's other writings, only one published piece of scholarship engages with the *Ave virgo* at any length.[31] As the surviving manuscript record and scholarly record together show, no established conceptual apparatus – modern or medieval – outside of Bodley 851 has brought the *Ave virgo* and the *De coniuge* together as objects of close analysis. They make use of separate poetic meters and literary styles, they originated in differing historical settings, and they pursue incommensurate rhetorical ends.

Nevertheless, a careful examination of these two poems together in Bodley 851 reveals a shared representation of feminine desire strange to the most common scholarly representations of misogamous discourse. In the better part of misogamous writings – as in Map, de Meun, and Chaucer – the material, feminine body is associated with sinfulness, while spirituality and reason are associated with a masculine pursuit of virtue. Most commonly, in patristic writings on wives and marriage, bodies are necessary for sex, and sex is almost invariably an instance of sin. As Augustine's partial response to Jerome in his paired tracts on marriage and virginity shows well enough, chaste marriage can only be considered a spiritual good in paling comparison with virginity: "whatever that is immodest, shameless, base, married persons do with one another, is the sin of the persons, not the fault of marriage," he writes, and elsewhere, "no fruitfulness of the flesh can be compared to holy virginity even of the flesh."[32] Following St. Paul's wish that "all men were even as

---

[29] E.g., Emma Lipton, *Affections of the Mind* (Notre Dame, IN: University of Notre Dame Press, 2011); Blamires, *The Case for Women*; Conor McCarthy, ed., *Love, Sex and Marriage in the Middle Ages* (New York: Routledge, 2004); and P. G. Walsh, "Antifeminism in the High Middle Ages", in *Satiric Advice on Women and Marriage*, ed. Smith, 222–42. Along with the *Apocalypsis goliae*, Rigg calls the *De coniuge* "ubiquitous" (*Anglo-Latin Literature*, 372n191).

[30] A. G. Rigg, "Golias and Other Pseudonyms," *Studi Medievali* 18.1 (1977): 65–109.

[31] Beryl Smalley, *English Friars and Antiquity in the Early Fourteenth Century* (Oxford: B. Blackwell, 1960), 50–1. Georgiana Donavin, "The Musical Mother Tongue in Anglo-Latin Poetry for Meditation" in *Scribit Mater* (Washington, DC: Catholic University of America Press, 2012), 115–62.

[32] Augustine, *On the Good of Marriage* §5 and *Of Holy Virginity* §8, trans. C.L. Cornish, *'On the Holy Trinity', Doctrinal Treatises, Moral Treatises*, ed. Philip Schaff,

myself" (that is, unmarried) and his subsequent admonition that "it is better to marry than to be burnt" (1 Cor. 7:7–9), heterosexual companionship was at best conceived as a means by which God's command in Genesis to "increase and multiply" (Gen. 1:28) might be fulfilled. The Middle Ages preserved this perspective: "The Lombard himself concluded that if a couple engage in sexual intercourse for the sake of offspring (*causa prolis*), then their coupling is free from blame (*sic excusatur coitus ut culpam non habeat*); however, if they are motivated by unbridled desire, then they fall into sin."[33] Although embodied sexuality was understood to incline both men and women ever into sin, marriage nevertheless could channel sexual appetites into an institution sanctioned by God and the church. In parallel with the patristic tradition, as Aristotelian philosophies increasingly associated womanhood and fleshliness with matter, so late-medieval misogamous discourse considered marriage almost exclusively in terms of the dangers women posed to men, since women were more intimately tied to embodied sexual desires.[34]

The *Ave virgo* and the *De coniuge*, however, associate sexuality and sinfulness more concretely with abstraction than embodiment, and they associate the body more concretely with purity than with filth. Between these poems, which bring together the durable influence of the patristic account and the rapidly expanding late-medieval cult of Mary, virginity is associated first with purification of the flesh, and then with purification of the spirit, while the absence of material piety informs spousal impurity, stereotypically rendered. Characterized foremost by insatiability, feminine desire is figured contrastingly as the highest expression of embodied spiritual purity (in the case of Mary in the *Ave virgo*) and as the most corrupt expression of disembodying earthly filth (in the case of wives in the *De coniuge*). A comparative reading of these two superficially incompatible poems demonstrates how feminine desire, as supported by the material, feminine, spousal body, could be required more fundamentally for devotion than for derision – how even in misogamous contexts, divinity itself might be found inextricably bound up rather with embodiment than with abstraction.

A Select Library of the Nicene and Post-Nicene Fathers of the Christian Church, Series 1, Vol. 3 (1887, repr., Peabody, MA: Hendrickson, 2004).

[33] Minnis, *Fallible Authors*, 285.

[34] Sandy Bardsley, *Women's Roles in the Middle Ages* (Westport, CT: Greenwood Press, 2007); Dyan Elliott, *Spiritual Marriage* (Princeton, NJ: Princeton University Press, 1993); Dyan Elliott, *The Bride of Christ Goes to Hell* (Philadelphia, PA: University of Pennsylvania Press, 2012); Henry Ansgar Kelly, *Love and Marriage in the Age of Chaucer* (Ithaca, NY: Cornell University Press, 1975). See also Ruth Evans, "Virginities" and Dyan Elliot, "Marriage," in *The Cambridge Companion to Medieval Women's Writing*, eds. Carolyn Dinshaw and David Wallace (Cambridge: Cambridge University Press, 2003), 21–39, 40–57.

Two Daughters of the Horseleech

Any sufficiently robust theoretical configuration may yield multiplying approaches to discovering aspects of a textual unconscious.[35] In attending to the codicological unconscious of the texts preserved on fols. 78ra–81va of Bodley 851, I will begin with a reference that both poems share to Proverbs 30:15–16:

> The horseleech hath two daughters that say: Bring, bring. There are three things that never are satisfied, and the fourth never saith: It is enough. Hell and the mouth of the womb, and the earth which is not satisfied with water: and the fire never saith: It is enough.[36]

The verse is notoriously enigmatic – so enigmatic, in fact, that so perspicacious a reader as St. Augustine cited it specifically as the most obvious biblical example of enigma, which he understood as a subcategory of allegory.[37] References to the "two daughters of the horseleech saying, 'bring, bring'" proliferate in late-medieval religious writings. Jerome famously declares that the leech ("sanguisuga") is the devil ("diabolus est"), and this basic interpretation endures throughout the medieval period, as in the writings of Bede, Sedulius Scotus, Alexander of Hales, and William of Newburgh.[38]

Most medieval references to Proverbs 30:15–16, however, take an allegorical approach to its meaning, understanding the "two daughters" to stand in for abstracted forms of concupiscence. The most common phrasing renders the "two daughters" as "avaritia et luxuria" ("avarice and licentiousness"), a dyad used in a wide array of patristic commentaries to describe sins of the flesh, as in Augustine's litany of virginal powers to abstain from "murders, devilish sacrifices and abominations, thefts, rapines, frauds, perjuries, drunkennesses,

---

[35] Paul Strohm, *Theory and the Premodern Text* (Minneapolis, MN: University of Minnesota Press, 2000), 165–81.

[36] "15 sanguisugae duae sunt filiae dicentes, adfer adfer / tria sunt insaturabilia et quartum quod numquam dicit sufficit // 16 infernus et os vulvae et terra quae non satiatur aqua / ignis vero numquan dicit sufficit" (Proverbs 30:15–16, *Biblia Sacra*, ed. Robert Weber [Stuttgart: Württembergische Bibelanstalt, 1969], 984). Weber's apparatus refers to Isaiah 5:14: "Therefore hath hell enlarged her soul, and opened her mouth without any bounds, and their strong ones, and their people, and their high and glorious ones shall go down into it." Remaining citations from the Vulgate are given parenthetically by book, chapter, and verse.

[37] Augustine, *On the Holy Trinity*, 15.9. For a review of the influence of "enigma" on medieval Christian thought, see Curtis A. Gruenler, *Piers Plowman and the Poetics of Enigma* (Notre Dame, IN: University of Notre Dame Press, 2017).

[38] *Adversus Jovinian*, 1.28, quoted in translation from Hanna and Lawler, *Jankyn's Book*, 1:188.

and all *luxury and avarice*, hatreds, emulations, impieties, cruelties."[39] This pair was commonly modified by later writers. Bede's commentary on Proverbs reads "luxoria et filargiria" ("licentiousness and greed") a phrasing adopted also by Sedulius Scotus in the ninth century and the Augustinian, Alexander of Ashby, in the late twelfth century.[40] The phrase "gula et luxuria" ("gluttony and licentiousness") was used to signify sins of the flesh in many contexts, often with mention of concupiscence lurking nearby; and this modified dyad can be found describing Proverbs 30 in an anonymous commentary on the *Apocalypse* dateable to the late thirteenth-century or early fourteenth century, as preserved among the works of Thomas Aquinas.[41] In contrast with the most common formulation combining "luxuria" with a more bodily sin, some writers interpreted the daughters of the horseleech as "vanitas et voluptas" ("vanity and lust"), including, most influentially, Bernard of Clairvaux.[42] Bernard's phrase is cited by Meister Eckhart and adopted by Aelred of Rievaulx, Gottfred of Admont, Gerric of Ignay, and Conrad of Eberbach in direct reference to Proverbs 30 – and by many others in discussion of fleshly desires in other contexts. In these most common formulations, the "two daughters" of the horseleech represent feminized figurations of bodily vices rather than actual, embodied women.

Reference to Proverbs 30:15–16 surfaces in both poems under discussion here, in each case obliquely (as is perhaps necessary for the categorically enigmatic) and in each case with vastly different implications. For all of their differences, the *Ave virgo* and the *De coniuge* both obsess over what it means to be a thing "never satisfied" like hell, the earth, fire, and the mouth of the womb. The following sequence of stanzas in the *De coniuge* represents one particularly extreme, though not necessarily uncommon, sexist interpretation of the enigma at Proverbs 30:

> Insaciabilis vulua no*n* deficit
> Nec vnam femina*m* vbi vnus afficit
> Fact*io* mulier se multis subicit
> Et adhuc siciens no*n* dicit sufficit

[39] Augustine, *Of Holy Virginity* §54 (emphasis mine).

[40] Beda Venerabilis, *In proverbia Salomonis libri iii* (CCSL 119B), ed. D. Hurst (Turnhout: Brepols, 1983), bk. 3, ch. 30, line 114.

[41] Anonymous, *Expositio Super Apocalypsim*, ch. 8 (www.corpusthomisticum.org/x2a08.html; last accessed 13 July 2023): "Prov. 30, *sanguisugae duae sunt filiae, dicentes affer affer*; gula scilicet et luxuria."

[42] Bernardus Clarauallensis, *Sermones de diuersis* in *Sancti Bernardi opera*, 9 vols., ed. J. Leclerq, Charles H. Talbot, and Henri Rochais (Rome: Editiones Cistercienses, 1957–98), Vol. 6.1 (1970), 169.

Quis satisfac*erit* illi p*er* coitum
Qui nimis coeunt inc*ur*runt obitu*m*
Si no*n* servierit quis*quam* ad libitu*m*
Ut reddat totiens carnale debitum

Idcirco plurime fiunt adult*ere*
Tedet quam plurimas maritos viv*ere*
Cum nullus femine possit sufficere
Dico qu*o*d nemini expedit nubere (fol. 80v; pl. 6; J9–J11)

Her insatiable womb never stops,
Nor, where one woman is, does one man act;
The wife lies down with many in the act
And thirsting, never yet has she said "enough!"

Who will leave her satisfied through sex?
Those who fuck too frequently rush into oblivion.
If no man serves her to her pleasure,
Then so many times he pays the carnal debt.

Therefore, most wives become adulterers,
And it wearies many that husbands live.
Since no one is able to satisfy a woman,
I say marriage benefits no one.

In Proverbs 30:15–16, hell, the earth, and the mouth of the womb are never satisfied, but it is fire, specifically, that never says "enough." In the *De coniuge* it is the woman who never says "enough," as the poem follows the syntax of its biblical source literally without preserving its final referent. Recalling rather the mouth of the womb (*os vulvae*) than the emphatic fire (*ignis vero*), the *De coniuge* shifts the ultimate subject of insatiability from the elemental to the feminine, from the fires associated with hell to the desires associated with imagined wives. In this transformation, the poem replicates Jerome's misreading in *Against Jovinian*, where "This is not said about a whore nor about an adulteress, but the love of woman in general is reproached here, that love which can never be satisfied... a wife is listed among the greatest of evils."[43] Where a casual observer might understand the verse to describe only *bad* wives, like Jerome the *De coniuge* takes the possibility of any possible sinfulness in any woman, real or imagined, as a sufficient argument for avoiding marriage altogether – since, after all, a single failure of judgment

---

[43] *Adversus Jovinian*, 1.28, quoted in translation from Hanna and Lawler, *Jankyn's Book* 1:188–190.

might lead any man toward those other things that are never sated, hell and the grave.

The *De coniuge* is less interested in making informed doctrinal, masculinist, or allegorical arguments than in repeatedly riffing on the same joke. Whereas Jerome frets over the possibility that women, like hell and the grave, are sure works of the devil, the *De coniuge* voices a more crass – and in this, presumably, more comic – concern: that every single woman imaginable is so interested in constantly having sex that any man foolish enough to take a wife will be exhausted himself, thrown headlong into oblivion.[44] The dilemma presented in the three stanzas quoted above – not specifically of being cuckolded or possibly damned, but of being worn out, of copulating (or being copulated) into catatonic indifference – surely suggested, for many audiences, a tongue planted firmly in cheek, a kind of flippancy about Last Things intended more to arouse laughter than to inspire self-reflection. It is possible Chaucer thought to imitate this brand of humor in writing *The Wife of Bath's Prologue*, as Alison's husbands fail both to satisfy her sexually and so to provide her with children, leaving her ultimately in control of their lives, their possessions, and their futurities.[45] Certainly the tone of the *De coniuge* carries us a long way from one early exegete's interpretation of Proverbs 30:15–16, where "every one who is the slave of sin in all the passions of the flesh… is never able to come to confession, and to the layer of regeneration, and like water and fire, never says 'It is enough.'"[46] In the *De coniuge*, the wife enjoys the fruits of "luxuria" and "voluptas," while the husband merely endures her insatiability.

In the textual tradition represented by Bodley 851, the husband's endless labors in the workplace are set in parallel with his wife's endless desire for sexual activity. In Bodley 851, these three "Insatiability Stanzas" are spoken not (as Rigg's edition has it) by the third angel, John, but by the first angel, Peter, whose verses otherwise tend to focus on the labors of married men rather than on their wives' inclination toward sexual deviancy. The three stanzas cited above are placed between the following two stanzas:

---

[44] For a parallel circumstance in Tudor verse, see Carissa M. Harris, "'All the Strete My Voyce Shall Heare': Gender, Voice, and Desire in the Lyrics of Bodleian MS Ashmole 176," *Journal of the Early Book Society* 20 (2017): 29–58, especially the acute observation that "antifeminist poems portray men's fears that women will sap their potency before rejecting them for their more virile and vigorous peers, and they give voice to the speakers' anxieties about intra-masculine competition" (35).

[45] Samantha Katz Seal, *Father Chaucer* (Oxford: Oxford University Press, 2019), 57–94.

[46] Hippolytus of Rome, *Commentary on Proverbs* in *The Ante-Nicene Fathers: Translations of the writings of the Fathers down to A.D. 325* vol.6, eds. by Alexander Roberts *et al.* (Grand Rapids, MI: Eerdmans), 320.

Instat laboribus causa pecunie
Ne fames urgeat ventres familie
Laborat iugit*er* et sine requie
Et cras incipiet quod fecit hodie

[…]

Vir lassus dormiens laborem sompniat
Sic q*ue* continuus labore se cruciat
Ut pascat coniugem qua*m* nu*n*q*uam* saciat
Guaterus igit*ur* vx*o*rem fugiat (fol. 80v; pl. 6; P9, P10; J9–J11 fall between)

The need for money sets him into labors
Lest hunger oppress his family's stomachs.
He labors perpetually without respite,
And tomorrow he will begin what he did today.

[…]

The exhausted man, sleeping, dreams about labor,
Thus continuously he torments himself with labor,
So that he might feed the spouse he never satisfies.
Let Walter, therefore, flee a wife!

Particularly at P10.3, where "quam nunquam saciat" ("whom he never satisfies") in another arrangement of stanzas (e.g., directly after P9) might provide only a counterpoint to the hunger of the stomach lamented in P9.2 ("fames urgeat ventres"), the intervening use of "insaciabilis" brings a further sexual connotation to the imagined husband's toil. Not only must the married man stave off literal hunger for his wife (and his family), but he must also satisfy – or fail to satisfy – another of her hungers as well, dreaming of the never-ending work he will inevitably continue in both the monetary and marital spheres. The sense of "saciat" suggests at once the imagined wife's gluttony and her lust, neither of which the husband can fulfill. In this setting, for the imagined husband, even the sexual pleasures of marriage become one more instance of work – not elevated, even, to sin, temptation, or devilish sign – something repeated endlessly and without enjoyment, day after day and night after night.

The use of Proverbs 30 in the *Ave virgo* could hardly diverge more sharply from its use in the *De coniuge*:

Tu celestis es irudo
Fauu*m* sugens plenitudo
Cui*us* no*n* ebibit*ur*

> Sugit deus fauu*m* tuu*m*
> Et tu sugis fauu*m* suu*m*
> Mel melle rependit*ur* (fol. 78v; 114)

> You are the leech of the heavens,
> sucking honeycomb, the plenitude
> of whom cannot be consumed;
> God sucked your honeycomb,
> and you sucked his honeycomb,
> honey with honey was repaid.

Much is familiar about the construction Wimborne adopts here, in the context of medieval Marian devotion. For example, references to honey and honeycomb, which surface eight times in the surrounding stanzas (110–120), were borrowed from *Song of Songs*, a text increasingly taken, over the course of the Middle Ages to refer allegorically both to Mary and God and to the Church and Christ (and, sometimes, confusingly, to Mary and Christ).[47] Scholarship abounds on Mary's transformation from a figure of power and authority in the early church to a figure of humility and desire in the late-medieval period, and this transformation is often linked to her increasing proximity to the bride described in that most erotic of biblical texts. Recent scholars with as diverse research purposes as Miri Rubin (history), Anne Matter (literary criticism), Sarah Jane Boss (theology), David J. Rothenberg (musicology), and Anna Russakoff (manuscript illumination) assign the *Song of Songs* a singularly prominent poetic role in the development of Marian devotion, specifically after the turn of the millennium, then particularly within monastic orders, and then especially for Cistercians following Bernard of Clairvaux and Franciscans following Francis of Assisi and Clare of Assisi.[48]

In the *Ave virgo*, a devotional poem by an English Franciscan, the fact of Mary's reciprocal position as chosen of God and chooser of God should

---

[47] Elliott, *Bride of Christ*; Newman, *God and the Goddesses*. See, e.g., "favus distillans labia tua sponsa mel et lac sub lingua tua / et odor vestimentorum tuorum sicut odor turis" and "messui murram meam cum aromatibus meis / comedi favum cum melle meo bibi vinum meum cum lacte meo" (*Song of Songs* 4:11, 5:1; " Thy lips, my spouse, are as a dropping honeycomb, honey and milk are under thy tongue; and the smell of thy garments, as the smell of frankincense"; and "I have gathered my myrrh, with my aromatical spices: I have eaten the honeycomb with my honey, I have drunk my wine with my milk").

[48] Miri Rubin, *Mother of God* (New Haven, CT: Yale University Press, 2009); E. Ann Matter, *The Voice of My Beloved* (Philadelphia, PA: University of Pennsylvania Press, 1990); Sarah Jane Boss, *Empress and Handmaid* (London: Cassell, 2000); David J. Rothenberg, *The Flower of Paradise* (Oxford: Oxford University Press, 2011); and Anna D. Russakoff, *Imagining the Miraculous* (Toronto: Pontifical Institute of Mediaeval Studies, 2019). See also Ann W. Astell, *The Song of Songs in the Middle Ages* (Ithaca, NY: Cornell University Press, 1990).

come as no surprise. As in the following stanza, she was understood under the aspect of singular *mediatrix* between man's sinfulness and God's purity:

> Ave nostra mediatrix
> Ave cuius tumet matrix
> Sine viri copula
> Tu pistrinum es habundum
> In quo deus munda mundum
> Panem pinsit pinsula (fol. 78v; 115)

> Hail, our lady mediator,
> hail, whose womb grows
> without the intercourse of man;
> your mill is abundant
> in which God with clean pestle
> grinds the bread of the world.

What is unusual in the *Ave virgo* is the poem's nearly obsessive description of physical intimacy between Mary and God. In this stanza, Wimborne emphasizes the procreational aspect of the mutual sucking ("sugens") that takes place between God and Mary in the stanza before. If Christ is the "bread of the world," Mary is the "mill," where God uses his "clean pestle" to grind that bread – himself, his son. Without the intercourse *of man*, Mary nevertheless comes to bear the Son of God. Accordingly, in the *Ave virgo* her relationship with God is erotic, physical, and procreative:

> Ave casta spousa dei
> Que pulsata pandis ei
> mentis ventris pessulum
> Dictis dulce das responsum
> Et admittis dulcem sponsum
> Ruentem in osculum (fol. 78v; 107)

> Hail, pure spouse of God
> You who, being battered, open to him
> passage to your mind and womb.[49]
> With these words, you sweetly give response,
> and you send your sweet spouse
> rushing toward your kiss.

---

[49] Or: "the gate of your womb's mind." Rigg gives "tue mentis pessulum" ("gate of your mind") or "tue ventris pessulum" ("gate of your womb"), positing that the reading in Bodley 851 "incorporates a gloss" (Rigg, *Walter of Wimborne*, 170). I translate as asyndeton. The use of "pessulum" recalls *Song of Songs* 5:6: "pessulum ostii aperui dilecto meo" ("I opened the bolt of my door to my beloved").

Elsewhere, the *Ave virgo* consistently employs the language of embodiment, and earlier stanzaic sequences often take the form of a litany of her fleshly beauties, such as: nose, neck, back, spine, teeth, canine teeth, gums, lips, eyelids, heel, joints, thighs, knees, shins, soles, stomach, hips, tendons, and windpipe (stanzas 89–92). In the *Ave virgo*, Mary's body is central to the depiction of her intimacy with God, her theological significance, and the quality of her status as woman and wife. What Mary and God do together is – in the Lombard's phrase – "causa prolis" ("for the sake of offspring"), mutually satisfying, and physically intimate.

The comparison of Mary to a leech found in stanza 114 – and unusual in late medieval literature (and, to my knowledge, any literature) – further uncovers the erotic pleasure that pervades the metaphors adopted by the *Ave virgo*. As is well known, ancient Greek and Latin sources indicate that leeches were used for medicinal bloodletting.[50] Medieval authorities appear to have little to say on the subject, however, perhaps because medical uses for leeches were so common. For example, Isidore of Seville makes no mention of the leech by the word "hirudo," referring to it instead as the more common word in post-classical Latin, "sanguisuga," a portmanteau "so named because it sucks blood (sanguinem sugere)" and discussing the animal not as part of his section on medicine but in his section on types of living things.[51] This reticence carries over as well into modern compendia of Anglo-Latin usage: DuCange defines "hirudo" only as "piscis genus" – that is, a kind of fish, a watery vermin – and the *DMLBS* cites the line under consideration from the *Ave virgo* as a literal usage under the translation, "leech," presumably meaning something along the lines of Isidore's vermin.[52] Grammarians sometimes provide etymological explanations for the semantic overlap between "sanguisuga" and "hirudo," as in Alexander Neckham's *Sacerdos ad altare*, where "hirudo" is derived from "haereo" ("to cling, to adhere").[53] Of course, the textual source most likely to be familiar to a literate friar of the thirteenth century or clerk of the fourteenth century was that under discussion here – Proverbs 30:15, the Vulgate's only

---

[50] Ian C. Beavis, "Worms, Leeches, Centipedes, Woodlice, Etc.," *Insects and Other Invertebrates in Classical Antiquity* (Liverpool: Liverpool University Press, 1988), 1–20.

[51] Isidore of Seville, *The Etymologies of Isidore of Seville*, ed. Stephen A. Barney (Cambridge: Cambridge University Press, 2006), XII.v.3: "The leech (sanguisuga) is a water vermin, so named because it sucks blood (sanguinem sugere). It lies in wait for creatures when they are drinking, and when it glides into their throat, or attaches itself somewhere, it drinks in their blood. When it is sated by too much blood, it vomits out what it has drunk so that it may once more suck in fresher blood."

[52] Du Cange, s.v. "hirudo"; *DMLBS*, s.v. "hirudo".

[53] Alexander Neckham, *Sacerdos ad altare* (CCCM 227), ed. C. McDonough (Turnhout: Brepols, 2010), II.383–6.

reference to a leech – where "sanguisugae" were generally understood to represent the transgressive desires of the flesh.

Unless we are to infer that Walter of Wimborne is accusing the Virgin Mary of concupiscence, it is more likely that he intended to reverse, rather than embrace, the usual verminous connotations between leeches and fleshly weakness. Unlike the lecher or the whore, each desiring without restraint what should not be desired at all, in this stanza Mary desires that which is the proper and inexhaustible object of desire, transforming a symbol of sinful indulgence into a symbol of spiritual exemplarity. Although the leech is hardly a common positive image for embodiment or sexuality, in Wimborne's imaginative devotional universe, it mediates between the cosmic import of Mary's relationship with the divine and the intimacy shared by Mary and God. Moreover, although no strict analogy is drawn, the repetition of "sugit" and "favum" in stanza 114 links what Mary does with the heavens to what Mary and God do with one another, suggesting in the final line not only the way intimacy acts as a form of recompense, but also a commensurate relationship between universality and intimacy by way of divinity. The inexhaustibility of the heavens becomes Mary's own plenitude, which none can exhaust. She occupies a position at once sexual and sinless. Mary's active body stands as a material figuration of devotional access to God and Christ, to inexhaustible blood and pure flesh, and to erotic communion with the divine.

By way of their shared intertext (Proverbs 30), the *Ave virgo* and the *De coniuge* share a formal obsession with overabundance and endlessness. In Wimborne's poem, the leech becomes rather a symbol of desire for erotic communion with the divine rather than of desire for sexual intercourse with men. Where the *De coniuge* worries over the possible effects of an erotic drive that may not ever be satisfied, the *Ave virgo* proposes a boundless and mutual satisfaction between virginal desire and divine superabundance: sucking honeycomb, the virgin mother of Christ and divine lover of God never says, "enough!" Wimborne transforms Jerome's claim that "the horse-leech is the devil" and so also contradicts the terms of mock-concern voiced by the *De coniuge*.[54] To pursue marriage with God is to be endlessly satisfied into life and to generate endlessly the grounds for future desire and future satisfaction. The virgin-mother Mary enjoys precisely the condition of interminable action from which the imagined husband of the *De coniuge* suffers, sating and being sated by the food of the divine (honeycomb) and participating erotically in the production and reproduction of that food (mill of the "bread of life"). The constant return to Mary's body in the *Ave virgo* signals wonder at and dependence on the role she, an enmattered and perfect wife, might play.

---

[54] *Adversus Jovinian* 1.28, cited from Hanna and Lawler, *Jankyn's Book* 1:188.

These two inverted references to Proverbs 30 establish a point of departure for describing how each poem goes about representing the material persons of its imagined female subjects. Where the *Ave virgo* not only acknowledges Mary's body (as material, as feminine, and as fundamentally generative) but relies upon that body in order to express complex devotional tropes, the *De coniuge* refuses to dwell upon the material bodies of its imagined wives while nevertheless insisting on their proclivity toward sins of the flesh. Although, in the *De coniuge* wives are assumed to lie, cheat, and steal, they always do these things generically or stereotypically – perhaps even archetypally – rather than in any particular bodily manifestation:

>   Sem*per* laborib*us* labores cumulat
>   Et laborem preterit *et* labor*em* pululat
>   Et hic est asinus que*m* vx*or* stimulat
>   Vt pascat filios quos ip*s*a baiulat
>
>   Longa coniugiu*m* est penitencia
>   Dolor continuus post pu*er*peria
>   Exp*er*ti coniuges horrent *con*iugia
>   Que crucem *pr*ep*ar*ant atq*ue* suppliciam.
>
>   Se semp*er* mulier infirma*m* asserit
>   Bibit *et* comedit mingit *et* egerit
>   Et vir laboribus multis atterit
>   Et tunc incipiet cu*m con*summaue*r*it (fol. 80v; pl. 6; P3, P6(A), P4(A))
>
>   Always labors pile upon labors,
>   He both sets work aside and brings forth more work.
>   And he is an ass whose wife spurs him on
>   To feed the children that she herself bears.
>
>   Long is the penitence of marriage,
>   A continuous sorrow after childbirth:
>   Experienced spouses recoil from marriage,
>   Which prepares a cross and tortures.
>
>   Always a woman claims that she is frail;
>   She drinks and eats, pisses and shits,
>   And a man wastes away in labors
>   And so work begins when he has consummated it.

The wife described here by no means lacks a body. Most visible thematically in her capacity as child-bearer – but equally in her capacity as consumer and excreter of food and drink – the wife in these stanzas has just enough of her own material person to irritate, offend, and burden the man fool enough to wed her. The wife must possess a body in order to bear and feed children, for example, but the embodied sites necessary for childbirth and the provision of sustenance do not themselves occupy the descriptions provided in the *De coniuge*. The total absence of mention of breasts, milk, or nourishment contrasts sharply with *Ave virgo*, which dedicates four of its final sixty stanzas (stanzas 105, 109, 112, 155) to the milk of Mary's breasts (that holy liquid nourishing Christ, Walter, and all of creation) and which lingers frequently, at times obsessively, on the swelling of her womb (stanzas 101, 105, 112, 115, 130, 157), the enticement of her kiss (stanza 107), and the glory of her body as fleshly residence or as holy sacrifice (stanzas 125, 161). In contrast, the *De coniuge* prefers to linger over the conditions of suffering that imagined wives bring upon their husbands, physically and psychologically. Comparison between husbands and various beasts of burden are not uncommon in the *De coniuge* (e.g., stanzas J2–J5). Moreover, the imagined wife of the *De coniuge* does not herself bear domestic burdens. Emphatically, from the perspective of the anti-matrimonial poem, wives are not themselves caretakers, only producers of cares for beleaguered husbands. The poem is concerned only with their relation to imagined husbands' perceived labors.

The double-vision adopted by the *De coniuge* of the bodies of its imagined wives holds as well in its discussion of specifically sexual labors, as in the "Insatiability Stanzas" quoted above. There, the first line identifies neither woman nor wife but the womb as the subject of unceasing and insatiable desire ("Insaciabilis vulva non deficit"), a subject that can then be taken as metonymically representative of any imagined woman, and so any wife, more generally. The shift from "vulva" to "feminam" and "feminam" to "mulier" signals an easy equivocation, familiar from Jerome and from Map, between who a wife is and what sexual functions her body performs. This collapse does not signal, however, a commensurate concern with any embodied conditions of her lived or imagined experience. In the eight stanzas cited from the *De coniuge* above, which largely describe wives who have sex, eat food, produce excrement, and bear children, it comes as something of a surprise that "vulva" is the only word that might refer to a specific part of the body, since the wife's imagined body is so frequently assumed in those stanzas to be a source of transgression, suffering, and remorse. In fashioning the archetypally imperfect wife, the *De coniuge* also excises any specific reference to her embodiment without abandoning the fundamental sinfulness that feminine embodiment is supposed to imply.

For the *De coniuge*, the bodies of its imagined wives are more filthy than fleshly, taking on significance only insofar as they can support the sinful and sexual act necessary for the poem's derision. For the *Ave virgo*, Mary's body is a source of divine significance, since it grounds the material, erotic, and procreative act necessary for communion with God. In both cases, the female, spousal body is imagined as a site of inexplicable insatiability, demanding something that no reader can give. Whether a coherent synthesis might be derived from this conceptual point of contact, where insatiability stretches from embodied perfection to disembodied transgression, forms the substance of the following section.

Misogamy and the Codicological Unconscious

The *Ave virgo mater christi* and the *De coniuge non ducenda* preserve a binary opposition between virginity and sexual transgression found in almost all antifeminist discourse, from Theophrastus to Jankyn, Augustine to de Meun. As in Warner's contention, above, that "there is no place in the conceptual architecture of Christian society for a single woman who is neither a virgin nor a whore," so in the two poems Scribe B copied into the quire ix of Bodley 851, no attempt is made to imagine any woman in terms apart from virginal purity on one hand and wanton fornication on the other.[55] Read together, however, the *Ave virgo* and the *De coniuge* do not preserve the strict association between sexual transgression and fleshly embodiment that typifies the misogamous literature of the clerkly tradition, as captured so enduringly by Chaucer's characterization of Jankyn and his book.

I do not suggest that, by inverting material associations with sinfulness, either poem operates outside of misogamist discourse. The *De coniuge* takes particular pleasure in representing wives and their desires as wholly degenerate in purpose and in practice. The poem's angelic authorities insist repeatedly that the dreaming protagonist flee marriage without providing for him any specific alternative course of action. Moreover, Wimborne's emphasis on Mary's singularity in the *Ave virgo* can be easily turned against less exceptional women, and so all women, by way of negative comparison. As the Wife of Bath observes in her own rendering of Jerome's modification to Proverbs 30, it is a small ideological step from "inferior" to "infernal": "Thou liknest eek wommenes love to helle," she complains, "Thou liknest it also to the wilde fyr" (*Wife of Bath's Prologue* III 371–3). To observe that these poems disrupt the usual terms of embodiment in misogamist discourse is not to extricate them from antifeminist discourse otherwise conceived. Rather, the disruption they signal suggests significant flexibilities in manuscript deployments of individual antifeminisms.

The *De coniuge* takes up and extends the extreme misogynist stance associated in scholarship with Map, Jerome, and Theophrastus. For Jerome, in *Against Jovinian* as in many of his other writings (such as his commentary on *Hosea*), marriage represents a compromise with sinful inadequacy, a shoddy

---

[55] Warner, *Alone of All Her Sex*, 235.

alternative to a rich spiritual life conducted in the absence of carnal obligations: "just to be in danger of" marriage to an odious woman is reason enough to remain unwed.[56] Even Jerome, however, leaves room for a woman both good and wed (as in the exemplary tales he furnishes from classical literature and mythology), with their imagined thirtyfold rewards. By refusing to consider virginity, contemplation, or chastity as spiritually efficacious alternatives to marriage, however, the *De coniuge* refuses any such alternative. In this, the rhetoric of the *De coniuge* overextends even that of Map, who – barely clearing the lowest imaginable discursive bar – at least refrains from identifying every instance of spousal transgression as a product of sexual transgression. As in R. Howard Bloch's much-disputed formulation that "the only true virgin is a dead virgin," for the *De coniuge*, unmarried women – even virgins – are always already becoming adulteresses ("fiunt adulterae"), since they are also always in peril of becoming wives.[57] If what is lost in between Jerome's arguments in *Against Jovinian* and in Map's *Dissuasio* is any functional concept of a "good woman" outside of virginity fanatically preserved, then what is lost in the *De coniuge* is any functional concept of a "good woman" at all.

Commentators on Proverbs 30 frequently sought to pre-empt the kind of extreme attitude toward feminine representation enacted by the *De coniuge*, usually by adopting allegorical or tropological readings that surpass the literal sense of the text. Above, I noted how the language of concupiscence surrounds Proverbs 30:15–16, so that the two daughters of the horseleech in Proverbs 30:15 are more commonly figured as allegorized vices than as embodied women. It should be noted, however, that the widely adopted phrase "concupiscentia oculorum" – used by Bede, Hrabanus Maurus, Peter Damien, and (later) Dionysius the Carthusian, among others – refers more directly to the sin of "curiositas" ("improper desire to know"; as Bede puts it, "scientes bonum et malum" ["knowing good and evil"]) than to any particular sexual transgression.[58] Mentions of whores ("meretrices"), while not infrequent – as in Peter de Celle's "duae meretrices sive sanguisugae" – are invoked far less frequently than discussions of vice in more general terms.[59] In this way, many interpretations of Proverbs 30 follow a common hermeneutic tradition, where any mention of sexual transgression might refer more adequately to the repentant (or unrepentant) soul and the Church sanctified (or belligerent) than to any specific sexual act undertaken by a specific human person. For

---

[56] *Adversus Jovinian*, 1.28, cited from Hanna and Lawler, *Jankyn's Book* 1:190.

[57] Bloch, *Medieval Misogyny*, 108.

[58] Beda Venerabilis, *Super epistulas catholicas expositio*, ed. D. Hurst, CCSL 121 (Turnhout: Brepols, 1983), 4.2.179. For the origin of "concupiscentia oculorum," see 1 John 2:16.

[59] Petrus Cellensis, *Commentaria in Ruth* (CCCM 54), ed. G. de Martel (Turnhout: Brepols, 1983), comm. 2, line 210.

example, in one early reading of Proverbs 30:20 – which describes the "way of an adulterous woman" ("via mulieris adulterae") and is frequently read alongside Proverbs 30:15–16 – Maximus of Turin (c. 400) preserves the binary between virginity and adultery but discards their literal referents:

> For this is the power of Christ the Lord, that even a sinner who washes himself in his water returns afresh to virginity and forgets what he had done before. And in his new birth he manifests the innocence of infancy, he does not know the sins of youth, and although he had been an adulterer because of the corruption of sin, he becomes a virgin because of faith in Christ.[60]

Maximos reverses the expectation that adulterers should be understood as negative *exempla*. He proposes the actions of the adulterous woman discussed in Proverbs 30:20 rather as a positive model for the soul in need of repentance than as a warning to prospective husbands (or wives). The former adulterer is most clearly identified by the "ardor of her faith" since she has "washed herself at the source" and "has no more awareness of her sin." Similarly, Origen compares the repentant fornicator favorably with the unrepentant fornicator as an exemplary spiritual subject, and Hippolytus of Rome declares that spiritual adultery and subsequent repentance are "the conduct of the Church."[61] Even in those cases where the material body is emphasized, the gendered figures of Proverbs 30 tend to take on tropological significance: on Proverbs 30:16, one manuscript tradition for the *Glossa ordinaria* acknowledges that "the body is not satisfied by delights, and the avaricious does not say, 'enough!'" but emphasizes how "others say this is the infernal devil, who is not satisfied in seducing humans" in order to associate the "way of the adulterous woman" with the "mind" practiced in transgression.[62] So too, along tropological lines, for Hippolytus of Rome in his discussion of Proverbs 30:20, "such is the conduct of the church that believes in Christ," which turns away from idolatry (signified by adultery) and engages in right religious practices (signified by repentance).[63]

---

[60] Maximus of Turin, *Sermon 22.3*, quoted in *Proverbs, Ecclesiastes, Song of Solomon*, ed. J. Robert Wright, no. 9 in *Ancient Christian Commentary on Scripture*, gen. ed. Thomas C. Oden (Downers Grove, IL: Intervarsity Press, 2005), 181.

[61] Origen, *Homilies on Jeremiah* and Hippolytus, *Fragments on Proverbs* both in *Proverbs*, ed. Wright, 180–1.

[62] "Corpus non satiatur deliciis, et avarus non dicit, sufficit; alii infernum dicunt diabolum, qui non satiatur seductione humana... Adultera quoque mens ut ea quae commemoravit, semper vaga est, quae ubi celare peccata poterit, negat se aliquid patrasse mali" (Walfridus Strabo, *Liber Proverbiorum*, ed. J. P. Migne, PL 1113 [Paris: 1852], 1113b–c).

[63] Hippolytus of Rome, *Fragments on Proverbs*, quoted in *Proverbs*, ed. Wright, 180.

The adulterous woman is understood to figure as a positive model for spiritual transformation, rather than a negative example to condemn absolutely.

In the most common readings, there remains little room for literal, material, human bodies, since "virgin" and "adulteress" describe more aptly a spiritual condition, whether individual or communal, than a social or physical condition. Rather than disparaging all women as inclined to sexual transgression, as in the *De coniuge* (or Map, or Jerome, or de Meun), allegorizing commentaries abandon gendered or sexed differentiation entirely in favor of explicating spiritual significance. Representations of feminine desire are in this way severed from imagined female subjects in order to be more securely associated with the soul or the Church. If Jerome's commentaries preclude thinking of any "good woman" outside of virginity, and if *De coniuge* precludes thinking of any "good woman" at all, then allegorical and tropological commentaries might be said to preclude any functional concept of "woman," generally. In this major tradition of biblical exegesis, the primary hermeneutic alternative to prejudice is not acceptance but abstraction.

As we observed above, however, the *Ave virgo* insists repeatedly on Mary as a woman, in emphatic possession of a woman's body, who both exists and is good. Rather aligning Mary with the figurative "sanguisugae" of Proverbs 30 than setting her in interpretive opposition to them, figuratively or sexually, the *Ave virgo* neither refuses Mary's status as material woman nor evacuates her of erotic desire in search of allegorical meaning. Nor does the devotional poem take Mary's sexual relationship with God as an opportunity for ribaldry or subversion.[64] In the *Ave virgo*, there is no competition between Mary and God, no binary opposition to be designated between word and flesh, universe and body, desire and reason, sexuality and divinity. As we saw above, Wimborne's poem takes Mary's body not only as a necessary part but as a primary grounds for understanding her relationship with divinity. She is holy precisely because she never ceases in her erotic and embodied communion with God. Her body does not stand in for disembodiment, nor is her unconstrained yearning a symptom of any need for repentance. She is neither virgin, insofar as virginity involves sexual abnegation, nor adulteress, insofar as adultery involves sexual transgression.

The *Ave virgo* does not categorically exclude any non-literal reading of Mary's significance, but neither does it demand such a reading. The common exegetical framing of reality as an imaginative, spiritual, and tropological discourse, wherein the condition of the self and the condition of the soul

---

[64] *Pace* Solberg, *Virgin Whore*, 7: "Mary had seduced God with her sexual charisma, bewitched his better judgment, and remade both the Word and the entire universe in her irresistibly attractive human image." Where Solberg posits a subversive role for Mary in her relationship with the divine, Wimborne understands conformity between divinity and her sexuality.

are most readily associated together over and against the condition of the body, allows the material contexts of Bodley 851 to inflect a critical understanding of Mary's place in medieval society almost wholly disconnected from discussions of marriage otherwise conceived. Indeed, by framing the real human condition not in terms of the social bonds of marriage but in terms of spiritual communion with God, the *Ave virgo* might have encouraged a tropological approach for some medieval audiences. As in many commentaries on the *Song of Songs* and many mystical expressions of divine union, so in Wimborne's poem Mary might represent the ideal example of a soul as virgin wife. She provides a perfect example for the enmattered soul seeking perfection and purification.[65] According to some of the more idealizing byways of mystical thought, her materiality might be construed more adequately as personhood, and the beauty of her imagined body – as with Dante's Beatrice or the *Pearl*-maiden – might be understood to represent the essential divinity of her imagined being. In this interpretive tradition, erotic and sexual language can figure not only for calls to repentance (as in the quotation from Maximus provided above) but also for exemplary formulations of desire, and so emerge in a doctrinally sanctioned ecclesiastical discourse. Readers are encouraged to imagine themselves as wives precisely as Mary is imagined as wife, material insofar as they are spiritual and erotic insofar as they might express devotion in spiritual terms.[66]

Where the *Ave virgo* might insist on materiality while allowing for dematerialized interpretation, the *De coniuge* repeatedly rejects both the materiality of carnal desire and the spiritual eroticism such desire might be understood to represent. There, it is precisely on account of the totalizing pervasiveness of sexual sin that marriage itself should be understood as burdensome and sinful. In commentaries on the *Song of Songs*, Mary is increasingly honored not only as mother of God but as a figuration of the Church, and so as bride of Christ – that is, in her capacity as spouse. So female monastics and mystics, for example, were encouraged to think of themselves as Brides of Christ, as were male monastics in the tradition of Bernard of Clairvaux or mystics such as Richard Rolle. But where such reading practices perceive spiritual marriage as an exemplary transformation of earthly marriage, and where the *Ave virgo* allows for Mary's physical eroticism to signify spiritual reality as well, the *De coniuge* refuses any version of marriage whatsoever, depicting not only sexual intimacy but the marriage state more generally – in every

---

[65] Amy M. Hollywood, *The Soul as Virgin Wife* (Notre Dame, IN: University of Notre Dame Press, 1995).

[66] For comparable readerly identifications, see Ryan McDermott, *Tropologies* (Notre Dame, IN: University of Notre Dame Press, 2016); Michelle Karnes, "Exercising Imagination," in *Imagination, Meditation, and Cognition in the Middle Ages* (Chicago, IL: University of Chicago Press, 2011), 141–78.

manifestation – as something to be resisted and avoided. What marriage *is*, most basically in the *De coniuge*, is an exemplary instance of subjection to sin. By refusing to acknowledge the fleshly grounds of its fleshly critique, however, the *De coniuge* also refuses the possibility of any transformation into spiritual terms. There is no room in the *De coniuge* for an ugly female body to represent a soul disfigured by sin, as in Alain of Lille's *Plaint of Nature*, Spenser's *Faerie Queene*, or D. W. Robertson's reading of *The Wife of Bath's Prologue* and *Tale*.[67] The more popular poem adopts, in short, a sort of pragmatic Gnosticism, and so rejects any rendering of spiritual marriage that might adopt as referent any unification of embodied persons whatsoever. If there is room in the *Ave virgo* for a sexual relationship in marriage, however spiritualized, there is no room in the *De coniuge* for any marriage whatsoever – sexual, chaste, or spiritual.

Read literally, read allegorically, read according to the terms of their source texts and the terms of their imagined audiences, the *Ave virgo* and the *De coniuge* consistently refuse the anthologizing logic modern readers often seek within medieval collections organized around shared generic features, thematic interests, or rhetorical aims. To examine these two poems closely is to rediscover constantly the terms of their thematic unlikeness and practical disagreement, rather than to uncover some overarching conformance to a broader cultural principle. Their material conjunction in Bodley 851 brings conceptual points of contact to the fore, which I have traced through their joint interest in insatiability. It does not therefore generate some hitherto unthought synthesis of the derogatory and the devotional in medieval thought.

Fragmented Prejudice and the Whole Book

As this chapter has described at length, two companion poems as unlikely and unlike as the *Ave virgo mater christi* and the *De coniuge non ducenda* can reveal much about why we must so often imagine, rather than examine, "books of wicked wives." Their conjunction lacks the imposed coherence of an imagined book like Jankyn's or a carefully structured poem like the *Rose*, and the state of their preservation in a fragmentary, composite manuscript at best evokes alternative cultural perspectives as muddled and obscure to the modern critic as they likely were to medieval scribes and readers. An examination of these poems as they are preserved in a single manuscript thus gives modern readers some access to, some purchase on, some hazy-yet-indicative features of the swirling, complex, and contradictory readerly motivations that might lead to their joint compilation, that might negotiate their impressions and invitations in conversation with one another, and that might perceive

---

[67] D. W. Robertson Jr., "The Wife of Bath and Midas," *SAC* 6 (1984): 1–20.

them – if only fleetingly – as textual objects capable of informing spiritual practice and practical contemplation in mutual relation.

In short, quire ix of Bodley 851 possesses a bewildering, illuminating, unsatisfying, and compelling codicological unconscious. To read its two poems together is not to arrive at a set of declarative or argumentative statements about one or more individual perspectives on Marian devotion, gendered social hierarchies, or the relation between physical sacraments and the condition of the soul. Much less does such an act of reading serve to upset or decenter the place of misogynist, misogamous, or antifeminist thought in medieval texts and their medieval books. Rather, to read these two poems together is to retrace the confused and contradictory byways of thought that conditioned the act of reading for a late-medieval English audience, to hold simultaneously two unfamiliar textual objects in our minds, and to glimpse, however inadequately and however temporarily, some perspective on the past strikingly different from the dominant tradition we know so well. There is room within quire ix of Bodley 851, between the *Ave virgo* and the *De coniuge*, for imagining innumerable women, not idealized and schematized – not made either virgin or whore (in the vein of Augustine and Jerome, Bloch and Warner) – but thought together, concretely, abstractly, and unequally, and in continuing disagreement.[68] The routine insistence on the necessity of embodiment for unification with God presented by the *Ave virgo* and rejected by the *De coniuge*, along with the poems' combined insistence on the correspondence between abstraction and transgression, do not amount to a competing ideology: if the implications we have been observing "were to be consciously noticed they would likely be disavowed."[69] They nevertheless can and should encourage new perspectives on deployments of antifeminist discourse in a wide variety of further texts.

As a brief closing example, we might return to that most familiar and embodied imagined reader of medieval misogamy, Chaucer's Wife of Bath. As Chaucerians know well, Alison's antagonistic relationship with Jankyn's habitual misogyny is often taken as the defining feature of her character. In two insightful formulations representative of a vast critical tradition, A. J. Minnis writes that, with the Wife of Bath, "the monster or the marvel – depending on how one wants to view her – comes alive, takes on flesh"; and Jamie C. Fumo refers to her as "ultimately a victim of the texts that have shaped her, a page torn out of a book to which she has no further rights."[70] Because she

[68] Bloch, *Medieval Misogyny*; Warner, *Alone of All Her Sex*.

[69] Sarah Kay, *Animal Skins and the Reading Self* (Chicago, IL: University of Chicago Press, 2017), 17.

[70] Minnis, *Fallible Authors*, 250; Jamie C. Fumo, "Argus' Eyes, Midas' Ears, and the Wife of Bath as Storyteller," in *Metamorphosis: The Changing Face of Ovid in Medieval and Early Modern Europe*, ed. Steven Rupp (Toronto: Centre for Reformation and Renaissance Studies, 2007), 150.

is anti-antifeminist, Alison takes pleasure in bodily delights, and because her pleasures are characterized by those of the flesh, she manifests – she embodies – rather than contradicts Jankyn's clerkly misogynist ideal. She is limited by the same discursive regime she opposes: there is no question that Alison's biography conforms to the terms of clerkish misogynist discourse, written as it is by Geoffrey Chaucer, a thoroughly clerkish medieval man. Yet, in view of the codicological unconscious of the fragmentary first part of the ninth quire of Bodley 851, we might glimpse the Wife of Bath in an unspoken, historicized, material perspective equally incommensurate to the monstrous and the marvelous – the virgin and the whore, the disfigured sinner and most pure servant of God. While acknowledging Alison as fiction, we might understand her complex embodied desires to characterize a mode of mediating what is muddled and human rather than what is idealized and infernal, of representing that insatiability which gives pleasure rather than that which exhausts.

When Alison of Bath tears apart Jankyn's fictional book, page by page, instead of dutifully patching it back together on Jankyn's behalf, literary historians might examine the more interesting, less comprehensive, and local records of "experience" that her less authoritative contemporaries left behind. Medieval manuscripts routinely compile overtly misogamist texts alongside less overtly prejudiced materials; and there is no shortage of neglected material – particularly in Anglo-Latin – that persists in surviving collections. A closer examination of historical practices outside of strictly canonical texts will lend critical insight to the pasts we inherit and trouble many narratives that modern readers, and especially modern scholars, tell about the present.

3

Recomposing Walter Map

This chapter examines the structure of Walter Map's *De nugis curialium* in order to ask how comparative approaches to a compiled book can inform comparative approaches to a compiled text. As we have seen, Part I of Bodley 851 preserves the sole surviving copy of Map's only life work (fols. 7ra–73v), a collection of historical accounts, folk tales, classical references, political jibes, and courtly witticisms (among other competing generic forms) in Latin prose, originally composed at the close of the twelfth century. Within Bodley 851, the *De nugis* is preserved in five distinctions, and each distinction is broken up into smaller chapters of disparate length. These textual divisions postdate Map's death.[1] One section of the *De nugis* circulated widely as the *Dissuasio Valerii ad Rufinum* (4.2–5), a fervently hyperbolic antifeminist epistle commonly attributed in manuscript witnesses to authoritative sources such as St. Jerome and Valerius Maximus.[2] In the version of the *Dissuasio* preserved within the *De nugis*, Map acknowledges the popularity of his epistle, noting that "it is snatched up greedily, copied passionately, and read with great delight" ("auide rapit*ur*; transcribit*ur* intente; plena iocunditate legit*ur*;"; fol. 47r, 4.5).[3] Immediately, he complains that "nevertheless, some people

---

[1] James Hinton, "Walter Map's De Nugis Curialium: Its Plan and Composition," *PMLA* 32.1 (1917): 81–132; Joshua Byron Smith, *Walter Map and the Matter of Britain* (Philadelphia, PA: University of Pennsylvania Press, 2017), esp. chapters 1–3.

[2] I refer to distinctions and chapters in the *De nugis curialium* using Walter Map, *De Nugis Curialium: Courtiers' Trifles*, rev. ed. and trans. M. R. James, Christopher N. L. Brooke and Roger A. B. Mynors (Oxford: Clarendon Press, 1983); cited as James *et al.* An alternative translation without edition is available as Walter Map, *Master Walter Map's Book, De Nugis Curialium (Courtier's Trifles)*, trans. Frederick Tupper and Marbury Bladen Ogle (London: Chatto & Windus, 1924). For discussion of the *Dissuasio* in terms of source, transmission, and commentary, see Ralph Hanna and Traugott Lawler, *Jankyn's Book of Wikked Wyves*, 2 vols. (Athens, GA: University of Georgia Press, 1997). For further discussion of Map's pseudonymous afterlives, see Chapter 4, especially pp. 157–9, 164–5.

[3] I cite and translate the *De nugis* directly from MS Bodley 851. I frequently provide a reference to James *et al.* for convenience. Because the revised edition reorganizes the text and occasionally takes liberties in translation that obscure Map's wordplay, whenever possible I have preserved in my transcription the orthography

– vulgar people! – deny that it is mine" ("mea*m* ta*men esse* q*uidam* sed de plebe negant."; fol.47r). Apart from the *Dissuasio*, Bodley 851 constitutes the only material evidence for any transmission of the *De nugis* – and so, too, for any possible medieval readership of Map's life work. Although Map's contemporaries lauded his wit, and although the manuscript record in England would come to attribute to Map a vast array of verse compositions that he did not actually write, there is no direct evidence for engagement from medieval readers of his text outside of the evidence presented by Bodley 851.[4] Indeed, the postauthorial division of the *De nugis* into distinctions and chapters may present the best evidence for medieval engagement with Map's text.

At the core of this chapter rests an extended reading of the contents of fols. 26r–27v, which relate, in three scribal chapters (2.11–2.13), a pair of fantastical stories about fairy-women and their progeny (2.11, 2.12), followed by a brief reflection on what those stories might reveal about God's providence (2.13). The most specific textual claim I advance about these scribal chapters is that when Walter Map narrates the story of a Briton named Triunein (2.11) followed by the story of an Anglo-Saxon named Alnoth (2.12), and then states the relevance of "this Alnoth and that Briton, discussed above" to his meditation on the presence of *fantasmata* and *fantastici* in the world ("hic alnodi *et* ille b*ri*tonu*m* de quo sup*er*ius"; fol. 27vb, 2.13), he intends to comment on the immediately preceding narratives of Alnoth and Triunein, discussed immediately prior. As I demonstrate below, this claim requires some significant substantiation, in light of previous critical engagements with the text.

The central interpretive claim of this chapter is that, in a carefully revised work of stylized literary fiction – here, the *De nugis curialium* – sequences of textual material substantially aligned in terms of genre, structure and theme should merit close literary attention. My formulation may strike the reader unfamiliar with academic discourse around Map as simplistic, if not redundant,

---

and conventions for punctuation present within Bodley 851. I treat the *point* as the modern comma (","), I treat single virgules as the modern sentence break ("."), and I preserve the appearance of the *punctus elevatus* (";" being an upside down rendition of the medieval mark) with its implications of continuity in sense and break in syntax; see *OUMEM*, xxxi; see also Suzanne Reynolds, *Medieval Reading: Grammar, Rhetoric, and the Classical Text* (Cambridge: Cambridge University Press, 1996). This punctuation need not have been Map's: it may belong to Scribe A, Scribe X, a prior exemplar, or – in some cases – a later reader. It may reflect the concerns of an oral culture. In any case, the manuscript represents one premodern attempt to make sense of Map's dense locutions, and my study responds to the manuscript's state.

[4] No new evidence has come to light that would alter Hinton's assessment nearly a century ago: "There is no affirmative evidence that *De Nugis Curialium* was known to medieval men of letters, that is, none except the existence of our unique mainuscript" ("Plan and Composition," 125).

and perhaps needlessly broad. After all, contemporary criticism usually takes for granted the relevance of literary quality (however construed) for literary inquiry (however pursued). It is nevertheless necessary, given past editorial and critical treatments of the *De nugis*, to demonstrate how *potential* points of contact between narrative sections of Map's text might cohere into *actual* grounds for literary interpretation. In fact, the critical tradition surrounding the *De nugis* requires some substantial revision of consensus perspectives on Walter Map and the scribes that copied his text in order to make relatively straightforward claims about the literary organization of his single surviving work in Bodley 851. Understanding how Map's narratives work in sequence allows us to understand how the construction of the material book affects the meaning of the written text. Close attention to scribal activity and authorial style together reveals a significant opportunity to read the *De nugis* as literature – not simply as a collection of isolated witticisms, but as a whole comprehensible only through careful consideration of the arrangement of its parts. The distribution of scribal rubricated chapter titles within Bodley 851, in particular, illuminates connections among sequential components of Map's text.

In this chapter, I first demonstrate how the material state of the *De nugis* in Bodley 851 can act as an interpretive guide for understanding arrangements of narrative components within Map's text. I build upon my analysis of Scribe A and Scribe X presented in Chapter 1. Second, I show how attention to the codicological unconscious – the hermeneutic intersection of how the book means and what its texts say – reveals not only structures of thought and imagination afforded by the material book but also contours of Map's own authorial project afforded by the literary work. The arguments of this chapter form a basis for my consideration of the afterlives of Map's authorial project for Bodley 851 in Chapter 4. Here, as in Chapter 2, I take the material manuscript book as interpretive guide to understanding its component parts. Unlike my analysis in the preceding chapter, which emphasizes topical incongruity between the construction of book and text might become, this chapter discovers a productive alignment between material evidence for the manuscript's production and textual evidence for the significance of the *De nugis*.

The present argument about how to understand Walter Map's literary fashioning in Bodley 851 constitutes also, therefore, a chapter about how forms of medieval authorship come to be silently categorized and pre-interpreted for modern readers, even – and most strikingly – where authorial activity occupies a substantial portion of relevant critical conversation. It is impossible to uncover the textual significance of the *De nugis* for Bodley 851 without first understanding how scribal agents made sense of Walter Map's work. Moreover, it is impossible to uncover any aspect of Map's complex relationship with the interpretation of his own writing without first understanding his canny proclivity for making simple yet misleading statements of fact. By examining manuscript, text, and author together, through extended engagement with the *De nugis*, this chapter addresses a set of broad methodological concerns in medieval literary study. It considers how modern critics might discern literary significance in the juxtaposition of textual units, determine the authority of material evidence for the purpose of representing a medieval work, and assess the interpretive affordances of medieval collections. This chapter thus raises about the *De nugis* the same question that *The Making and Meaning of a Medieval Manuscript* raises about its central manuscript: how can we discern literary affiliations within a collection of disparate textual materials? How do we go about reading a medieval book?

Editorial Encrustations

Like its sole surviving medieval witness, MS Bodley 851, Walter Map's *De nugis curialium* contains a variety of superficially mismatched textual units of uncertain relation. Unlike most of the other Latin texts preserved within Bodley 851, there is no dearth of academic writing on Map or his sole surviving literary corpus. Medievalists often excerpt Map's witty and erudite "nuggets" for the literary pleasures they bring and the historical perspectives they present. His oblique style welcomes the complexities of high theory, and his sprawling authorial reputation as courtier, romancer, and satirist invites a broad consideration of the generic affiliations of his literary output. Map's name appears regularly in important studies of medieval literary culture.[5] Critics have produced robust analyses of individual tales, literary scholars have examined shared literary influence in selected narrative comparisons (especially between Map and Gerald of Wales), and historians have collated a wide array of information from disparate regions of Map's book in studies of his political strategies, cultural affiliations, and political milieu.[6] From Map we learn that Cistercians in England made use of a kind of ecclesiastic eminent

[5] Medievalists might first encounter Map in a variety of guises, e.g.: as paradoxical authority in the first chapter of Alastair Minnis, *Medieval Theory of Authorship: Scholastic Literary Attitudes in the Later Middle Ages*, 2nd ed. (Philadelphia, PA: University of Pennsylvania Press, 2010); as arch-antifeminist throughout Carolyn Dinshaw, *Chaucer's Sexual Poetics* (Madison, WI: University of Wisconsin Press, 1989); as wry categorizer of the inexplicable in Benedicta Ward, *Miracles and the Medieval Mind: Theory, Record, and Event, 1000–1215* (Philadelphia, PA: University of Pennsylvania Press, 1982); or as literary phenom in any number of discussions of Chaucer and Langland, such as Hanna and Lawler, *Jankyn's Book*; or Morton W. Bloomfield, *Piers Plowman as a Fourteenth-Century Apocalypse* (New Brunswick, NJ: Rutgers University Press, 1962).

[6] Mentions of Map's relationship with Gerald are common. For a recent essay that primarily discusses Walter's relationship with Gerald, see Joshua Byron Smith, "Gerald of Wales, Walter Map and the Anglo-Saxon History of Lydbury North," in

domain (*De nugis* 1.24); from Map we confirm that the Waldensians were well-meaning dunces, schooled better in piety than doctrine (*De nugis* 1.31); and in Map we read that Henry II had working knowledge of every language used in Latin Christendom between the Atlantic and the Jordan (*De nugis* 5.6).

Perhaps because the contents of the *De nugis* are so thoroughly heterogenous, there is little consensus about how to categorize Map's text or affiliate its component textual parts. Map's individual narratives have been analyzed according to familiar generic affiliations, including historical writing, romance, folklore, and satire.[7] Indeed, the broader implications of these narratives do occasionally receive extended consideration.[8] Moreover, Map is discussed regularly in terms of networks of authors centered around the court of Henry II.[9] Mentions of Map occur more frequently in historical scholarship than in literary criticism, however, especially in treatments of the "twelfth century renaissance" and in discussions of the history of literature on the English border with Wales.[10] Overall, there is little disagreement that Map is "a figure who is central to several different literary histories of the Middle Ages."[11]

Gerald of Wales: New Perspectives on a Medieval Writer and Critic, ed. Georgia Henley and A. Joseph McMullen (Cardiff: University of Wales Press, 2018), 63–78.

[7] For examples of each mode, see, e.g., Victoria Flood, "Political Prodigies: Incubi and Succubi in Walter Map's *De Nugis Curialium* and Gerald of Wales's *Itinerarium Cambriae*," *Nottingham Medieval Studies* 57 (2013): 21–46; Ralph Hanna, "The Matter of Fulk: Romance and History in the Marches," *The Journal of English and Germanic Philology* 110.3 (2011): 337–58; Stephen Gordon, "Monstrous Words, Monstrous Bodies: Irony and the Walking Dead in Walter Map's De Nugis Curialium," *English Studies* 96.4 (2015): 379–402; and Margaret Sinex, "Echoic Irony in Walter Map's Satire against the Cistercians," *Comparative Literature* 54.4 (2002): 275–90.

[8] For example, Neil Cartlidge, "'Vinegar upon Nitre'? Walter Map's Romance of Sadius and Galo," in *Cultural Translations in Medieval Romance*, eds. Victoria Flood and Megan G. Leitch (Cambridge: D. S. Brewer, 2022), 117–34; and Siân Echard, "Clothes Make the Man: The Importance of Appearance in Walter Map's De Gadone Milite Strenuissimo," in *Anglo-Latin and Its Heritage*, eds Siân Echard and Gernot R. Wieland (Turnhout: Brepols, 2001), 93–108. A major recent exception is Richard Firth Green, *Elf Queens and Holy Friars: Fairy Beliefs and the Medieval Church* (Philadelphia, PA: University of Pennsylvania Press, 2016), which returns to Map's text repeatedly and fruitfully.

[9] E.g., Neil Cartlidge, "Masters in the Art of Lying? The Literary Relationship between Hugh of Rhuddlan and Walter Map," *The Modern Language Review* 106.1 (2011): 1–16.

[10] For example, see Lindy Brady, *Writing the Welsh Borderlands in Anglo-Saxon England* (Manchester: Manchester University Press, 2017); Graham Seal, *Outlaw Heroes in Myth and History* (New York: Anthem Press, 2011); and Monika Otter, *Inventiones: Fiction and Referentiality in Twelfth-Century English Historical Writing* (Chapel Hill, NC: University of North Carolina Press, 1996).

[11] Neil Cartlidge, "*Walter Map and the Matter of Britain* by Joshua Byron Smith (Review)," *Digital Philology: A Journal of Medieval Cultures* 8, no. 1 (2019): 145–8, at 146.

Although treatments of Map's work show little consensus in terms of topic or theme, critical readers are nearly unanimous in observing in Map a unique and characteristically oblique authorial mode. A significant strain of criticism understands Map's narrative style to undergird a nearly post-modern theoretical position on the conditions of authorship more generally.[12] Many critical readers have identified wry deflection as the hallmark of Map's wit. Echard identifies Map as uniquely interested "in the operations and implications of writing" among his peers at the Angevin Court, observing that as part of his authorial persona Map "both subverts and asserts his own *auctoritas*."[13] Expanding upon Echard's theory, Edwards devises for Map a theory of "counter-authorship," defined as "a form of authorial self-definition that exists in virtue of its differences from official literary roles, the higher genres of literary discourse, and the sociopolitical imaginary that those roles and genres sustain."[14] And in their landmark inquiry into the primary sources of Chaucer's *Wife of Bath's Prologue*, Hanna and Lawler write of the *Dissuasio*, that "Map satirically challenges the veridical nature both of philosophic claims and of his own verbal construction."[15] Almost every reader to have engaged at any length with Map's oblique literary style has come away with some impression that he never quite means exactly what he says – and probably means something he refuses to say, besides. It is nevertheless immensely difficult to identify any specific moment in his writing where such rhetorical duplicity is inarguably present (or inarguably absent). Moreover, as Stephen Gordon writes, "the meaning of the written or spoken text is *other than*, rather than *opposite of*, its literal form."[16] The range of what Map *could mean* based on what he *has said* is remarkably broad.

For an exemplary case of Map's narrative style, consider the following summary of *De nugis* 2.4, a miracle-story Map heard about Peter of Tarentaise from an acquaintance, Master Serlo of Wilton:

> A monk at the house of Cîteaux, born with a deformed foot, requests healing from Peter. Taking the monk's foot in his hands, Peter prays

---

[12] On Map as a nearly post-modern author, see Sebastian Coxon, "Wit, Laughter, and Authority in Walter Map's *De Nugis Curialium* (*Courtiers' Trifles*)," in *Author, Reader, Book: Medieval Authorship in Theory and Practice*, eds Stephen Partridge and Erik Kwakkel (Toronto: University of Toronto Press, 2012), 38–55; Robert Edwards, "Walter Map: Authorship and the Space of Writing," *New Literary History* 38.2 (2007): 273–92; Mark Philpott, "Haunting the Middle Ages," in *Writing and Fantasy*, eds. Ceri Sullivan and Barbara White (New York: Longman, 1999), 48–61; and Siân Echard, "Map's Metafiction: Author, Narrator and Reader in De Nugis Curialum," *Exemplaria* 8.2 (1996): 287–314.
[13] Echard, "Map's Metafiction," 288–9, 313.
[14] Edwards, "Space of Writing," 277.
[15] Hanna and Lawler, *Jankyn's Book*, 1:55. See also Smith, *WMMB*, 173.
[16] Gordon, "Monstrous Words," 381.

for a while, then refuses to heal him, exclaiming that the man would be better entering the kingdom of heaven with one good foot than being cast into hell with two good feet. Later, the same monk confesses to his abbot that he was from a noble and beautiful family ("cu*m* gen*er*osus *et* pulcher*ri*me p*r*osapie sim"), and that he only became a monk because he had been ashamed of his deformity. In fact, the monk confesses, for a moment he had begun to experience healing in his deformed foot. In that moment, immediately he began to think about returning home with joy to the place he had left in shameful sadness. (fol. 24v)

The narrative ends with the monk's admission; no further explanation or reflection is provided. Nor is any explanation truly necessary, in the sense typical of miracle-stories broadly considered, given that no miraculous event has taken place. A "miracle" in its typical sense abrogates or contravenes the natural course of events. Here, instead, the natural course of events is maintained. Yet Map places this narrative at the center of three consecutive tales about miraculous healings accomplished by the same Peter: in *De nugis* 2.3, he heals a lunatic of his madness, and in *De nugis* 2.5, he frees a man from the enduring grasp of a demonic lizard. Both surrounding chapters describe an event that is miraculous in the usual sense. In the present story, however, the miracle is precisely that there is no miracle. Peter discerns through prayer that if the monk's deformity were to be healed, he would depart from the monastery and lose his faith (or, at least, break his vows). The cost of physical healing would be spiritual suffering, a foot gained and a soul lost. In this context, the natural course of events (leaving the foot the way it is) is itself made miraculous, accomplishing something of greater importance (healing the soul) than an interruption would have accomplished (healing the foot).

There are multiple levels of jest to be considered: at the expense of nobility, at the expense of those who would eavesdrop on confession, at the expense of puffed-up churchmen – all favorite targets of Map's – and perhaps in parody of the miracle-story genre itself. But the broad force of the overarching lesson is not therefore insincere. To deny that Map has related a miracle is to deny the efficacious working of God's servants in the world; and to interpret the narrative as a miracle is to understand that miracles and the normal course of events – the way things simply *are* – are deeply intertwined. "The structure of the piece," as Echard writes of another section of the *De nugis*, "suggests a preoccupation with the reception of the story."[17] In *De nugis* 2.4, as is common elsewhere within Map's wry productions, while the terms of the joke are apparent, the full significance of the joke is difficult to pin down. His ostensibly jovial authorial stance invites complex engagements with the narratives he relates.

---

[17] Echard, "Map's Metafiction," 311.

Map's readers tend to agree, then, that his writings merit close interpretive attention. From sustained critical consensus that understands Map as author of oblique and heterogenous material, however, has followed only intermittent concern with the material arrangement of the *De nugis* within its sole manuscript context, Bodley 851. Critical readers tend to harvest a wide cross-section of material from the *De nugis* according to generic, thematic, or historiographical interests prevalent in academic scholarship.[18] Accordingly, even the most sensitive treatments of the *De nugis* are little concerned with whether harvested selections have bearing on one another within the text's own structure.

Indeed, the better part of scholarship on the *De nugis* denies that the text preserved within Bodley 851 has structure enough to merit literary attention. One exceptional article, published by James Hinton in 1917, borrowed the idea of "fragments" from the Chaucerians in order to create a chronology of Map's authorial process in composing the text.[19] Hinton further proposed several hypotheses for how chronologically misplaced textual pieces might have been rearranged, whether intentionally or accidentally, by Map and by later scribes working with his rough papers. Ultimately, according to Hinton, "it is evident that Walter Map left his materials in a[n]... at best half-edited, state."[20] Indeed, though there is much to praise within individual components of the *De nugis*, "its excellence would never have been in its larger architecture, but in the charm of its component parts."[21] Hinton's conclusion – that Map's own working copy of the *De nugis* was characterized more by whimsical disarray than careful organization, only later to be disrupted by scribal reception beyond recuperation – has been cited widely by readers and editors alike.

Critical consensus about Map's style and editorial consensus about the arrangement of Map's work is perhaps best captured by the word "untidy" – as in the single most widely cited description of the text, wittily penned by its most recent editors, that the *De nugis* is "the untidy legacy of an untidy mind."[22] Hinton's conclusion in this way describes and anticipates the legacy of modern approaches to the *De nugis* on the whole. M. R. James, for example, praised the breadth of Map's reading but criticized a lack of organization within the text: "as to the plan and date of the *de Nugis*, nothing

---

[18] See nn5–12 on pp. 121–3, above.
[19] Hinton, "Plan and Composition,".
[20] Hinton, "Plan and Composition," 93.
[21] Hinton, "Plan and Composition," 132.
[22] James *et al.*, xxx. Variations on the "untidy" theme can be heard throughout the editors' preface. For citations of this quip, see, e.g., Gordon, "Parody, Sarcasm, and Invective," 82; Echard, "Map's Metafiction," 291; Smith, *WMBB*, 6.

can be clearer than that there is no plan."[23] In this, he followed the opinion of Thomas Wright, who described "the whole book" in his *editio princeps* as "one mass of contemporary anecdote, romance, and popular legend," so that Map routinely "goes on stringing together stories and legends which have no intimate connection."[24] More recently, having posited the text's total untidiness, C. N. L. Brooke and R. A. B. Mynors determine that the *De nugis* "never makes up its mind which way to jump," and so must be considered "a ragbag of different kinds of cloth."[25] For example, in their discussion of how *De nugis* 4.1, given the chapter heading "Prologus," and *De nugis* 4.2, given the chapter heading "Epilogus," came to sit back to back, Brooke and Mynors write: "The epilogue's present place, however, is inexplicable. Since it was evidently written on a loose slip or bifolium, it is possible that Map, finding his prologue unhappily sandwiched in the middle of the book, with gay abandon attached the epilogue to it."[26] According to the assessment shared by each of Map's modern editors, the disastrous material state of *De nugis* as it is uniquely preserved within Bodley 851 must preclude any examination of the narrative arrangement of its parts. Any relation between contiguous chapters need be thought accidental, and so negligible, for understanding the work on the whole.

Joshua Byron Smith has produced a persuasive alternative vision of how Map's book arrived at its current material state. To the hypothesis ventured by Brooke and Mynors about 4.1–4.2, Smith retorts: "Just to be clear, what Brooke and Mynors propose is that Walter wrote a coherent book, cut it in half so that it began with the satire on the court, neglected to discard his first draft of said satire on the court, perhaps placed an epilogue in the now middle of the work because that is where his prologue lay, and afterward inserted a few stories here and there."[27] Smith finds this degree of ineptitude implausible. By attending closely to the role scribes and annotators played in the transmission of Map's text, Smith argues convincingly that a considerable part of the material untidiness now associated with the *De nugis* is better associated with historical agents other than Walter himself. In this view, "the *De nugis curialium* is a collection of Walter's papers containing a few complete texts, earlier draft material, and some work in progress. It was never intended to be a complete book. This false impression has been created by later scribal

---

[23] Walter Map, *De nugis curialium*, ed. M. R. James (Oxford: Clarendon Press, 1914), xxiv.

[24] Walter Map, *De Nugis Curialium*, ed. Thomas Wright (London: Camden Society, 1850), v, x.

[25] James *et al.*, xlii.

[26] James *et al.*, xxix.

[27] Smith, *WMMB*, 41.

interference."[28] While not every aspect of the text now preserved in fols. 7r–73v of Bodley 851 need be taken to represent Map's authorial discretion, neither should Map's role in the construction of his sole surviving text be discounted on account of the exigencies of its transmission: "It is hardly [Map's] fault that the only surviving copy of his work has been taken as the definitive testament of his literary talents."[29] If there is untidiness to be accounted for in the *De nugis*, it is not in Map's mind but in the minds of his readers, medieval and modern.

Smith's formulation, like Hinton's a century prior, bears the hallmarks of Chaucerian attention. ("As is well known, *The Canterbury Tales* is a mess.")[30] Yet readers of the *Tales* do not abandon any attempt to understand the *Tales* in relation to one another due to signs of textual fragmentation. Nor need we attribute every gap in sense to a shuffling of parchment. Chaucerians view with some skepticism the idea that "fragments" determined by editorial procedure might be found in fragmentary physical form anywhere in the manuscript record.[31] Like the *Tales*, the *De nugis* frequently contains moments of textual discontinuity that need not be derived from some prior material discontinuity. Accordingly, even supposing that Map's working papers were left in total disarray at the time of his death, it does not necessarily follow that the state of Map's text after his death was in any material sense "fragmentary."[32] Scribal chapter headings and distinction breaks in particular need not transparently signal some irreparable material disjuncture within the text. As Chaucerians know well, so too should we recall in studies of Walter Map that the appearance of fragmentation, discontinuity, and interruption can arise from sources other than errors in scribal copying, especially as artifacts of authorial praxis and editorial presentation. Moreover, apparent disruptions can serve multiple and contradictory rhetorical ends.

As Smith has demonstrated recently, the mass of text now titled the *De nugis curialium* must have grown and shifted under Walter Map's supervision over the course of at least a decade. Furthermore, as Hinton demonstrated over

---

[28] Smith, *WMMB*, 75

[29] Smith, *WMMB*, 39.

[30] Daniel Wakelin, *Immaterial Texts in Late Medieval England: Making English Literary Manuscripts, 1400–1500* (Cambridge: Cambridge University Press, 2022), 221. Wakelin continues: "It shows stages of authorial revision; it was left incomplete; it survives in fragments, but maybe not fixed ones. The divergent copies that emerged betray the messy state of the text at Chaucer's death. This was a problem caused by physical copies: rough papers, perhaps in awkward formats such as added leaves, with visually confusing revisions." Apart from the implication of multiple surviving manuscript witnesses, the description could as easily apply to Walter.

[31] Robert J. Meyer-Lee, "Abandon the Fragments," *SAC* 35 (2013): 47–83.

[32] Hinton, "Plan and Composition," 93.

a century ago, much of the apparent continuity of presentation in Bodley 851 and in modern editions (such as the connectedness of his five distinctions), as well as some of the apparent fragmentation (such as the many chapter headings that break up the text or the penwork initials that precede them), are byproducts of textual transmission rather than lingering traces of authorial untidiness. The current situation in scholarship, wherein Map is excerpted frequently but interpreted only rarely, depends upon common misunderstandings about the material implications of his surviving text. Accordingly, even given the multiple successes of editions produced by Wright (1850), James (1914), and Brooke and Mynors (1983), it is no exaggeration to say that, in the intervening century between Hinton's article and Smith's monograph, little if any attention has been given to analyzing literary sequences within the *De nugis*, rather than literary nuggets, in terms of their thematic or narrative coherence.

In order to capture the significance of one potent literary sequence in the *De nugis*, this chapter further complicates Smith's assessment of Map's authorial praxis through an examination of how textual sequences intersect with manuscript production in Bodley 851. If, as Matthew Fisher has argued, "the work of the scribe is ultimately the variously blurry lens through which the work of the author can, and must, be seen," in Map's case the work itself is already kaleidoscopic, such that scribal alterations to its material preservation compound, rather than simply blear, the frustrating complexity of arranging its component parts.[33] Scribal chapter headings, in particular, simultaneously declare in their contents continuity between successive narrative moments and imply in their placement discontinuity between one chapter and another. By breaking Map's authorial text into sequential parts, they provide a medieval commentary upon the coherence of sequential content.

The textual situation for the *De nugis* in its sole manuscript copy is well known and well studied. Walter Map's authorial persona is well known and well studied. Yet the complex arrangements of narrative, implication, and imagination presented by Map within the *De nugis* remain almost wholly neglected in modern criticism. Most commonly, scholarship on the *De nugis* has treated the book as an impediment to understanding the text's significance. Whether on account of Map's ostensibly impenetrable obliqueness or on account of scribal corruptions of the same, editors and critics have mostly disregarded the construction of the manuscript (Bodley 851) as evidence for construing meaning in the text (*De nugis*). In this way, scholarship has by and large discarded the collaborative work of Scribe A and Scribe X, and so the specific material contexts of Bodley 851, in surveying the significance of the *De nugis*. This chapter aims to uncover a more productive relationship between Bodley 851, Walter Map, and the scribal tradition of the *De nugis*

---

[33] Matthew Fisher, *Scribal Authorship and the Writing of History in Medieval England* (Columbus, OH: Ohio State University Press, 2012), 37–8.

culminating in Scribe A and Scribe X, in which surviving material evidence refracts a complex, parodic, and self-deprecating authorial project.

The codicological unconscious of Bodley 851 thus can be understood to intersect "untidily" with the textual unconscious of the *De nugis curialium*, such that the construction of the material book both clarifies and disrupts the compiled components of its compiled text. In making this particular book, scribal agents undertook to present Map's authorial habit through non-authorial structures of organization and interpretation. Ostensible textual discontinuities within the *De nugis* present a bounty of interpretive possibilities commonly obscured by editorial assumptions about its author.

Of course, I do not assume that every contiguous section of text contained between fols. 7r–73v of Bodley 851 will necessarily contain hitherto unthought interpretive riches. Sometimes, a disjuncture is just a disjuncture. The *De nugis* shows many signs of inarguable fragmentation. Careful analysis will not benefit from ignoring its most obvious and uncontestable discontinuities. But criticism will not benefit, either, from ignoring the possibility that apparent discontinuity and stylistic "untidiness" might serve an array of underlying purposes. Fragmentation – in Map's book, in medieval manuscripts, and in the study of texts more generally – forms an invitation to robust interpretation, rather than an insurmountable obstacle to the act of literary inquiry.[34] Indeed, attention to the codicological unconscious of Map's manuscript may yield insight into further interpretive possibilities within Map's book. The compiled book – as literary object and as material object – has the potential to illuminate what Map's the text alone might otherwise make wholly obscure.

Scribal Clarifications

What can the scribal chapter headings included throughout the *De nugis* reveal about the meaning of Walter Map's text within the context of Bodley 851? As Hinton and Smith have shown, many elements that survive within the *De nugis* can be attributed safely to agents other than Map himself. Following a pattern common in late-medieval copying in England, annotations and marginal notes frequently made their way into Map's authorial text.[35] Chapter titles, in particular, derive from a tradition of reception and interpretation.[36]

---

[34] See Arthur Bahr, *Fragments and Assemblages: Forming Compilations of Medieval London* (Chicago, IL: University of Chicago Press, 2013). See also Bahr's striking response to Meyer-Lee, "Abandon the Fragments," in "Celebrate Fragments," *New Chaucer Society Blog* (5 December 2013), https://newchaucersociety.org/blog/entry/celebrate-fragments (last accessed 7 February 2021).

[35] Smith, *WMBB*, 68–73. For the frequency of such movement from margin to body, see also Wakelin, *Immaterial Texts*, 165.

[36] Smith, *WMBB*, 65–8.

As I demonstrated in Chapter 1, however, the scribes of Bodley 851 considered chapter titles and distinction breaks integral to the text's construction. Scribe A carefully plotted space for chapter titles in his arrangement of layout for the main text, and he wrote out the chapter titles in inked text for the table of contents at the close of the *De nugis*. Afterward, Scribe X wrote rubricated chapter titles into the main text; and he further modified the table of contents according to a shared scheme. In both respects, Scribe X undertook to complete a coherent program that Scribe A began.

Table 3. Comparison of chapter titles for a section of Distinction 2 of the *De nugis curialium* between the table of contents, imposed by Scribe A, and the rubrications for the main text, imposed by Scribe X.

	Main Text fols. 25r–28v (Scribe X)	Table of Contents fols. 72v–73v (Scribe A)
De nugis 2.7	De luca hungaro	De luca hungaro
De nugis 2.8	De i*n*discreta deuoc*ion*e Walensiu*m*	De i*n*discreta deuoc*ion*e Walensiu*m*
De nugis 2.9	De Helya heremita Wale*n*siu*m*	De Helya her*[e]*mita Walensi
De nugis 2.10	De Cadoco Rege Walensi	De Cadoco rege Walensi
De nugis 2.11	De a*paricion*ibus fa*n*tasticis	De ap*paricion*ibus fantasticis
De nugis 2.12	It*em* de eisd*em* a*paricion*ib*us*	It*em* de eisd*em* ap*paricion*ib*us*
De nugis 2.13	It*em* de eisd*em* a*paricion*ib*us*	It*em* de eisd*em* ap*paricion*ib*us*
De nugis 2.14	Item de eisd*em* a*paricion*ib*us*	Item de eisd*em* ap*paricion*ib*us*
De nugis 2.15	Item de eisd*em* a*paricion*ib*us*	Item de eisd*em* ap*paricion*ib*us*
De nugis 2.16	Item de eisd*em* a*paricion*ib*us*	Item de eisd*em* ap*paricion*ib*us*
De nugis 2.17	De gradone milite strenuissimo	De gadone milite strenu*issi*mo

Moreover, scribal chapter headings are consistent between the main text of the *De nugis* (fols. 25r–28v) and the table of contents at its close (fols. 72v–73v; pl. 5). Consider the titles surrounding *De nugis* 2.11–2.13 (Table 3). The first thing to notice is how consistent the chapter titles are between disparate locations. The only two differences in this sampling are in *De nugis* 2.9 and

De nugis 2.17. For *De nugis* 2.9, Scribe X gives "Walensium" in the main text, while Scribe A gives "Walensi" in the table of contents. For *De nugis* 2.17, where Scribe X's main text has "gradone," Scribe A's table of contents has "gadone." (In this second example, the table of contents is correct: the knight for most of the relevant tale is, indeed, "Gado" and not "Grado." Scribe X likely responds to the spelling used in the chapter's first sentence, itself presumably an error: "Gradone*m* mira*mini*" [fol. 28v].) Such consistency of lection reflects the relationship between in-text titles and titles in the table of contents for the *De nugis* on the whole. They suggest that Scribe A and Scribe X were working from a common copy; or, possibly, that Scribe X was working directly from Scribe A's labor.

The second thing to notice, however, is that patterns of scribal abbreviation differ frequently between the two locations. Scribe A, for example, uses two **p**'s in his spelling of "apparicionibus," including the conventional crossbar abbreviation for "par" on the descender for the second **p**. Scribe X, on the other hand, either omits the second **p** (as I have transcribed above) or considers the crossbar abbreviation sufficient to indicate the reduplication for audiences who might expect it (i.e., "a*ppari*cio*ni*bu*s*"). Another example is the handling of "Item." Scribe A alters his approach to the word across these entries, at first including a superscript squiggle to indicate abbreviated graphs (*De nugis* 2.12–13, table of contents), but then writing out the entire word for the final three entries of the same title (*De nugis* 2.14–16, table of contents). Scribe X, however, is consistent throughout, relying upon the same superscript squiggle in every case (*De nugis* 2.12–16, main text). Both scribes abbreviate "eisdem" in precisely the same way throughout. Neither scribe seems to be copying mechanically from some other source (shared or separate). Instead, each applies familiar conventions to the material as he conducts his work as copyist.

These chapter headings also tell a coherent story about shared contents between the chapters they describe. There is a declared triad of "Welsh" stories, for example, which reflects the ethnic status of the main characters within each, signaled by "Walensi" or "Walensium." A concern with the religious and political customs of the Welsh re-emerges later in the second distinction, again signaled by the same key words in the chapter titles. The Welsh stories are set off from the prior narrative, itself a continuation of prior narratives about holy men. And the string of six consecutive narratives about apparitions are united in many cases by a single repeated title, held distinctively in content from the tale of Gado, that most vigorous of knights.

If it is the case that these chapter titles are not authorial, it is also the case that they reflect measured readerly consideration of textual content. Chapter divisions occur reliably at moments of rhetorical separation in the text. So, the chapter title between *De nugis* 2.11 and 2.12 occurs just before the sentence, "The one about Edricus Wilde is similar" ("Simile*m* huic e*st* q*uo*d edric*us* wilde," fol. 26v). Even if Walter Map did not personally write, "Again of the same apparitions," the title responds to both the narrative content and the rhetorical construction of that content within the main body of the text. A finer gloss is made by the preceding chapter title (to *De nugis* 2.11), which links the matter of Welsh ethnicity prominent in the story of Cadog (*De nugis* 2.10), to the problem of apparitions that will trouble Map more directly. Where *De nugis* 2.10 ends, "So much for Cadog Brenin" ("H*ec* de cado*co* brenin," fol. 26r), *De nugis* 2.11 begins, "The Welsh tell us another – not a miracle but a prodigy" ("Aliud no*n* miraculu*m* se*d* portentu*m* nobis Walenses referu*nt*," fol. 26r). As Map's rhetorical construction signals a shift in narrative focus on the Welsh to a focus on otherworldly events – what Map himself calls "fantasma" – so too do scribal chapter headings highlight the strangeness of the narrative over the foreignness of its main characters. This same concern extends in the chapter titles through *De nugis* 2.16, which reflect Map's own rhetorical signals: "Isn't this another *fantasm*?" ("N*un*quid no*n et* hoc fantasma e*st*," fol. 28r). If in some sense the narrative focus has shifted, some emphasis nevertheless remains on that which is unusual: "You wonder at Grado" ("Gradon*em* mira*mini*," fol. 28v). Chapter titles break the text into sections without necessarily disrupting thematic continuity.

The interpretive crux central to the present chapter comes with the transition between *De nugis* 2.12 ("Again of these same apparitions") and *De nugis* 2.13 ("Again of these same apparitions"). The relevant passage reads:

> ...et in eius obsequiis residuum uite peregrinus expendit. [*De nugis* 2.13] A fantasia quod est aparicio transiens dicitur fantasma.
>
> ...and he spent the rest of his life as a pilgrim in service to Him. [*De nugis* 2.13] From fantasia – that is, a transient apparition – something is called fantasma.

The current critical consensus is that *De nugis* 2.13 marks a break from the interconnected narratives *De nugis* 2.12 and *De nugis* 2.11. As I explain in detail below, editors have posited sharp division in narrative referent, so that when Map refers to "the one before" ("de quo superius") in the midst of *De nugis* 2.13, he cannot be understood to refer to the closing subject of *De nugis* 2.12 – he who devotes himself as pilgrim to Christ. Instead, Map is understood to refer to *De nugis* 4.8 and 4.10, composed for this section of the manuscript but shuffled untidily, either by Map or by later scribes, into a wholly separate distinction.[37]

The state of the manuscript book, however, provides a contrary perspective. Scribal chapter headings draw a clear connection between Map's chosen

---

[37] Hinton, "Plan and Composition," 86–9, 91, 104, 111; James *et al.*, xxviii–xxix; Smith, *WMBB*, 59.

terminology ("A fantasia... dicitur fantasma") and the interest in apparitions ("aparicio transiens") that fills the surrounding chapters. Having established that scribal authorship need not be totally disparaged as scribal interference, we might ask: what can the close connection between scribal titles for these consecutive authorial units reveal about their literary significance?

It is my position in this chapter that scribal divisions and chapter titles capture textual significance latent within the authorial work and crucial to understanding the literary sequence preserved within Bodley 851. The medieval scribes who encountered Map's work, it turns out, were apt readers of his organization. Even setting aside authorial concerns, however, the underlying examination of the codicological unconscious remains: that the state of Bodley 851 offers an opportunity to think critically with the only surviving witness to Map's work about one coherent literary sequence within the *De nugis* (2.11–2.13). Following Map's scribes, I will show how the many structural similarities shared by *De nugis* 2.11 and *De nugis* 2.12 correspond exactly to Map's subsequent topical reference in *De nugis* 2.13. When Map refers to "Alnoth and that other Briton" ("hic alnodi *et* ille b*ri*tonu*m*") in a compact contemplation on "fantastic occurrences who remain and successfully perpetuate their lineage" ("de his fantasticis dicend*um* casib*us*, qui mane*nt et* bona se successione p*er*petuant," fol. 27vb), he means precisely the subject of *De nugis* 2.12 and the subject of *De nugis* 2.11. Through its topical interest in the fates of fairy-children as relatively mundane agents in the world, this particular sequence, *De nugis* 2.11–13 performs Map's tendency to complicate any hard distinction between the natural and the supernatural, the miraculous and the mundane.

Alnoth the Pious (*De nugis* 2.12)

A summary of the narrative contained in *De nugis* 2.12 will be clarifying. The reader should be advised that this tale, along with the tale of Triunein below, contains sexual violence and rape:

> Eadric Wild, returning home from the hunt, comes across a strange building at dusk. Within he sees a great number of ladies dancing, each nigh-unbelievably beautiful. He is inflamed with desire for one lady in particular; and despite knowing many moral stories that would cause him to behave otherwise ("Gentiu*m* errores audierat noctu*r*nas q*ue* phalanges demonu*m et* mortiferas eorum uisiones"), he resolves to "ravish her by whom he is ravished" ("ip*s*am rapit a qua rapit*ur*").[38] He bursts into the hall, fights off the other women, drags the most beautiful woman into the woods, and rapes her repeatedly for three

---

[38] For the latter citation, the original inked text reads "aqua rapit" and has been corrected, likely by Scribe X, to the given reading.

days and nights ("*et* ea p*ro* voto t*ri*bus dieb*us* et noctib*us* usus"). On the fourth day, she proposes that they marry. She promises to bring him health and prosperity until the day he is rude to her or her sisters. They are wed before a crowd, and her extraordinary beauty is relayed even to William the Conqueror ("wills bast*ardus*"), who summons them both to London. The king's court believes that she must be of non-human origin, since no woman was ever so beautiful ("maximu*m* erat fatalitatis argumentu*m* i*n*uisa p*ri*us *et* in audita species mulieris"). Some years later, Eadric returns once more from hunting and inappropriately mentions her sisters, breaking his oath. Immediately, she disappears ("disp*ar*uit"), leaving him a single heir and child of the inhuman woman, Alnoth, who suffers from palsy. Eadric mourns continuously until his unhappy death. Alnoth, being very pious, presents himself to St. Aethelbert at Hereford. He is made healthy, and in gratitude he donates his Lydbury estate ("Ledebiriam sua*m*") to the bishop there, which estate even at time of Map's writing yields its lords thirty pounds yearly ("t*ri*ginta libras a*n*nuas"). (fols. 26v–28v)

Scholarship has uncovered a great deal of historical context for this tale, most commonly referred to in modern critical writing as the "tale of Eadric the Wild." Eadric himself has been identified either as an Anglo-Saxon thegn or as a Welshman who led at least one rebellion against English/Anglo-Norman rule; and his legacy has been associated in legend with the Wild Hunt.[39] The specific source for the narrative Map gives is unknown, but it may once have advertised some affinity for Welsh, Galfridian myth set in opposition to Anglo-Norman rule; and it may also have been devised partly in order to shore up the bishopric of Hereford's claim to the distant estate of Lydbury North.[40] In Map's rendition, any precise political resonances are obscured, however, and it is difficult to say with any confidence whether Map muffles folkloric elements out of ignorance or wit.[41] Moreover, Map's is not the only rendition of Eadric's legend.[42] Since the *De nugis* does not appear to have circulated widely, if at all, it seems likely that there were competing variants of the Eadric-narrative outside of Map's work. Certainly, the broad narrative structure Map follows – man returns from hunt near midnight, encounters dancing women, makes and breaks arbitrary oath, etc. – is familiar from any

---

[39] Green, *EQHF*, 172-8; Susan Reynolds, "Eadric Silvaticus and the English Resistance," *Historical Research* 54.129 (1981): 102–5.

[40] Smith, "History of Lydbury North."

[41] Flood, "Political Prodigies."

[42] Franco Mormando, "Bernardino of Siena, Popular Preacher and Witch-Hunter: A 1426 Witch Trial in Rome," *Fifteenth Century Studies* 24 (1998): 95–6. Cp. Cartlidge's supposition that Sadius and Galo circulated as a romance ("Vinegar upon Nitre," 131–2).

number of authors from the twelfth century onward. The word chosen by Map for William's court to describe Eadric's wife, *fatalitas*, signals clear debts to an emerging romance tradition and its enduring interest in otherworldly beings.[43]

Unlike his modern readers, however, Walter Map is more interested in the significance of Alnoth the Pious than that of Eadric the Wild. The final paragraph of *De nugis* 2.12 transitions into a more complex discussion of ontological categories:

> Audiuimus demones. incubos *et* succubos; *et* concubitus eorum periculosos. heredes an eorum. aut sobolem felici fine beatam; in antiquis hystorijs. aut raro aut nunquam legimus, ut alnodi qui totam hereditatem suam, xristo pro sanitate sua retribuit; *et in* eius obsequiis, residuum uite, peregrinus expendit. [*De nugis* 2.13] A fantasia quod est aparicio transiens dicitur fantasma... (fol. 27v)

> We have heard of demons: *incubi* and *succubi*, and the perils of copulation with them. Have we heard of their heirs? Or the blessed posterity of a happy ending, in ancient histories? Either rarely or never do we read this, as of Alnoth who repaid his entire inheritance to Christ for his own health; and in following him, he expended the remainder of his life as a pilgrim. [*De nugis* 2.13] From *fantasia* – that is, a transient apparition – something is called *fantasma*...

With this reflection on Alnoth's origin and end, Map draws a correlation between the infernal and the otherworldly and between devils and the fay. In the twelfth century, *incubi* and *succubi* were commonly understood as incorporeal beings that constituted a specific sub-class of the angels who fell from heaven with Satan. These fallen spirits gave themselves the illusion of human attractiveness in order to lure men and women into sexual deviance. Their prevalence in fictional and ecclesiastical writing establishes what Caroline Walker Bynum has called a "near obsession with fairy-human or demon-human sex" in the high Middle Ages.[44] Famously, Merlin was the son of a mortal woman and an *incubus*, and "not only the Lusignans, but also the English house of Plantagenet owed their origins" to "overbreeding" between *incubi* and human women.[45] Cultural historians often understand such entities to have fulfilled a social need for an unwed woman to explain an unwanted pregnancy.[46] Victoria Flood notes that the "obsession" Bynum

---

[43] Green, *EQHF*, 79.

[44] Caroline Walker Bynum, *Metamorphosis and Identity* (New York: Zone Books, 2001), 1000.

[45] Green, *EQHF*, 99.

[46] "The incubus here comes as an answer to something of a riddle: the existence of a fatherless boy" (Flood, "Incubi and Succubi," 25); "fairy insemination offered

identifies is characteristic of "the products of writers with an ecclesiastical education, including a theological concern with the corporeal status of incubi and allied phenomena, and a courtly-clerical fascination with the meaning, particularly the political meaning, of dreams and visions."[47] But it is important to recall that the same "obsession" also had folkloric and intellectual roots, as Richard Firth Green demonstrates in *Elf Queens and Holy Friars*, so that "for much of the Middle Ages the word 'incubus,' whatever its connotations in clerical discourse, meant simply 'fairy.'"[48] In Map, as was so often the case in Latin writings, "incubi and succubi" traversed the fuzzy boundaries between inhuman entities of some power.

In underscoring Alnoth's mother's *fatalitas*, Walter Map is not interested in the usual problems that clerics brought to such beings, whether demonic or fay. For example, he makes no mention of corporeality (how semen might have been transported at body temperature by an incorporeal *incubus*, how a *succubus* might go about giving birth to an embodied infant), or legitimacy (how a descendant of a human and a demon might be classified within a social or ontological hierarchy). He pointedly skips over what a casual modern reader might mistake as the point of interest in this reflection, namely whether *incubi* and *succubi* exist at all. For Map, the existence of demons, fairies, *incubi*, and *succubi*, however distinguished among other inhuman agents, was by no means an uninteresting topic. But such existence, alone, does not form sufficient grounds for Map's relaying of such a remarkable narrative.[49] Nor is the trouble with Alnoth the more general observation, exactly, that he "lived an exemplary life and survived to an advanced age."[50] For Map, it is certainly not the case that "any frisson of Otherness about Eadric's liaison is expelled by Alnoth's personal holiness and by the bishop's acceptance of his properties."[51] In fact, as we have seen, Map declares the significance of Alnoth in *De nugis* 2.12 to be precisely the opposite: Alnoth is of interest because his origin leads to sincere piety accepted by the church. Otherness is sanctified

---

medieval women a convenient way to account for any pregnancy that, for whatever social reasons, could not safely be attributed to a specific human father" (Green, *EQFH*, 84).

[47] Flood, "Incubi and Succubi," 30.

[48] Green, *EQHF*, 79.

[49] Jacques Le Goff, "The Marvelous in the Medieval West," *The Medieval Imagination*, trans. Arthur Goldhammer (Chicago, IL: University of Chicago Press, 1988), 33: "What is perhaps most troubling about medieval marvels is precisely the fact that they merge so easily with everyday life that no one bothers to question their reality."

[50] Green, *EQHF*, 58.

[51] Hanna, "The Matter of Fulk," 348; see note 4. Hanna's casual use of "halfelven son" to describe Alnoth glosses over the precise phenomenon that Map draws attention to.

rather than expelled. What bothers Walter – what will provoke his sincere, satirical, pious inquiry into the relation between *fantasia* and lived experience – is not that a fairy woman was discovered, abducted, wed, or verified in kind ("fatalitas") before the king of England, nor that the child of such a being could be transformed into a functioning member of a religious community. As Walter notes, and as his readers know, and as Eadric ought to know full well, this sort of thing happens all the time ("Audiuim*us* demones. *in*cubos *et* succubos; *et* co*n*cubit*us* eo*rum* pe*r*iculosos," *De nugis* 2.12; fol. 27v).

Walter is most pointedly concerned that such a fairy woman – a *succubus* – produced a landowning heir still remembered specifically for his devotion to the Christian faith; and that this holy, wise, and propertied heir of fay parentage was subject to miraculous healing under the influence of an English saint, was responsible for generating considerable wealth for the bishopric of Hereford, and – as, we shall see, is made exceptionally clear in *De nugis* 2.13 – left behind him any number of children and grandchildren, "now a multitude." Monika Otter's observation is germane here, that for Map, "what makes history almost impossible to narrate is not its pastness but its presentness."[52] The difficulty in relating Alnoth's tale is not the fantastic event but its enduring ramifications on a real social and religious community. The trouble Map raises is not that "that the products of unions between humans and fairies are rarely successful."[53] Instead, the implication of *De nugis* 2.12 runs the other way around. As far as Map knows, such relations are so common as to have produced an indistinguishable multitude of people with demonic lineage. Had Alnoth disappeared along with his mother, or had he come to a disturbing end, his story would be so much the less remarkable. But Alnoth *lives*, and bears multitudes, and gains a reputation for piety. Alnoth's tale is of interest to Walter because his legacy is so mundane: the sons of demons walk among us, propagating, tithing, and receiving blessings from God and His saints.

Alnoth and that Other Briton (*De nugis* 2.11 and 2.12)

The structural similarities between the tale of Eadric and Alnoth told in *De nugis* 2.12 and the tale of Gwestin and Triunein told just before, in *De nugis* 2.11, emerge clearly in summary. Here is a brief account of *De nugis* 2.11:

> Gwestin Gwestiniog lives near a lake, and on three consecutive nights he sees a great number of women dancing together in his fields. On the fourth night he ("ille raptor") learns from their whispers ("m*u*rmu-ra*n*tes") how one could be captured ("adepta sit"). He captures one lady, and she agrees to marry him and serve him until the day that he should strike her with his bridle. She bears him many children, but

---

[52] Otter, *Inventiones*, 128.
[53] Green, *EQHF*, 58.

one day she is struck by his bridle ("ab eo freno percussa est"). She flees with all their children, and he grabs ("arripuit") only one of his sons, Triunein Vagelauc. (fols. 26r–26v)

Once more we find a Welsh knight, a crowd of women dancing in the middle of the night, a woman abducted, a marriage construed as consensual but only according to some arbitrary oath, the bearing of children, the breaking of the oath, the disappearance of the woman, and the single son left behind. As with the story of Alnoth that follows, the folkloric elements of Triunein's story are evident. Again, Map is less interested in the existence of *succubi/* fairy-women or the terms of otherworldly oaths than he is in the implications of how any offspring of such inhuman agents directly affect the real world of human relations.

Into the general structure shared by Alnoth's origin and Triunein's, Map weaves a long adventure story, in which Triunein joins the court of King Deheubarth (a political opponent of his own king in the Brecons), incites a war between these two kings, and disappears in the ensuing battle. The inner narrative concludes with a decisive political victory for King Brychan, legendary forerunner of twelfth-century Welsh leadership familiar to Map and the court of Henry II. *De nugis* 2.11 ends alongside the end of the battle: in parallel with *De nugis* 2.12, no further mention is made of Triunein's father. Of Triunein's ultimate fate, Map writes:

> Quod autem aiunt triunein a matre sua seruatum. et cum ipsam in lacu illo uiuere. vnde supra mencio est; imo et mendacium puto, quod de non inuento fingi potuit error huiosmodi. [*De nugis* 2.12] Simile huic est quod Edricus Wilde... (fol. 26vb)

> And they say that Triunein was saved by his mother, and that he lives with her in that lake, the one mentioned above. Yet, I believe it a lie, since an error of this kind could be made up about someone lost. [*De nugis* 2.12] Similar to this is the one about Eadric Wild...

Critical responses to Map's quip generally evade the question of what actually did happen to Triunein for the understandable reason that Map fails to say what actually did happen to Triunein. Smith, in a rare moment of agreement with Brooke and Mynors, takes the open-endedness of Map's statement at the close of *De nugis* 2.12 as evidence that Triunein "dies without any mention of his offspring."[54] Flood understands Map's "dismissal of the tale's conclusion as a popular fable" to reflect his lack of concern for folkloric narrative.[55]

---

[54] Smith, *WMMB*, 59.
[55] Flood, "Political Prodigies," 32

Green describes Map's uncertainty as participating in a "popular tradition" that "regularly assigned those who had disappeared on the battlefield a place in fairyland" and suggests that Map may have staged a joke at the expense of the monks at Glastonbury touting their discovery of Arthur's tomb, satirizing an emergent Plantagenet mythology.[56] By the same logic, though with different parodic implications, A. G. Rigg suggests that Map might also make reference to the more famous empty tomb of Christ.[57] Each of these interpretations agrees that, whatever happened with Triunein, he must have disappeared.

Looking forward to the close of Alnoth's story, however, we might propose an end for Triunein "similar to" that of Alnoth – just as Map tells us it is similar. Rather than placing Triunein in fairyland or the realm of the dead, the pairing suggests that Triunein (like Alnoth) could not be found because he was alive and well, and that he and his heirs lived on in the world in anonymity. As with Alnoth, although his lineage could be traced to a fairy/*succubus* mother, Triunein's further actions have been made indistinguishable from the mass of humanity that forms the subject of history.

Tales and Summaries: 2.11 and 4.8, 2.12 and 4.10

Crucially, for the narrative sequence under discussion, Map acknowledges the many similarities between Triunein's tale in *De nugis* 2.11 and Alnoth's tale in *De nugis* 2.12 at the close of *De nugis* 2.13:

> *Et quid de his fantasticis dicendum casibus, qui manent et bona se successione perpetuant, ut hic alnodi et ille britonum de quo superius, in quo dicitur miles quidam uxorem suam sepellisse reuera mortuam, et a chorea rediduisse raptam, et postmodum ex ea filios et nepotes suscepisse, et perdurare sobolem in diem istum, et eos qui traxerunt mihi originem in multitudinem factos, qui omnes ideo filii mortue dicuntur?* (fol. 27v)

> And what should we say about these fantastic occurrences who remain and successfully perpetuate their lineage, as with this Alnoth and that other Briton (discussed above), where it is said that a certain knight truly had buried his own dead wife, had dragged her home again from a dance against her will, and afterward by her had had sons and grandsons, and had preserved this lineage until this very day? And

---

[56] Green, *EQHF*, 156–8.
[57] See A. G. Rigg, "Walter Map, the Shaggy Dog Story, and the Quaestio Disputata," in *Roma, Magistra Mundi* (Louvain-la-Neuve: Fédération Internationale des Instituts d'Etudes Médiévales, 1998), 2:723–5. For the pressing legal issues raised by missing persons, see Elizabeth Papp Kamali, "Tales of the Living Dead: Dealing with Doubt in Medieval English Law," *Speculum* 96.2 (2021): 367–417.

what of those who have conveyed their origin to me, now made a multitude, who all for this reason are called sons of a dead woman?

Editors and critics of the *De nugis* have rejected Alnoth and Triunein together as referents of "Alnoth and that other Briton" on account of the fact that both relevant narratives lack an element crucial to Map's summary in *De nugis* 2.13: namely that "a certain knight" had "truly buried his own dead wife," then found her again and had children by her, such that their progeny would be called "sons of a dead woman." On account of this omitted detail, Map's declared interest in the fantastic in *De nugis* 2.13 has been rejected as integral to the narratives he tells immediately beforehand, and the narratives have been rejected as integral to the meditation on *fantasia* and *fantasma* that follows. The critical situation is accentuated by the fact that every modern edition has preserved the scribal chapter breaks in Bodley 851 without accounting for their interpretive significance.

The editorial supposition that the disparity between *De nugis* 2.13 and *De nugis* 2.12 forms a rather obvious and typical omission – i.e., that Map forgets to include in his long-form narratives the single most remarkable detail from subsequent summary – is commonly understood to correspond to the characteristic "untidiness" assumed by editors for the *De nugis* on the whole (see above). On account of a later reference to Alnoth in *De nugis* 4.10, it was Hinton who first proposed the need for a major editorial invention to solve a narrative problem that Walter inadvertently introduced in *De nugis* 2.13.[58] In Hinton's view, the whole of Distinction 4 originally must have been placed somewhere in the middle of Distinction 1, so as to make sense of Map's omission in *De nugis* 2.12.[59] Accordingly, if Distinction 4 was originally placed prior to Distinction 2, then the reference ("discussed above") could be easily rectified: if the book weren't such a mess, *De nugis* 4.10 would occur immediately before *De nugis* 2.13, not *De nugis* 2.12.[60] Surpassing Hinton, Brooke and Mynors took Map's omission as evidence of "a simpler and more fundamental derangement," i.e., the sandwiching of wholly unrelated narrative parts discussed above.[61] For its most recent editors, the *De nugis* is such a mess that it would not matter where Map had placed which narratives: in any iteration, only deranged untidiness can be found.

Even Smith, the most ardent defender of Walter's acuity in revision, concedes that the tales of Triunein and Alnoth already related (as *De nugis* 2.11 and 2.12) and the description given (in *De nugis* 2.13) do not align. He attributes what is in his view the most indicative tag, "discussed above" ("de quo superius"), to scribal misplacement of a marginal note at some point

---

[58] Hinton, "Plan and Composition," 86.
[59] Hinton, "Plan and Composition," 88–9.
[60] Hinton, "Plan and Composition," 91; cp. 104, 111.
[61] James *et al.*, xxviii–xxix.

in the line of scribal transmission. Accordingly, Smith sees "no convincing evidence to reconsider this brief discussion of the sons of a dead woman as a revision of the thematically similar tale in *distinctio* 4 [i.e., *De nugis* 4.8]."[62] With Hinton, Brooke, and Mynors, Smith agrees that the narrative given in *De nugis* 4.8 better corresponds to the reference in *De nugis* 2.13; and, according to the vagaries of scribal transmission endemic to Map's disorganized text, that the narrative provided in *De nugis* 4.8 has been tangled up with the story of Alnoth, about whom "discussed above" makes perfect sense. Thus, in the published reading most generous to Walter's organizational capacities (Smith's), there is Alnoth "discussed above" and some other Briton, about whom a brief summary is sufficient, requiring no prior narrative, whether in Distinction 2 or in Distinction 4.

The reader may be forgiven for experiencing some confusion at the contorted critical situation I have just described. To sum up: in those views least generous to Map and his book, the putative reference to *De nugis* 4.8 in *De nugis* 2.13 signals a material disorder present within the text so chaotic as to make reading its component parts according to any coherent literary program impossible. In the most generous perspective, these narratives are understood to be related contiguously by accident, on account of scribal interference rather than authorial purpose, such that the apparent external reference in *De nugis* 2.13 in fact stands on its own.

Each of these explanations misunderstands Map's careful use of narrative detail to provoke interpretive ambiguity and to reveal, with characteristic wryness, what was before the reader's eyes all along. No published interpretation sufficiently accounts for the rendition of Triunein's tale at *De nugis* 4.8, which provides an abbreviated version of the narrative now recounted as *De nugis* 2.11, or the rendition of Alnoth's tale provided at *De nugis* 4.10, which provides an abbreviated version of the narrative now recounted as *De nugis* 2.12.

I argue that "Alnoth and that other Briton" in *De nugis* 2.13 stands as a direct reference to the narratives immediately preceding, already described (*De nugis* 2.11–12), which tell the stories of Alnoth and then another knight (Gwestin). Because prior critical approaches have insisted upon the relevance of Distinction 4 to *De nugis* 2.13, I will show how each account in Distinction 2 corresponds to its summary version in Distinction 4. Accordingly, I will demonstrate how both the long versions (*De nugis* 2.11, 2.12) and their abbreviations (*De nugis* 4.8, 4.10) make sense in terms of Map's acute meditation on fantastic beings in the world. As above, I begin with Alnoth and continue on to Triunein.

---

[62] Smith, *WMMB*, 59. Elsewhere, Smith acknowledges the repetition of Alnoth's story (Smith, "Lydbury North").

The summary version of the story of Eadric and Alnoth told in *De nugis* 4.10 shares with the longer account in *De nugis* 2.12 a particular interest in Alnoth as a holy figure with a *succubus* mother. In fact, in *De nugis* 4.10, Map fails to name Eadric at all:

> alnodi... viri cuius mater in auras euanuit; manifesta visione multorum. indignanter inproperium viri sui ferens; quod eam a mortuis rapuisset. (fol. 52r)

> Alnoth... whose mother vanished into the air in the plain sight of a multitude, bearing indignantly her husband's uncouth suggestion that he had raped her from among the dead.

The few differences between *De nugis* 4.10 and *De nugis* 2.12 are easy to identify. In *De nugis* 4.10, what Map writes in *De nugis* 2.13 ("filii mortue") is displaced into indirect statement from her husband ("a mortuis rapuisset"), the man by whom she had been caught out of a company of women dancing in the woods at midnight ("de cetu nocturno feminarum choreancium pulcherrimam rapuit," *De nugis* 4.10; fol. 52r). The complaint is formulated differently from that voiced by Eadric in *De nugis* 2.12, when once more returning from the hunt, he demands to know, "What now, have you been detained by your sisters for so long?" ("Numquid a sororibus tuis tam diu detenta es," *De nugis* 2.12; fol. 27r). In both cases, however, the result is the same: she disappears ("disparuit," "evanuit"). Accordingly, Alnoth's story in *De nugis* 2.12 conforms to Map's summary in *De nugis* 4.10 at nearly every point – aside from the mention of a dead mother. Supposing the Alnoth born of a woman snatched from a midnight dance in the woods who appears before the king of England and disappears when reprimanded by her husband (*De nugis* 2.12) to be the same person as the Alnoth born of a woman snatched from a midnight dance in the woods who appears before the king of England and disappears when reprimanded by her husband (*De nugis* 4.10), we can confidently consider these two sections to render different versions of the same tale. We might also, therefore, ask whether Eadric's two criticisms of Alnoth's mother – (1) detained by your sisters, (2) raped from among the dead – share a common insult.

For the substance of this common insult, Green's *Elf Queens and Holy Friars* provides an elegant solution. Green demonstrates that, however specific lines of transmission may have been constructed, "fairyland" and "purgatory" operated as comparable locations where people went once they had died, or once they had been supposed to die, in what Green calls the "great" and "little" traditions.[63] Readers of folklore more broadly will immediately recognize midnight – the hour when both Eadric and Gwestin come across their erstwhile

---

[63] Green, *EQHF*, 178–93.

brides – as a time when the realms of the natural and the supernatural grow closest together. Michelle Karnes notes that "beautiful women gathering in fields at night" routinely populate late-medieval marvels associated with the fay and with the dead.[64] And, as discussed above, Map's omission in *De nugis* 2.12 and his indirect statement in *De nugis* 4.10 both gesture toward the same general conflation between *incubus, succubus,* "demon," and "fairy" noted above while suggesting – without endorsing – the overall affiliation between the otherworld of the fay and the realm of the dead. Putting all of these pieces together, we might recognize that for Map (or for the tradition he parodies), there is little distinction between "the dead" and "the inhuman." To name Alnoth's mother's sisters (*De nugis* 2.12) and to name a company of the dead (*De nugis* 4.10) are to name, in fact, the same entities. In her refusal of her husband's claim that she had some unnatural origin, Alnoth's mother vanishes into thin air, confirming that whatever she might be, she both is not human and bears some affiliation with the numbers of the dead.

Therefore, the small differences in narration observable in *De nugis* 4.10 point toward the most obvious reading for *De nugis* 2.12–2.13: that when Walter Map names Alnoth as the subject of the "matter above" and refers to "sons of a dead mother," he means to name Alnoth as the son of a dead mother, as evident from his rendition of the story immediately preceding. Indeed, Map appears to confirm Green's argument from other sources that, in the context of a fantastic tale, any group of indescribably beautiful women discovered dancing at midnight can be associated reasonably with the realm of the dead.

The same pattern of implication holds for the other narrative under consideration, that of Gwestin and his son Triunein. Although neither Triunein nor Gwestin is named in *De nugis* 4.8, there is clear evidence that *De nugis* 4.8 corresponds to the narrative given in *De nugis* 2.11 and acts as a kind of epitome of Map's interests in the earlier narrative, much as *De nugis* 4.10 acts as an epitome of Map's concerns in *De nugis* 2.12. In fact, the similarity between *De nugis* 4.8 and the brief narrative reference in *De nugis* 2.13 is already well established.[65] Less well-established is the similarity between *De nugis* 4.8 and the longer story of Triunein given in *De nugis* 2.11. Nevertheless, the narratives align substantially in structure: a knight finds a company of women in the night ("*in magno feminarum cetu de nocte*"), resolves to seize her who has caught his attention ("*certo proponit animo rapere*"), does so ("*rapit eam igitur*"), and has children by her ("*ex ipsa suscepit liberos*") who now have many descendants ("*quorum hodie progenies magna est*"; *De nugis* 4.8, fol. 51r). In the knight's resolution to capture his dead wife, we hear

---

[64] Michelle Karnes, "The Possibilities of Medieval Fiction," *New Literary History* 51.1 (2020): 217–18.

[65] James *et al.*, 344n1: "This [*De nugis* 4.8] is apparently the story referred to in Dist. ii. 13."

echoes of the formulaic three days of effort by Gwestin in *De nugis* 2.11, and in the emphasis on his descendants, we glimpse the exact concern that Map reiterates at the close of *De nugis* 2.12 and that forms the substance of his meditation in *De nugis* 2.13.

It is unnecessary to rehearse in full what has been established above concerning the overlapping conceptual regions between companies of nocturnal women, fairies, *succubi*, and the dead. Nevertheless, for corroboration we might note that, in *De nugis* 4.8, Map himself describes the company of women as "fairies" (*fatis*), and describes his now-anonymous knight as worrying that he might be deceived by a *fantasm* ("a fantasmate fallat*ur*," fol. 51r) when endeavoring to capture one of them. Finally, in *De nugis* 4.8 Map uses the same eponym, "sons of a dead mother," as in *De nugis* 2.13 ("filii mortue") to describe the child.

Although some details of Triunein's narrative are omitted, the only potentially contradictory detail is that of location. Where the story related in *De nugis* 2.11 clearly takes place in Wales, pitting a northern political group against a southern group, and where *De nugis* 2.13 refers to "this Alnoth and that other Briton" ("hic alnodi *et* ille b*ritonum* de quo sup*erius*"; fol. 27vb, 2.13), *De nugis* 4.8 refers only to a soldier from Brittany ("miles quidam britannie minoris," fol. 51r). James *et al.* sidestep the problem entirely by taking "britonum" in *De nugis* 2.13 to refer to *De nugis* 4.10, rather than *De nugis* 4.8, and so omit any specific referent apart from Alnoth himself. But the apparent contradiction is easily resolved. Almost certainly, "britonum" at *De nugis* 2.13 means "of Britain" (one who lives in Britain) rather than "Breton" (one who lives in Brittany), although both meanings are available: English authors routinely refer to the Welsh, Cornish, Scots, and Picts as "britones," and occasionally to Bretons by the same designator.[66] If the *De nugis* 4.10 characterizes Triunein as a Breton, the contradiction must stand. If, however, the soldier identified in *De nugis* 4.10 is rather Gwestin than Triunein, then the matter is easily resolved: Gwestin, at some time from Brittany, finds his dead wife in Wales, where Triunein (a "Briton") undertakes his adventure. On the whole, if the current editorial position must stand and if one designation or the other must constitute an inaccuracy, it is an inaccuracy that could arise simply from orthographic confusion or scribal transmission. Given the many features of the two narratives that *do* correspond, the suggestion that either the knight or his wife may once conceivably have been "of Brittany" is hardly sufficient evidence to fully sever the narrative connection between *De nugis* 2.11 and *De nugis* 4.8. Moreover, the subsequent summary of *De nugis* 2.12

---

[66] *DMLBS*, s.v. "Brito."

at *De nugis* 4.10 confirms that these two sections bore some relation to one another in Map's process of composition.[67]

In short, *De nugis* 2.13 refers to *De nugis* 2.11 directly and *De nugis* 4.8 only indirectly, as separate renditions of the same narrative. Rather than disjunction, we might read Map's economical allusion to Triunein's tale in *De nugis* 2.13 as clarifying the important details for his readers. "*In case you missed it*," Map insists to his unyieldingly stubborn audience (chiefly, it appears, modern scholars), "the fairy woman was Gwestin's dead wife *all along*." But this is no plot twist. Rather, it is only a restatement of fact for an audience that should have been prepared to understand Map's meaning in the first place. When, in *De nugis* 2.13, Map refers to "Alnoth and that Briton, discussed above," he means Alnoth (2.12) and Triunein (2.11), discussed above.

Map's Literary Sequence

For the modern critical reader unfamiliar with Map's work and reputation, the conclusion I have taken such time to defend is apt to feel a bit disappointing, if not redundant. It is hardly groundbreaking, much less theoretically inspiring, to suggest that a celebrated author (like Walter Map) might compose interrelated but distinct narratives in sequence (as in *De nugis* 2.11–13) without explicitly announcing the underlying topics or themes which might best serve to understand their relation (e.g., the endurance of holy demon-children). Or, rather than "explicitly announcing," we might better say "repeatedly announcing," since Map does in fact declare, in *De nugis* 2.13, precisely that he is most interested in "fantastic occurrences who remain and successfully perpetuate their lineage, as with this Alnoth and that other Briton" – i.e., the subjects of *De nugis* 2.12 and *De nugis* 2.11.

We expect indirection from literary writing. Literary readers take pleasure in formulating educated hypotheses that might fill the gaps and fissures in many of our most beloved works. The history of critical scholarship on the *De nugis*, however, would deny the validity of any such critical work to readers of Walter Map, based on the putatively intractable material condition of the text within its sole manuscript copy. In the current critical landscape of approaches to Map's text, themselves representative of unnecessarily conservative approaches to manuscript evidence further afield, many of the basic assumptions which ground literary criticism must themselves be argued.

Future engagements with the *De nugis* will benefit from an openness to discovering literary coherence according to the terms of inquiry and interest

---

[67] Smith argues in favor of the view that *De nugis* 2.12 is a later expansion of *De nugis* 4.10 (Smith, "Lydbury North," 66). While I find his case persuasive, the order of composition has no bearing on the argument I put forward here.

that its sequences declare. Currently, absent strong arguments in favor of literary continuity, the assumption of material discontinuity and authorial untidiness acts as a default stance toward Map's collected narrative materials. Two contrary critical trends emerge from such assumptions. On one hand, the *De nugis* has been read as a series of discontinuities that can only be analyzed in terms of its disparate individual parts, such that its chapters need not be related to their surrounding materials in order to be interpreted. On the other, the *De nugis* has been read as an untidy bundle of textual components that can be serviceably critiqued in any rearrangement the critic might choose. In both cases, working from flawed editorial and codicological assumptions, readers of Walter Map have been forced to assume – against all signs to the contrary – that as clear a reflection as is *De nugis* 2.13 on *De nugis* 2.11–12 must, in fact, be read in either isolation from those narratives which directly precede it or else in conversation with every possible comparable moment within the work.

Methodologically, this chapter proposes a middle way, in which neither discontinuity (debilitating untidiness) nor continuity (total aesthetic unity) must be assumed. Rather, the potential significance of obscure affiliation or unlikeness can act as a catalyst for closer inspection. Not *every* contiguous arrangement of narrative text need be a literary sequence; but neither need the mere possibility of cogent literary sequences in the *De nugis* be dismissed out of hand. As with medieval books in general, so with Map's book specifically: material and textual compilations should be considered carefully for the features they share (or refuse to share) according to evidence for their arrangement by different agents over time.

Fantasms Made Flesh (*De nugis* 2.13)

The matter of textual sequence settled, I now turn to the significance of Map's meditation in *De nugis* (2.13) for understanding the narratives of Triunein and Alnoth that precede it. In *De nugis* 2.1, Map declares his own interest in coming to understand "the miracles that we know or believe" ("*et* que scim*us* a*ut* credim*us* miracu*l*a; p*r*emittam*us*"; fol. 24r). In *De nugis* 2.13, Walter ponders the significance of his narrative project in relation to the etymological and philosophical significance of *fantasia* and *fantasm* (now usually rendered *phantasia* and *phantasm*). Reflecting specifically upon the paired narratives he has related in *De nugis* 2.11–12, Map emphasizes how the effects of *fantasia* endure in the world – how unnatural and divine works and deeds linger on, not only in the imagination but also in the flesh. Moving beyond the credulous conclusion he provides to Alnoth's tale, he places *fantasia*, miracle, marvel, and prodigy in conversation, asking not only how we can identify inhuman progeny in the world but also how a pious reader ought to interpret extraordinary events that seem simultaneously to demand interpretation and to defy meaning-making.

Immediately following the conclusion to the tale of Alnoth, Map meditates with characteristic wit on the relation between *fantasia*, *fantasma*, and the fantastic:

> A fantasia quod est aparicio transiens dicitur fantasma. ille enim aparencie quas aliquibus interdum demones per se faciunt a deo prius accepta licencia aut innocenter transeunt aut nocenter secundum quod dominus inducens eas aut conseruat aut deserit et temptari permittit. (fol. 27v)[68]

> From *fantasia* – that is, a transient apparition – something is called *fantasma*. Indeed, these are appearances that demons every now and again fashion of their own power for some people – with permission being acquired beforehand from God – and they happen harmlessly or harmfully, according to how God guiding them protects them, forsakes them, or allows them to be tempted.

Although his syntax is complex, the idea Map expresses here is straightforward in summary. He claims that the two words *fantasia* and *fantasma* are related, that this relation has to do with the interplay between divine authority and demonic powers, and that appearances themselves ("illae apparentiae"; i.e., *fantasms*) can serve any number of purposes according to God's will. They can protect, isolate, or tempt, sometimes causing pain and sometimes not. At the forefront of this explanation is the casual use of *fantasia*, which emphasizes its transience by way of the root shared between "apparition" ("apparitio") and "appearance" ("apparentia"). This more familiar medieval word was used by later scribes and readers in many chapter headings throughout Distinction 2 (i.e., "Item de eisdem aparitionibus"). As with Map's wordplay in the prologue and conclusion, ambiguity in meaning carries over into the following sentences.

---

[68] James et al., 160. Because the text of Bodley 851 is faded at this point, it is difficult to assess the accuracy of transcription in James, Brooke, and Mynors and nearly impossible at many locations to judge confidently between scribal annotations, punctuations, and otiose strokes. Moreover, due to the spread of SARS-COV-2, I was unable to examine this section of the manuscript in person in July 2020 as I had intended. Lacking immediate access to the manuscript itself, I have confirmed by way of representations stored online at the *Digital Bodleian*, as best as I am able, that this transcription corresponds to what survives in the manuscript. Accordingly, I cite this specific section from the revised edition (1983) with limited editorial changes. I include the italicization of scribal abbreviations only where they are clearly visible in digital copy.

In order to understand this ambiguity, a brief terminological detour will be useful. Map denies that the story of Triunein (2.11) is a miracle, declaring, "Here's another one, not a miracle but a prodigy" ("Aliud non miraculum sed portentum," fol. 26r). Map's use of *fantasia* and *fantasma* at the close of Alnoth's tale (*De nugis* 2.12), however, signals another concern adjacent to that of interpreting such events: namely, that of identifying their origins and functions. Generally speaking, as Robert Bartlett summarizes, *fantasmata* were understood by a wide range of medieval thinkers as "images impressed on the mind but without physical reality."[69] Theological inquiries into magic, witchcraft, and demonic forces frequently expressed concern that such images, while lacking the ability to cause physical effects, might nevertheless effect change in human agents. How could an incorporeal spirit, like a demon, have bodily effects on corporeal beings? If demons are real but lacking a physical body, what is the scope of their ability to act upon the material world? These were pressing moral and social problems: as Michelle Karnes notes, "We might equate physicality with existence, but medieval writers typically do not."[70] Karnes further observes that in Neoplatonic commentaries on Aristotle, the imagination "was often subdivided into a lower and higher power, sometimes called the *virtus imaginativa* or *imaginatio* and *phantasia* in Latin."[71] In implementations of Aristotelian thought, as part of the faculty of the imagination, *fantasia* came to play a prominent role in comprehending miracles and marvels (*mirabilia*) – generally, "unusual events that resist explanation." *Fantasia* was "a sensory faculty that performs a wide, potentially incoherent range of functions according to medieval philosophy" that "helped to explain how marvels could mean more than the events that constitute them" – specifically "by troubling the crucial boundary between things that exist objectively within the soul and those in the world outside."[72]

While many uses of *fantasia* and *fantasma* lacked technical distinctions, broadly speaking *fantasma* tended to take on instrumental meaning correlative with the abstracted meaning of *fantasia*. *Fantasmata* were based on received sense data for the purpose of presentation to the intellect.[73] Roughly summarizing, we might characterize *fantasia* as experience and *fantasma* as experiential record, where the Neoplatonic tradition, with its prominent concern for interrogating dreams and visions, would leave room to locate the generation

---

[69] Robert Bartlett, *The Natural and the Supernatural in the Middle Ages* (Cambridge: Cambridge University Press, 2008), 80.

[70] Karnes, "Medieval Imagination," 330.

[71] Karnes, "Medieval Imagination," 328.

[72] Karnes, "Medieval Imagination," 327–9.

[73] Michelle Karnes, *Imagination, Meditation, and Cognition in the Middle Ages* (Chicago, IL: University of Chicago Press, 2011), 88–9.

of *fantasmata* outside the individual (with, say, demons or with God);[74] and where the Aristotelian tradition, with its prominent concern for comprehending the mechanics of experience, would locate the generation of *fantasmata* more strictly within the sphere of the soul's activities.

As a product of and participant in what has been influentially termed "the renaissance of the twelfth century," Map's use of *fantasia* and *fantasma* most likely suggests a version of the casual understanding tinged by his proximity to academic debates, but it is not necessarily defined by them.[75] Mary Carruthers renders M. D. Chenu's description of technical usage of language concerning the soul in the twelfth century as "the continual sliding of word-forms over each other" ("les glissements continuels des vocables les uns sur les autres"), an apt characterization of the present formulation.[76] Nevertheless, according to any major Latinate usage, Map's opening to *De nugis* 2.13 briefly confuses the relationship between *fantasia* and *fantasma*, where he explains *fantasia*, not *fantasma*, as a "transient apparition." As with so much of the *De nugis*, it is not immediately clear whether this confusion derives from Map's own misunderstanding or whether it signals some more subtle, or parodic, rhetorical purpose. It is possible that Map deploys a joke at the expense of perceived academic hair-splitting in his own age. Bynum and Rigg have voiced their intuitions that Map was more attuned to contemporary currents in the intellectual activity of northern Europe than he lets on;[77] and Carey Nederman has

---

[74] See also Barbara Newman, "What Did It Mean to Say 'I Saw'? The Clash between Theory and Practice in Medieval Visionary Culture," *Speculum* 80.1 (2005): 1–43.

[75] By invoking the "twelfth-century renaissance," I mean only to signal familiar historical and intellectual contexts for Map's literary activity, rather than to embrace any connotations the term "renaissance" carries. I discuss Map's own attitude towards the inferior accomplishments of his own day above, pp. 119–20. Map's pessimism – his wry refusal to die for fame corresponds well with the trend described in C. Stephen Jaeger, "Pessimism in the Twelfth-Century 'Renaissance,'" *Speculum* 78.4 (2003): 1151–83.

[76] Chenu, "Le vocabulaire de l'ame," 212; cited by M. Carruthers in "Fantasye," *Chaucer Encyclopedia*, eds. Richard Newhauser *et al.* (Hoboken, NJ: Wiley, 2022), 708–10.

[77] In discussion of *De nugis* 2.14, Bynum writes, "It is hard not to suspect a spoof of university debates when he comments that we should feel no surprise at Christ's Ascension since we see fairies depart through the roof" ("Miracles and Marvels: The Limits of Alterity," in *Vita Religiosa Im Mittelalter*, ed. Franz Felten and Nikolas Jaspert [Berlin, 1999], 810). For a closer examination of Map's use of academic forms in non-academic texts, see Rigg, "Shaggy Dog Story." See also Minnis, *Theory of Authorship*, 10–13, wherein Map's reflection upon the infelicity of his own existence for authorial fame is tacitly understood to operate broadly within the context of academic study in the twelfth century.

demonstrated that some friction between Platonic and Aristotelian frameworks would have been available to medieval thinkers well before the development of scholasticism, fully-fledged, in the thirteenth century.[78] As these critics suggest, Map need not have adopted university forms in order to poke fun at university debates.

It is also possible the explanatory tag ("quod est aparicio transiens") itself originates with a scribal copyist.[79] If the tag is scribal, rather than authorial, then Map's original text would have defined the most basic relation between a generative power and what it generates: "An image is said to be from the imagination." Moreover, the scribal addition would provide further evidence for conscious alignment between the chapter heading ("Item de eisdem apparicionibus") and the body of the text. The explanation itself could signal one instance of the kind of interpretation Map's text constantly invites.

By introducing a proliferating number of grammatical subjects and objects – *fantasia, fantasma*, human beholders, demonic agents, and a permissive God – the close of the second sentence introduces further ambiguity of interpretation. Who is it ("eas") that God protects, forsakes, or allows to be tempted? Taken out of context, the overarching sense of the passage might suggest that the people to whom appearances are made to appear are also governed by the will of God. The casual reader might assume that God protects *people*, as the observing subjects of fantastic occurrences. This reading is available. But in the specific context of Triunein and Alnoth, children of demons whose progeny are now a multitude, the possibility that God guides apparitions themselves comes to the forefront of Map's concern:

> *Et quid de his fantasticis dicendum casibus, qui manent et bona se successione perpetuant, ut hic alnodi et ille britonum de quo superius, in quo dicitur miles quidam uxorem suam sepellisse reuera mortuam, et a chorea rediuisse raptam, et postmodum ex ea filios et nepotes suscepisse, et perdurare sobolem in diem istum, et eos qui traxerunt mihi originem in multitudinem factos, qui omnes ideo filii mortue dicuntur?* (fol. 27v; reproduced here as above, p. 139)

> And what should we say about these fantastic occurrences who remain and successfully perpetuate their lineage, as with this Alnoth and that other Briton (discussed above), where it is said that a certain knight

---

[78] Cary J. Nederman, "The Meaning of 'Aristotelianism' in Medieval Moral and Political Thought," *Journal of the History of Ideas* 57.4 (1996), 572–3.

[79] James *et al.* correct the mistake, translating, "*Fantasma* is derived from *fantasia*, i.e., a passing apparition" (*De nugis*, 161); as do Tupper and Ogle, translating "Phantom is derived from 'phantasy,' that is, a passing apparition" (97). This instance is not included in the preliminary appendix of interpolated glosses provided at Smith, *WMBB*, 175–6.

truly had buried his own dead wife, had dragged her home again from a dance against her will, and afterward by her had had sons and grandsons, and had preserved this lineage until this very day? And what of those who have conveyed their origin to me, now made a multitude, who all for this reason are called sons of a dead woman?

This construction suggests that the antecedent for "eas" is "apparentiae" ("the appearances") with which the chapter begins, and which the chapter headings underscore, rather than the human subjects observing them or the demonic powers which fashion their appearance.[80] Map implies that God, in fact, protects, forsakes, and allows to be tempted the appearances themselves, as they – like all of creation – are ultimately generated by his power and governed by his authority. Temporarily bracketing the reality, or at least physicality, of demonic influence, Map further introduces a third term (*fantasticis*) alongside his original two (*fantasia* and *fantasma*) in order to ask how it is that something illusory or ephemeral might nevertheless continue to act in the world. These appearances act on specific beholders of dubious visions, thus emphasizing *fantasia* as a power of the soul or a demonic power over beset individuals. More importantly, these appearances produce heirs, own property, and engage in biographical self-reportage on the subject of their origin, thus emphasizing the effects of *fantasia* on external conditions of experience. Map transforms immaterial images (Bartlett's "images... without physical reality") into human agents, and further complicates the general question of how fantastic events come to pass. *Fantasmata* might have bearing not only on some non-fantastic observer but also on the *fantasticis* or *apparentiae* themselves.

Crucially, as we have seen, the "fantastic occurrences" designate "Alnoth and that other Briton" – which is not to say dreams or misunderstood visions or some non-physical mental image generated by the soul, but actual people, whose identities can be ascertained and whose existences can be confirmed. The indisputable realities of such people further blur any distinction between *fantasia* and *fantasma*, since they can only be understood as enduring, corporeal products of incorporeal experiences. Moreover, they provide an unsettling answer to the syntactic question posed above: who does God protect, forsake, or allow to be tempted? As *fantasms* made flesh, heirs of demonic activity such as Alnoth and that other Briton come to pass ("transeunt") and so to live either harmfully or harmlessly.

If the origins for *fantasm*-humans are fantastic, these hybrid persons nevertheless survive and interact regularly with the quotidian world of sense, bearing

---

[80] Map's habitual blurring of subject and object may have played a role in his belated association with "goliardic" literature; for comparable moments of medieval satire as reliant upon syntactical reflexivity see Jill Mann, "Satiric Subject and Satiric Object in Goliardic Literature," *Mittellateinisches Jahrbuch* 15 (1980): 63–86.

further children and propagating upon the earth without any specific need of supernatural aid, demonic or divine. The etymology and the paradigmatic story of Alnoth's ancestry (*succubus* mother and human father) are now considered alongside one another, linked by a knowledge of infernal and celestial powers in what appears to be a fair bit of confusion about how real apparitions are, exactly, and according to what grounding assumptions about reality. Within the context of *De nugis* 2.13, the marvelous can only be distinguished from the unremarkable by means of narrative inquiry and interpretive effort, along with a great deal of research into local family histories.

In a pious conclusion to this foray into how the fantastic might be understood to relate to the quotidian, Map adopts a well-protected, if wholly unsatisfying, interpretive position, by asserting God's essential role as guarantor of knowledge and experience alike:

> Audienda sunt opera et permissiones domini cum omni paciencia, et ipse laudandus in singulis, quia sicut ipse incomprehensibilis est, sic opera sua nostras transcendunt inquisiciones et disputaciones euadunt, et quicquid de puritate ipsius a nobis excogitari potest aut sciri, si quid scimus, id videtur habere, cum totus ipse sit vera puritas et pura veritas. (fol. 27vb, *De nugis* 2.13)

> It is necessary to hear the works and permissions of the Lord with all patience, and he will be praised in every one of them, because just as he is incomprehensible, so too do his works transcend our own questions and escape our arguments; and whatever is able to be thought or known by us about his own purity – if we know *anything* – this he is known to have as his very own, that he is true purity and pure truth.

In his conflation of the remarkable and the unexceptional, Map could be said to follow Augustine's assertion that creation itself constitutes the most "unique wonder, that miracle of miracles, the world itself"; since, in Benedicta Ward's summary, "there is only one miracle, that of creation" such that "all creation was, therefore, both 'natural' and 'miraculous.'"[81] We might recall *De nugis* 2.4, discussed early in this chapter, where the real spiritual miracle (the preservation of monastic vows) turned out to be the fact that no physical miracle (healing the deformed foot) took place at all. Responding to the immensely difficult problem of how to distinguish the imaginary from the real, when fantasy, *fantasm*, and the fantastic so freely populate the earth, Map returns to a pat statement of faith already implicit at the beginning of *De nugis* 2.13. He leaves aside entirely the demonic powers first introduced as cause of fantastic visions ("demones per se faciunt") and, in a triumph of the soul ("anime triumphus est"; *De nugis* 2.1), renders unto God that which is God's. Which is to say, he abandons the whole problem of sorting out fact

---

[81] Ward, *Miracles and the Medieval Mind*, 2–3.

from *fantasm*, of distinguishing the believable and the unbelievable, and of identifying the "sons of death" ("filii mortue") who populate the world as distinct from people more generally.

De nugis 2.13 is concerned not with the crafting of interpretations, but with the conveyance of narrative realities. As Map declares in *De nugis* 2.32, he is but the huntsman, who brings forth from the wilds of narrative the gamey meat of fantastic occurrences, and it is not for him to make meals of his labor.[82] Moreover, any such crafting of interpretive dishes must derive from God's omnipotent truth and purity ("vera puritas et pura veritas"), not from the natural powers of human thought ("nostras inquisitiones et disputationes"). In the final line of *De nugis* 2.13, Map questions whether we can "know anything," given God's incomprehensible powers to protect and forsake: there is no bright line between hermeneutics and epistemology. When faced with the continued and obvious presence of the impossible – when faced with Alnoth and Triunein and their multiplying, anonymous, pious, Welsh and English heirs – Map is left with little else to do other than to throw his interpretive hands in the air and leave the hard work of distinguishing pure truths from pure appearances to God – or, at any event, to the interested reader. These *fantasms*-made-flesh are self-evidently existent, as physical and social agents at work in the world. The conditions of their existence lead Map to declare that no interpretation is necessary at the precise moment when the need for careful interpretation has become most apparent.

Turning the logic of an explanatory fable on its head – wherein a supposedly fantastic event can be explained by means of rational causes – Map insists at every turn that day-to-day life is filled to the brim with the effects of fantastic causes. Any perceived normality in the quotidian affair of living and being in England is shot through with the multiplying effects of *fantasmata* as beings and agents. If the world itself is a *miraculum* in its own way, then the such incomprehensible existence cannot be fathomed without acknowledging the mundane presence of demon-descendants walking in broad daylight down every familiar street.

Readers at least passingly familiar with Walter Map will find it difficult to take his exaggerated conclusion to *De nugis* 2.13 at face value. In this textual sequence, Map repeatedly raises difficult questions about experience, the natural, and the unnatural, suggesting but never saying outright that many clear distinctions the average reader might draw between human action and supernatural activity actually may be insufficient for any competent understanding of reality or the experience of reality. Map nevertheless deflects the further implications his narratives might have for his readers' understanding of divine authority, demonic power, or human experience.

If one side of Map's speech is captured by a literal exposition of his words, it is nearly impossible to pinpoint with any clarity what the other

---

[82] See Echard, "Map's Metafiction," 305–6.

side of his duplicitous speech might be. Steven Justice has observed that Eucharistic miracles "show how easily the practices of piety could foster a benign inattention that avoids the hardness of hard truth."[83] In *De nugis* 2.13, we might describe Map as undermining any confidence in "benign inattention" by enacting a blatantly insufficient version of it. The baldness of the rhetorical move demands a less credulous meaning than the pious declaration at its close. Yet the section, taken alone as I have presented it here, gives little sense of what that less credulous meaning might be – what the "hardness of hard truth" might look like; or what the content of "*other than*" is, apart from Map's blandly pious closing comments. Moreover, any focus on the content of "other than" runs the risk of ignoring Map's own insistence that he sincerely means exactly what he *does say*. We do not doubt that Map, a member of the secular clergy with clearly defined religious training, has some sincere faith in God as "true purity and pure truth." We have good reason to doubt, however, that such piety captures fully his reflections on the difficult questions he raises.

A less nimble author than Walter might be concerned with the demystification of that which appears inexplicable or incomprehensible in the world. There where the uneducated and superstitious find evidence of demonic activity, he might urge the more rational observer to discern the natural beauty, human and inhuman, present in God's creation. But Walter knows better than to doubt God's powers in this way. He has heard of demons, *incubi* and *succubi*, and he has heard their descendants yet walk among us. He will not err in judgment as do Eadric and Gwestin, mistaking undead-fairy-women for women and becoming enraptured by them. Rather, with the knowledge of old stories well in hand, he occupies himself with filling the day-to-day experience of the world with wonder. For Map, miracles and marvels are everywhere, performed and withheld according to the judgment of God's servants in innumerable, chaotic, untidy ways. There where the unimaginative and stubborn might perceive only the quotidian and disorganized workings of human society, the careful reader of the *De nugis curialium* might better discern the enduring evidence of otherworldly activity in the brave, holy, perfectly normal actions of the children of the dead, now a multitude – propagating, tithing, and giving praise to God and his saints.

Rewarding Obfuscations

Map's hazy, mediated relationship with the organization of his text is a boon to critical inquiry, not its bane. In Map we encounter a twelfth-century member of the secular clergy and infamous member of the Angevin literary scene

---

[83] Steven Justice, "Eucharistic Miracle and Eucharistic Doubt," *JMEMS* 42.2 (2012): 316. See also Justice's much-cited article, "Did the Middle Ages Believe in Their Miracles?," *Representations* 103.1 (2008): 1–29.

foregrounding one complex problem of the field that we now call literary formalism by way of a text made more complex by the exigencies of its material transmission than the author could have anticipated. In Bodley 851, we encounter a representation of Map's life work at once sensitive to Map's authorial project and non-identical with the originary authorial composition we call the *De nugis curialium*. A literary-critical approach to the *De nugis* must account for multiplying aspects of the text's ambiguity – unequal mixtures of intentional obscurity in arrangement and unintentional obscurity in transmission – understanding its value as an object of interpretation within a broad set of thematic and topical contexts. In the analysis I have proposed, Map's specific subject matter includes the otherworldly, the marvelous, and the mundane. Elsewhere in the *De nugis* he ranges into history, historiography, doctrine, theology, political machinations, Welsh indigeneity, religious hierarchy, classical mythology, romance, the court, authorship, and household management, among other diverse subjects and topics. Map has been compared to Wodehouse, Waugh, and Stevenson; but in his use of digression, understatement, and not-insincere moralization – neither credulous nor disingenuous, meaning precisely what it says and, while suggesting a great deal else, nothing more – his most significant literary successor may well be Laurence Sterne. Map thrives on the apparently incidental, the nonchalant omission of what is most important, and the casual suggestion of what some of his readers would not, or could not, venture to think at all. In this way, Walter Map was an architect of the unconscious of his age, drawing to the fore the quotidian implications of widely accepted marvelous thought.

The collaborative attention given to the *De nugis curialium* by Scribe A and Scribe X only heightens the need for examination of material evidence and literary evidence together when reading Map's work. I have argued throughout this chapter that the thread of coherence connecting *De nugis* 2.11–2.13 as a literary sequence originated with its author, Walter Map, and was preserved and embellished in sense by the scribes who transmitted his work, in particular Scribe A and Scribe X. How exactly each of those individuals – Walter, Scribe A, and Scribe X – understood the significance of intersecting narrative and exposition within that literary sequence remains an open, and indeed unanswerable question. Attention to the codicological unconscious does not amount to the reading of minds. Moreover, whether the literary sequence repays literary inquiry is a question nearly tautological in form, answerable only by the inquirer. We cannot know whether Scribe A or Scribe X understood *De nugis* 2.11–2.13 in the way I have proposed, as an object of interpretation, nor can we ascertain that Map intended by it precisely what I have argued concerning its significance.

Whether the contiguous narratives are constructed so as to invite consideration together within the manuscript book, however – that is, whether *De nugis* 2.11–2.13 might plausibly be considered a literary sequence at all – is a question substantially answerable through consideration of the material evidence for textual arrangement and transmission within Bodley 851. For the *De nugis curialium*, as throughout Bodley 851 and the manuscript record generally, material form and textual significance are inextricable. Where examination of textual production alone may suggest irrecuperable "untidiness," either on the part of Walter Map or the scribes who transmitted his text, examination of the production and arrangement of the *De nugis* points instead towards numerous possibilities for reading complex literary sequences throughout the work. Scribal arrangements of organizational material direct attention to possible continuities in narrative structure. In the case of *De nugis* 2.11–2.13, I have argued for a general agreement between the codicological evidence and evidence for authorial intention, insofar as both substantiate underlying narrative continuity. In this way, although the copy of the *De nugis* preserved within Bodley 851 was not produced under Map's direction or in his lifetime, the manuscript witness will nevertheless serve as a productive site for examining codicological intentionalism.[84] Moreover, as I demonstrate in Chapter 4, attention the codicological unconscious of Bodley 851 reveals further implications for scribal perceptions of a pseudonymous authorial project long associated with Walter Map. The significance of *De nugis* 2.11–2.13 within Map's work in Bodley 851 aligns suggestively with the significance of *De nugis curialium* within Bodley 851 on the whole.

Of course, not every instance of contiguity in layout will reward literary inspection. Potential literary complexity suggested by manuscript evidence must be confirmed by close analysis of the lexical text. It is nevertheless the case that manuscript arrangement acts as a prompt to inquire into whether and how opportunities for understanding literary sequence might emerge from shifting conditions of textual possibility. As with many apparent discontinuities in Map's *De nugis*, the apparent discontinuities between and among textual "fragments" in its single manuscript witness should draw close attention, rather than dismissal, from literary scholars. That the sole surviving manuscript of a text so thoroughly invested in misdirection as the *De nugis curialium* should present its own forms of material misdirection, however unintentionally, ought to compound rather than negate our interest in the literary arrangement of that text. It is in this precise sense that Bodley 851 itself – the book containing Map's book – holds such potential.

---

[84] Sebastian Sobecki, "The Author's Three Bodies: Codicological Intentionalism and the Medieval Text," *JMEMS* 53, no. 3 (2023): 573–96; "Authorised Realities: The Gesta Romanorum and Thomas Hoccleve's Poetics of Autobiography," *Speculum* 98, no. 2 (2023): 536–58. See also my own contribution: Thomas C. Sawyer, "Book Work: Towards an Extended Codicological Intentionalism," *JMEMS* 55.2 (2025): 159–84.

4

Walter Map's *Piers Plowman*

For centuries, readers of medieval romances, satires, and anonymous lyrics in Latin, French, and English attributed to Walter Map a vast corpus of literature that he almost certainly did not write. As we have seen, his longest piece of writing did not circulate widely among medieval audiences (*De nugis curialium*; hence, *De nugis*). His most successful piece of writing – indeed, one of the most widely copied texts in late-medieval Europe – circulated commonly under names other than his own (*Dissuasio Valerii ad Rufinum*). If Map found humorously vexing some confusion between his compositions and such authorities as St. Jerome and Valerius Maximus, one can only imagine him succumbing to virtual hysterics upon learning that he himself had been summoned as an authorizing force for the entirety of the French *Lancelot-Grail Cycle*, a large quantity of satirical Anglo-Latin poetry, and the textual production of any number of persons living in England or France after the death of Henry II so unfortunate as to have composed while being named Walter.[1] In Chapter 3, I showed how Map thought subtly about the possible consequences of fairy offspring acting out the most mundane aspects of quotidian experience. Fittingly, the many dubious heirs of his own authority still lingering within the surviving textual record pay tribute, with uncanny accuracy, to his own authorial fascinations. Bodley 851 itself reflects Walter's own obsession with what is manifest yet marvelous, with those lingering human and archival authorities at once inescapable, revealing, informative, and false.

This chapter takes the material association between Walter Map and the Z-text of *Piers Plowman* as a point of departure for considering Map's

---

[1] "Scimus hanc placuisse multis. Auide rapitur. transcribitur intente; plena iocunditate legitur. meam tamen esse quidam sed de plebe negant" (fol. 47r; James *et al.*, 313): "I know this [letter] has pleased many. It is snatched up greedily, copied passionately, and read with great delight. Nevertheless, some people – vulgar people! – deny that it is mine." Walter goes on to complain that authorship is only granted to the dead, a problem he has no intention of solving – as influentially discussed in Alastair Minnis, *Medieval Theory of Authorship: Scholastic Literary Attitudes in the Later Middle Ages*, 2nd ed. (Philadelphia, PA: University of Pennsylvania Press, 2010). For an overview of how "Walter" was used as a broad authorial tag in late-medieval manuscripts, see A. G. Rigg, "Golias and Other Pseudonyms," *Studi Medievali* 18.1 (1977): 65–109.

pseudonymous influence on the production of Bodley 851. The material contents of Bodley 851 bring *Piers* into conversation with a tradition of satirical poetry in Anglo-Latin thriving in England at the turn of the fifteenth century and precisely captured – albeit inaccurately captured – by the authorial persona of Walter Map. Of course, the *Piers*-author's debts to the schools are well-established.[2] The compilation of Bodley 851, however, reveals debts to a tradition of educated Anglo-Latin poetry composed more for entertainment than for self-improvement. This chapter traces specific textual debts the Z-text preserves alongside broader generic debts too often neglected in scholarly engagements with the *Piers* tradition. As with so many other manuscripts of *Piers*, Bodley 851 bears signs of interest in the poem's contents alongside its form, underscoring topical and thematic resonances (e.g., economies of grace, misogamy, and the fantastical) and formal similarities (e.g., language, alliteration, narrative frame).[3] Indeed, as I show in this chapter, practices in decoration and rubrication reveal an affinity between the pseudonymous ghost of Walter Map and medieval perspectives on textual similarity more broadly. The production and modification of Bodley 851 draw together authorship and genre in a single compilational sweep. Within Bodley 851, what it means for a poem to be ascribed to Walter Map and how a poem by Walter Map goes about meaning are, ultimately, inextricable from one another.

The comparative points of contact that I identify between a twelfth-century courtly wit known for his Anglo-Latin production and an anonymous fourteenth-century alliterative poem in Middle English emerge tenuously but suggestively from Bodley 851 as modified by the overarching presence of Scribe X in his capacity as editor, rubricator, copyist, and reader. Scribe X transformed this repository of disparate textual materials into a coherent and presentable literary collection. For Scribe X, Bodley 851 either was or was to become a Mappean manuscript. As with so many other texts of uncertain authorship, for broad swathes of late-medieval audiences, so here we find evidence that *Piers*, specifically, was read in Bodley 851 as though it were

---

[2] See Andrew Galloway, "*Piers Plowman* and the Schools," *YLS* 6 (1992): 89–107; John A. Alford, "Langland's Learning," *YLS* 9 (1995): 1–17; Ralph Hanna, "School and Scorn: Gender in *Piers Plowman*," in *New Medieval Literatures III*, eds. David Lawton, Wendy Scase, and Rita Copeland (Oxford: Oxford University Press, 1999), 213–27; Katharine Breen, *Imagining an English Reading Public, 1150–1400* (Cambridge: Cambridge University Press, 2010); Traugott Lawler, "Langland Versificator," *YLS* 25 (2011): 37–76; and Christopher Cannon, *From Literacy to Literature: England, 1300–1400* (Oxford: Oxford University Press, 2016).

[3] See Anne Middleton, "The Audience and Public of *Piers Plowman*," in *Middle English Alliterative Poetry and Its Literary Background: Seven Essays*, ed. David Lawton (Cambridge: D. S. Brewer, 1982), 101–23; Sarah Wood, *Piers Plowman and its Manuscript Tradition* (York: York Medieval Press, 2022).

written by Walter Map. By attending to Scribe X's labor, we can understand what it was like, late in the fourteenth century, to read Walter Map's *Piers Plowman*.

Of course, I will not argue that Walter Map actually wrote *Piers*, a claim easily disproven by any superficial historical or textual analysis of the poem. I will argue, however, that there is good reason to believe Scribe X thought as much – that if posed the question, "Whose poem begins 'In a somer sesoun'?" he might plausibly have answered "Walter Map's" (Z.Prol.1).[4] At the very least, Scribe X's scribal labor on Bodley 851 demonstrates that he understood his transcription of the Z-text of *Piers* to participate in a broader discursive field of textual materials best described by their belated, persistent, and inaccurate associations with Walter Map. It is not only plausible but likely that Scribe X added the Z-text of *Piers* to Bodley 851 as a sincere, informed, and literate contribution to a collection of material already present in that manuscript and loosely organized around the idea of Mappean authorship.

From the standpoint of modern scholarship, it is easy to demonstrate that Scribe X was incorrect. Yet Scribe X is no longer capable of learning from his mistakes. We, however, can learn a great deal about the historical reception of *Piers* around the turn of the fifteenth century from his choices in compiling the sole surviving manuscript containing Map's work. Scribal labor on Bodley 851 encourages us to read *Piers* in the way that medieval readers read things that they thought were Walter Map's.

How to Read the Z-text of Piers Plowman

In order to recapture some of the ways in which a late-medieval reader (Scribe X) may have encountered one strange rendition of a notoriously eccentric fourteenth-century poem (*Piers*) under the sign of a twelfth-century courtly wit (Walter Map), I place *Piers* in conversation with the specific group of Anglo-Latin texts that Scribe X received, modified, and contributed within the material compilation of Bodley 851. Although we cannot recreate any medieval experience of reading this medieval book, we can uncover some of the literary habits, cultural assumptions, and structural forms common between texts too-often considered unrelated on account of their differing languages, origins, and narrative contents. If Scribe X was, factually, incorrect about what texts Map wrote, the manuscript he compiled nevertheless provides insight into a wide range of comparative reading practices available to each of the poems contained within.

---

[4] I cite *Piers Plowman* parenthetically from William Langland, *Piers Plowman: A Parallel-Text Edition of the A, B, C and Z Versions*, ed. A.V.C Schmidt (New York: Longman, 1995). For citations from the Z-text, I have also consulted William Langland, *Piers Plowman: The Z Version*, eds. Charlotte Brewer and A. G. Rigg (Toronto: Pontifical Institute of Mediaeval Studies, 1983), along with the manuscript itself.

The material circumstances surrounding the production of Bodley 851 place the reception of the Z-text not in conversation with the development of the many versions, revisions, and renditions of *Piers* over time but rather in conversation with the assortment of miscellaneous texts gathered alongside a single witness to the poem in a single manuscript copy – the scribal version specific to this manuscript. In 1986, Anne Middleton observed that "the meaning and standing of 'scribal versions' have been central to all textual discussion and editorial debate on the poem," and returning to a similar line of argument in her review of the Athlone C-text with the *Piers Electronic Archive* in 2001, she further argued that "the editorial search for the original text is inseparable from the pursuit of the immediate verbal and institutional conditions that motivated and informed it."[5] Although editors of *Piers* have responded admirably to Middleton's call to consider manuscript contexts as paramount for understanding the poem's textual construction, literary critics have been much slower to approach individual copies of *Piers* as objects of interpretation motivated by the immediate textual conditions of their production.[6] Of course, perspectives on the authorial status of the Z-text and its place within the transmission of *Piers* abound.[7] Yet, critical attention has

[5] Anne Middleton, "*Piers Plowman*," in *A Manual of the Writings in Middle English, 1050–1500, VII*, ed. Albert E. Hartung (Hamden: Archon Books, 1986), 2211; "Editing Terminable and Interminable," *Huntington Library Quarterly* 64.1/2 (2001): 161–86. Middleton's term "scribal versions" refers to a major editorial and interpretive problem in scholarship on *Piers Plowman*, namely that nearly every copy of the poem differs in some way, however major or minor, in terms of structure, organization, and lection from every other copy of the poem. Following Walter Skeat, editors have divided manuscript witnesses into three or four main versions (A, B, C; and sometimes Z, the present text); but within each version can be found substantial variation. To assess "the poem," one must account for local differences and variations preserved by individual scribes in their copies, or "scribal versions."

[6] Scholars of Middle English will readily identify exceptions to this trend, especially from the perspective of codicology, as in many studies conducted by Ralph Hanna, Simon Horobin, and Sarah Wood. Of great value for my thinking in this chapter has been Noelle Phillips, "Compilational Reading: Richard Osbarn and Huntington Library MS HM 114," *YLS* 28 (2014): 65–104. An important precursor to the method I propose is Karrie Fuller, "The Craft of the 'Z-Maker': Reading the Z Text's Unique Lines in Context," *YLS* 27 (2013). Nevertheless, the vast majority of scholarly treatments of individual manuscripts of *Piers Plowman* – themselves representing a minority critical approach to the text of *Piers Plowman* – consider the poem primarily with editorial or authorial concerns in mind, seeking to relate individual copies of the poem to its own broader poetic tradition rather than to any specific texts compiled alongside it in manuscript copy.

[7] George Kane, *Piers Plowman: The Evidence for Authorship* (London: Athlone Press, 1965); A. V. C. Schmidt, "The Authenticity of the Z Text of *Piers Plowman*: A Metrical Examination," *Medium Aevum* 53.2 (1984): 295–300; George Kane, "Review

never been paid to how the compilation of texts preserved within Bodley 851 might be made central to understanding the received meaning of the Z-text. In order to understand this literary object in historically grounded literary conversation, criticism will benefit from an examination of the poem and its textual companions *as texts* in placed conversation with one another on codicological grounds.

A fruitful interpretive approach, comparable to my own, has been explored by Karrie Fuller, who argues that the unique lines of the Z-text yield some sense of the Z-maker's literary investments and social identity. Fuller helpfully distinguishes between the person who revised the *Piers*-author's work into its present form (the Z-maker, or Z-redactor) and the person who transcribed the resulting revision into Bodley 851 (the Z-scribe, or Scribe X).[8] Fuller's approach follows Kathryn Kerby-Fulton's work on the material circulation and cultural influences evident for Bodley 851 as well as Ralph Hanna's suggestion that the text is "of considerable interest for Rezeptionsästhetik."[9] Fuller's attention to the literary effects of the Z-maker's alterations uncovers some unexpected commitments in the text, not least of which being his substantial patience with clerical malfeasance – an attitude uncharacteristic of other variants of *Piers*. Her work makes the welcome observation that the Z-text might go about meaning in ways foreign to the main body of scholarship on *Piers*.

Article: The 'Z Version' of Piers Plowman," *Speculum* 60.4 (1985): 910–30; Hoyt N. Duggan, "The Authenticity of the Z Text of 'Piers Plowman': Further Notes on Metrical Evidence," *Medium Ævum* 56.1 (1987): 25–45; Charlotte Brewer, *Editing Piers Plowman: The Evolution of the Text* (Cambridge: Cambridge University Press, 1996); Ralph Hanna, "MS Bodley 851 and the Dissemination of *Piers Plowman*," in *Pursuing History: Middle English Manuscripts and Their Texts* (Stanford, CA: Stanford University Press, 1996); and Sarah Wood, "Monologic Langland: Contentiousness and the 'Z Version' of *Piers Plowman*," *The Review of English Studies* 68.284 (2017): 224–43.

[8] See also Richard Firth Green, "The Lost Exemplar of the Z-Text of *Piers Plowman* and Its 20-Line Pages," *Medium Aevum* 56.2 (1987): 307–10.

[9] Fuller, "Craft of Z-Maker"; Kathryn Kerby-Fulton, "Confronting the Scribe-Poet Binary," in *New Directions in Medieval Manuscript Studies and Reading Practices: Essays in Honor of Derek Pearsall*, eds. Kathryn Kerby-Fulton et al. (Notre Dame, IN: University of Notre Dame Press, 2014); Hanna, "Dissemination," 201. See also Kathryn Kerby-Fulton, "Oxford," in *Europe: A Literary History, 1348–1418*, ed. David Wallace (Oxford: Oxford University Press, 2016), 208–226; and Kathryn Kerby-Fulton, "Professional Readers of Langland at Home and Abroad: New Directions in the Political and Bureaucratic Codicology of *Piers Plowman*," in *New Directions in Later Medieval Manuscript Studies: Essays from the 1998 Harvard Conference*, ed. Derek Pearsall (York: York Medieval Press, 2000), 103–29.

Even as Fuller addresses the specific language of the Z-text, however, her argument does not take into account the specific manuscript contexts of Bodley 851. Arguing that the Z-maker's alterations to his received text of *Piers* by and large serve as "deradicalization of Langland's thought," Fuller observes that "Bodley 851 contains a significant amount of harsh anticlerical and antimendicant debate as well as politically charged texts, such as the 'Apocalypsis Goliae,' an excerpt from the 'Epistola Sathanae ad universalem ecclesiam'..., and John of Bridlington's *Prophecy*."[10] Though mention is made of these companion texts to the Z-text, Fuller's article does not attempt to account for their own literary subtleties and, more importantly, misrepresents the cultural status they had achieved. It is crucial to recognize that none of the three texts Fuller mentions was preserved singularly for an "elite, privileged class of readers allowed to encounter radical thought."[11] Most of these texts were widely circulated and consumed in a variety of contexts. Indeed, some of them (e.g., *Apocalypsis goliae episcopi* and the *De coniuge non ducenda*, neither "politically charged" nor "antimendicant") may count among the most commonly encountered written and oral vernacular texts in late-medieval England. In her tendency to read the Z-text in comparison with the A-, B-, and C-texts, rather than in direct conversation with, e.g., the *Apocalypsis*, the *Speculum stultorum*, or the Bridlington *Prophecy*, Fuller's approach might be taken as representative of a prevailing trend in criticism on *Piers*, which – with significant exceptions – takes each variant text rather as a response to other variant texts (and their reconstructed archetypes, read by no medieval person) than as a response to the local conditions of production and representation made evident by that variant text.

I locate the argument of this chapter in the specific material contingencies of Bodley 851, rather than the broad textual contingencies of the *Piers* tradition. To borrow Fuller's terminology, I attend rather to the craft of the "Z-compiler" than that of the "Z-maker." While I will argue that one poem in Bodley 851, the *Apocalypsis goliae episcopi*, was a source for the Z-text, and so must have been known to the Z-redactor, it does not necessarily follow that the Z-compiler (Scribe X) copied the *Apocalypsis goliae* into Bodley 851 alongside the Z-text specifically *because* the poem was a source for the Z-redactor. Nor is it necessary to argue that the Z-compiler (Scribe X) perceived precisely the same conceptual resonances in his compiling as the Z-redactor perceived in his redacting. Rather, like the Z-redactor, Scribe X may have held any number of half-formed, contradictory, private motives – all inaccessible to the modern scholar, just as they would have been for any other medieval agent – for placing these two texts side by side.

---

[10] Fuller, "Craft of Z-maker," 32.
[11] Fuller, "Craft of Z-maker," 32.

To investigate relations among texts as they appear together within Bodley 851 thus requires close attention to the codicological unconscious – what I described in the introduction as "a mode of attending to the medieval book that allows scholars to consider interactions between medieval texts according to how those texts were constructed – and as they are now preserved – within the context of the production of their extant medieval manuscripts" that is "neither exclusive of considerations of agency nor dependent upon the recovery of authorial, scribal, or readerly intention."[12] This chapter aims to discover how this specific text of *Piers*, the so-called Z-text, might be understood within the larger field of material texts compiled alongside it. The critical positions established below are intended to approximate possibilities latent within the granular textual construction of the medieval book (as in Chapter 2). The analysis undertaken below also takes as methodological principle that the material arrangement of texts in their manuscript contexts should inform literary approaches to their contents (as in Chapter 3). Comparative readings of the Z-text in light of its companion texts demonstrate how this unique version of *Piers* might be inflected by the history of (false) Mappean authorship unevenly and at varying scales, by way of textual resemblance and topical affiliation. An examination of the manuscript conditions surrounding the text of *Piers* yields insight into the construction and reception of the fourteenth century's most baffling poem.

Though more connections might be discovered between the Z-text of *Piers* and its companion-texts in Bodley 851 than those outlined below, I focus my argument in this chapter on the collection of texts with the closest ties, in the surviving manuscript record, to Walter Map. Following a brief summary of how Scribe X's contributions to the manuscript create an illusion of authorship for the texts he collected, I offer two case studies in pseudo-Mappean influences on *Piers*. First, I analyze the Hunger episode of *Piers* in terms of its textual and thematic debts to the *Apocalypsis goliae*, a text that Scribe X ascribed to Walter Map. Then, I analyze Z-text's deployment of misogyny in conversation with Map's *Dissuasio Valerii ad Rufinum* (attributed to Map by Scribe X) and the pseudo-Mappean *De coniuge* (for which no author is given, in Bodley 851, and which was commonly ascribed to Map in the late-fourteenth century and throughout the fifteenth century). The ascription of the *Apocalypsis goliae* and the *De coniuge* to Map, made commonly in late-medieval and early modern productions, would only be seriously questioned in 1841, in the context of Thomas Wright's anthology of *Latin Poems Commonly Attributed to Walter Mapes*.[13] Finally, in closing, I turn to the opening lines of the Z-text as exemplary of fantastical uncertainties present throughout Map's actual text, the *De nugis*. My close analysis thus proceeds from particularity, through

---

[12] See pp. 23–4.

[13] Thomas Wright, *The Latin Poems Commonly Attributed to Walter Mapes* (London: Camden Society, 1841).

topicality, and into one suggestive intersection of authorship and genre – all yielded by close attention to the construction of Bodley 851.

Since Scribe X and his fellow readers did not limit themselves to reading lines unique to the Z-text, among competing versions of *Piers*, neither do I: my analyses will treat the text as it appears, in full, in its single manuscript copy. In fact, it is worth emphasizing that most medieval readers – Scribe X and otherwise – would have been hard-pressed to identify lines specific to the Z-text (or any text) against lines present in multiple other archetypal versions.[14] Moreover, I do not make any strong editorial claim about the significance of the Z-text within the broader history of the transmission of *Piers*. I do, however, restrict my attention to lines of the Z-text present in Bodley 851 before the textual continuations that begin on fol. 139r (in the hand of Scribe Q), since these continuations were added later – possibly several decades later – than the work of Scribe X and his contemporaries. In sum, I consider any text transcribed, corrected, or rubricated under the direction of Scribe X to be pertinent to the present analysis. I do not consider any text that was added subsequent to Scribe X's rubrication. What is important to the method I adopt throughout this chapter remains the material text of *Piers* present in Bodley 851, rather than the status of the lexical Z-text of *Piers* in view of textual criticism.

Scribe X's Walter Map

It would be difficult to overstate the role Scribe X played in unifying and modifying the disparate material parts of the manuscript we now call MS Bodley 851 (see Chapter 1). When Scribe X acquired the manuscript materials now bound together in a single codex, those materials lacked much of the scribal work now present. Along with transcribing the Z-text of *Piers*, Scribe X was responsible for applying all rubricated headings, all paraph marks, all penwork initials, and all decorations in red and blue penwork throughout the manuscript. He was not the last agent to contribute textual material to the manuscript's constituent parts, which were most likely bound after his involvement had concluded. Nevertheless, for any critical study of the manuscript's reception, use, and alteration over time, it is the presence of Scribe X as reader and compiler that must be accounted for most fully.

Without Scribe X's labor on Part I of Bodley 851, the *De nugis* itself might count among the great mass of texts only skeptically and incompletely considered Mappeana. In Part I, Scribe A had written the *De nugis curialium*

---

[14] Unless, as Brewer and Rigg argued, the Z-maker was, in fact, the *Piers*-author – in which case many of the points of comparison identified below are indicative not only of manuscript affiliation but of the process of composition informing all versions of the poem (*A Facsimile of the Z-Text*).

and its table of contents, followed by the "Fall of Carthage." The final four bifolia of Part I remained blank. At the time of Scribe A's copying, none of the rubricated chapter titles for the *De nugis* had been added in red ink (fols. 7ra–72vb), nor had the work's formal attribution to Walter Map been penned (fol. 7ra; pl. 1). All such material was added by Scribe X, along with numerous corrections to the text of the *De nugis*.[15] It is worth emphasizing that subsequent readers have referred to the *De nugis* as Map's work primarily on the authority of Scribe X's rubricated heading. Left only with the work of earlier scribes, limited internal evidence might corroborate the assumption that Walter Map – meaning, the historical personage associated variously with Oxford, Hereford, and Lincolnshire in service to Henry II – was author of the many sections of the *De nugis*. The notion that every preserved chapter could be taken authoritatively as Map's would be less readily accepted.

In fact, at the conclusion of Scribe X's work, the only rubricated claims to authorship made within the whole of Bodley 851 were those ascribing texts to Walter Map. Before applying any rubricated material (headings, *capitulae*, paraph marks, etc.), Scribe X added the *Debate between heart and eye* directly following the incomplete *De coniuge* (fol. 81va; pl. 7).[16] He allowed for five blank pages to follow the *Speculum stultorum* (116r–118r) before adding the *Apocalypsis goliae* (fols. 118va–120vb; pl. 11) and six blank pages to follow the *Apocalypsis goliae* (121r–123v). If he had not already written what is now called the Z-text of *Piers*, he did so at this time, in a new booklet that would become fols. 124r–139r. In his copy of *Piers*, Scribe X left room for block letters at the beginning of each passus, provided section headers at passus breaks, and planned for a large puzzle initial ("I"), which would run alongside the first seventeen lines of the text in a curving taper (pl. 12). For all of the manuscript's texts copied at this time, except the *De coniuge*, the *Debate between heart and eye* (directly following the *De coniuge*), and the Z-text of *Piers*, Scribe X added rubricated headers in the same style as the chapter titles and numbers for the *De nugis*. (I leave aside the *Ave virgo mater christi*, since its incipit has been lost; although there is manuscript evidence for Walter of Wimborne's poems being mistakenly ascribed to Map.)[17] He

---

[15] A second layer of corrections and annotations in a nearly black ink and in a secretary hand with no Anglicana features was added later.

[16] There is no reason to believe Scribe X would have thought the *Debate between heart and eye* was written by Philip the Chancellor, an ascription made only recently; see Peter Dronke, "The Lyrical Compositions of Philip the Chancellor," *Studi Medievali* 28 (1987): 563–92.

[17] As collected by John Bale, *Scriptorum Illustrium Maioris Brytannie* (Basil, 1557), 253–5; see A. G. Rigg, "Medieval Latin Poetic Anthologies (I)," *Mediaeval Studies* 39 (1977): 281–330.

ascribed both the *De nugis* and the *Apocalypsis goliae* to Walter Map ("Gauteri Mahap," fol. 7ra, pl. 1; "Galteri Mahap," fol. 118va, pl. 11). He did not make any authorial ascriptions to any of the other texts present in Bodley 851, nor would any such ascriptions be added to the manuscript until the annotations of postmedieval readers.

We can place all existing decoration, not only rubricated incipits and explicits, within the chronological span of Scribe X's activity. After he had written out the *Debate between heart and eye*, the *Apocalypsis goliae* and the Z-text, Scribe X also imposed two rubrication schemes in parallel. As I demonstrated in Chapter 1, at this moment in the production of Bodley 851, Parts I, II, and III could be considered for the first time a coherent textual unit, unified by a single overarching contributor. Scribe X had imposed a single paraph scheme on the table of contents to Map's work (the *De nugis*), which apart from the short entry now called *The Fall of Carthage*, would have concluded all written material in Part I at the time. Scribe X had read and corrected the better part of the *De nugis*, decorating it according to a single scheme and attributing it to Walter Map; he had added the *Apocalypsis goliae*, decorating it according to the same scheme and attributing it to Walter Map; and, immediately following the *Apocalypsis goliae*, he had added the Z-text of *Piers*, decorating it according to the same scheme but omitting any attribution whatsoever. He did not copy any text in the few pages lying between the *Apocalypsis goliae* and *Piers*, nor had he, for any other text present in the manuscript, named any other author. For none of the remaining texts is it the case that a full examination of their manuscript witnesses otherwise presents a unified set of authorial ascriptions.

When the work of Scribe X was complete, he had taken a collection of texts beginning and ending with pseudonymous Mappean material (the *De coniuge* and the *Apocalypsis goliae* in Part II) and bookended those texts with the sole surviving copy of Walter Map's *De nugis* on one side (Part I) and the unique Z-text of *Piers* on the other (Part III). No texts yet intervened between the *De nugis* and the *De coniuge* or between the *Apocalypsis goliae* and *Piers*. To imagine Bodley 851 in its fullest state of inscription, rubrication, and decoration by Scribe X is to imagine a disparate collection of textual materials affiliated loosely but concretely by the illusory authorial presence of Walter Map. With Scribe X, we ask: how do we read Walter Map's *Piers Plowman*?

Scribe X's Piers Plowman

Map's Hunger

The *Apocalypsis goliae* immediately precedes the Z-text in Bodley 851, is decorated according to the same scheme, and is explicitly ascribed to Walter Map. The pseudo-Mappean affiliations between the Z-text and the *Apocalypsis goliae*, while present at many moments in the text, can be seen most clearly in the Hunger episode that occupies the better part of passus Z.7. With the *Apocalypsis goliae*, the Z-text of *Piers* reflects sincerely and humorously upon practical economies of charity and transgression within an implied social and eschatological order. Though it does seem likely that the *Apocalypsis goliae* was known to the *Piers*-author, on account of its general popularity and on account of the textual debts traced below, what concerns this chapter are the local affiliations made evident between one satirical poem and another within the context of Scribe X's modifications to Bodley 851. The likelihood that the Z-text of *Piers* borrows directly from the *Apocalypsis goliae* strengthens the connection between these two texts in their manuscript context. Such citation is not strictly necessary, however, for the observation of manuscript affiliation undertaken in this section. Manuscript affiliation between these two poems establishes parallel forms of duplicity between two of their most memorable figures: Hunger, in *Piers*, and the deacon, in the *Apocalypsis goliae*.

Scholars have long recognized borrowings from the *Apocalypsis goliae* in *Piers*. After Scribe X, it appears to have been Walter Skeat who first recognized the *Apocalypsis goliae* as a possible influence on *Piers*. Skeat made note of the poem as a source for the Feast of Patience, a scene not present in Scribe X's Z-text, based on the emphasis on depraved and gluttonous behavior nowhere prominent in the biblical book of Revelation but the subject of long description in the satirical vision often attributed to Map.[18] Skeat's note may have led Jeanne Krochalis and Edward H. Peters to include an early seventeenth-century translation of the poem in their collection of source-texts for *Piers*, called *The World of Piers Plowman*.[19] Jill Mann, in *Chaucer and Medieval Estates Satire*, notes the poem's connections to Map and its massive pan-European popularity, before comparing Chaucer's "knowledge of Goliardic satire" specifically to that of the *Piers*-author;[20] and Andrew Galloway's *Penn Commentary* on the first four passūs of *Piers* mentions the *Apocalypsis goliae* as exemplary of "estates satires" produced in the twelfth and thirteenth centuries: as "the narrator's flight to heaven in a vision leads to his chance to read about the vices of the clergy," so too does the narrator's vision in *Piers* lead to his

---

[18] For a full discussion of the reference, see Ben Parsons, "An Unrecognized Reference to a Latin Satire in Langland's *Piers Plowman*," *Notes and Queries* 57.1 (2010): 27–9. The Feast of Patience scene appears, of course, in the C-text continuation of *Piers* later added to Bodley 851 by Scribe Q.

[19] Jeanne Krochalis and Edward H. Peters, eds. *The World of Piers Plowman* (Philadelphia, PA: University of Pennsylvania Press, 1975).

[20] Jill Mann, *Chaucer and Medieval Estates Satire* (Cambridge: Cambridge University Press, 1973), 298, 301, and 310.

chance to critique social formations of his own day.[21] The poem's ubiquity in the manuscript record, the subjects of its satire, and its status as a vision all point to some indebtedness to the *Apocalypsis goliae* on the part of *Piers*.

In fact, *Piers* owes one of Hunger's more baffling remarks to an allegorical pun made repeatedly in the pseudo-Mappean *Apocalypsis goliae* – a debt made most obvious in the details of the Z-text. Partway through the second vision, Piers, concerned that he might be held spiritually accountable for Hunger's proposed plan to starve beggars and poor folk into right religious action, asks Hunger simply and starkly, "Myght Y synneles do as thow seyst?" (Z.7.213).[22] Hunger affirms not only that he might but that he must, citing the books of Genesis and Wisdom as evidence that one should not consume without first having labored. Hunger then cites the book of Matthew in order to give a rendition of the parable of the talents – a reference to a specific gospel which has confused several commentators, since the language used in this passage must come specifically from the account in the book of Luke. Introducing the parable, he says "Mathew *wyth the mannes face* mowtheth these wordus," but in conclusion, having provided an English gloss on the parable's concluding verse, he refuses to properly interpret the terms of the parable he recounts: "Of thys matere Y myght make a longe tale / Ac h[i]t fallet nat for me, *for Y am no dekne* / To preche the peple wat that poynt menes" (Z.7.230–2; emphasis mine; the second and third lines are unique to the Z-text).

It is worth noting that the parable's significance is clear in context. Piers worries that his refusal to feed those whom he has afflicted with Hunger might be counted as sin, and Hunger wants to convince him that it would, in fact, be a greater sin to feed those who have not labored for their reward. In Hunger's rough allegorical reading of the parable, just as the iniquitous servant would expect gratitude from his master for doing no labor with his monetary gift, so too do beggars desire food from society where they have not earned any with their bodily gifts. The conclusion follows that, as with the lord in the parable of the talents, in the same way also should Piers look without favor on members of society who refuse to make use of their gifts. Nevertheless, Hunger refuses to say as much in so many words – to "preche the peple what that poynt menes" – since, after all, he is "no dekne."

---

[21] Andrew Galloway, *The Penn Commentary on Piers Plowman*, vol. 1 (Philadelphia, PA: University of Pennsylvania Press, 2006), 53.

[22] This line is the source of David Aers's influential assertion of Hunger's "wobble," a possible "abandonment of the punitive surveillance involved in the discriminatory relief he had begun" ("*Piers Plowman:* Poverty, Work, and Community," in *Community, Gender, and Individual Identity: English Writing, 1360–1430* [New York: Routledge, 1988], 46). See also the response to Aers's "wobble" proposed by Jill Mann in "The Nature of Need Revisited." *YLS* 18 (2004): 3–29.

Some note has been made of the first formulaic tag ("Matthew with the man's face") in commentaries on *Piers* generally, since it appears also in A- and B-texts. Ralph Hanna notes that this is "the traditional symbol of the evangelist," following language found in Revelations 4:7 (as borrowed from Ezekiel 1:10), since "[Matthew's] gospel begins with an outline of Jesus' human genealogy."[23] For this information Hanna cites only Schmidt's commentary in the parallel text edition, which in turn cites only Gertrud Schiller's *Iconography of Christian Art*.[24] Schiller's study, however, makes no reference to any specific textual source, instead providing examples of how the four Evangelists were commonly depicted in conjunction with the four beasts named in both Ezekiel and Revelation, such that Mark might be associated with a lion, Luke with a bull, and John with an eagle. There, Matthew's apocalyptic symbol is not a man, *per se*, but an angel, an entity otherwise-than-human (hence a "beast") but in many ways appearing to resemble a human ("having the face of a human"). Typologically, Matthew is represented in his capacity as gospel-writer by a humanoid figure with identifying wings, halo, and heavenly book.[25]

For the specific interpretation Hanna provides (citing Schmidt, citing Schiller) that associates Matthew with Jesus' human genealogy, however, we must also look to an alternative interpretive source, rather than limiting our attentions to any prevalent or particular trend in iconographic depictions of Matthew. One such source commonly read in medieval Europe was Jerome's preface to his *Commentary on Matthew*. In Jerome's reading, "The first face of a man signifies Matthew, who began his narrative as though about a man."[26] Though I have found no study tracing the precise effects of Jerome's intervention, the reading resurfaces occasionally (but not uniformly) in later patristic and scholastic commentaries on Matthew, finding some significant

---

[23] Ralph Hanna, *Penn Commentary on Piers Plowman*, vol.2 (Philadelphia, PA: University of Pennsylvania Press, 2017), 267.

[24] Schmidt, *Piers Plowman vol. II.2*, 557a cites Gertrud Schiller, *Iconography of Christian Art*, 2 vols. (Greenwich: New York Graphic Society, 1971), vol. 1, pl. 172. But Schiller's index of depictions of Matthew, whether alone or with the other three Evangelists, includes over twenty plates between the two volumes, and would likely only have included more should her proposed third volume have been completed (Schiller, *Iconography*, 1:671, s.v. "Evangelist's symbols, Four beasts").

[25] Cf. especially Schiller, *Iconography*, vol. 1, pls. 53, 76, 379, 405.

[26] Jerome, *Commentary on Matthew*, ed. and trans. by Thomas P. Scheck (Washington, DC: Catholic University of America Press, 2008), 55. According to Scheck, Jerome's schema of matching Evangelists with apocalyptic beasts follows Irenaeus, a source omitted from Jerome's otherwise near-comprehensive list of previous commentaries on *Matthew* (55n37, 56–7); Augustine, for example, pairs Matthew not with the Man but with the Lion (55n37).

purchase in the work of the Victorines, most notably in Richard of St. Victor.[27] Further expositions commonly link the "man" of Revelation 4:7 with the human nature of Christ, sometimes citing Philippians 2:6–8 (an important crux for Trinitarian theology), where Christ is humbly made a servant, taking the likeness of humanity. In patristic sources and in Victorine sources, then, the face of the angelic figure signifies some correlation between divinity and mankind; and Matthew's interest in the human genealogy of Christ associates him with that man-faced angel. The formulaic description at *Piers* Z.7.221 might thus be easily explained, as a poetic turn of phrase, by the *Piers*-author's familiarity with Jerome or with typological figurations of the four evangelists in art on display in public venues, especially churches.[28]

The even stranger declaration that Hunger cannot provide any exegetical interpretation for his own parable because he is "not a deacon" does not rely upon Jerome, however, nor does it relate in any way to the terms of Jerome's allegorical reading of Matthew. Jerome's reading depends upon Matthew's opening interest in the genealogy of Christ as an allegorical referent for the "likeness of man," since Christ afterward took upon himself the likeness of man but was nevertheless also divine: likeness, for Jerome, signals the mystery of the Incarnation, not any sinful deceit lurking within the Son of Man. It is possible, as Schmidt suggests, that Hunger signals some small concern for preaching outside of his station, since it was considered heretical to preach at all unless one had advanced in one's orders to the rank of deacon.[29] Yet, Hunger has already been preaching: he provides matter from Genesis and Wisdom, advocates a specific course of action for spiritual benefit, and asserts social authority on textual grounds. As Hanna points out, Hunger's further argument from Kynde Wyt (Z.7.233) to Psalm 127:2 ("*Labores manuum tuarum quia manducabis*"; Z.7.23) reflects Holy Church's earlier preaching on moderation.[30] Hunger's declaration appears a contradiction in terms.

Hunger's rhetorical deflection finds specific reference not in biblical exegesis but in the *Apocalypsis goliae episcopi*. For although the exact association between the fourth beast of Revelation 4 and the clerical office of deacon is not found in any patristic or scholastic authority, it can be found clearly in the *Apocalypsis goliae*. There, the same verses discussed by Jerome

---

[27] "Tertium animal, id est Matthaeus, quasi faciem hominis habuit, quia ipse in principio Evangelii sui dixit: Liber generationis Jesu Christi (Matth. I), per quod incarnationem Verbi non figuraliter significavit, sed patenter enarravit" (J. P. Migne, ed., "In Apocalypsim Joannis," in *Richardus S. Victoris*, PL 196 [Paris, 1855], 750).

[28] See C. David Benson, *Public Piers Plowman: Modern Scholarship and Late Medieval English Culture* (University Park, PA: Pennsylvania State University Press, 2004).

[29] Schmidt, *Piers Plowman*, vol. II.2, 557a.

[30] Hanna, *Penn Commentary*, vol. 2, 268.

in his preface to his *Commentary on Matthew* (Ez. 1:10; Rev. 4:7) provide a governing structure for its first four visions of the corruption of clergy. The *Apocalypsis goliae* borrows the fourfold creature in order to symbolize not the four Evangelists but four hierarchical positions within the institution of the church (stanzas 23–30).[31] On the beast in the likeness of a man, the *Apocalypsis goliae* has:

> Est qui induitur humana facie,
> Decanus tacite plena versucie,
> Qui fraudes operit forma iusticie,
> Pium que simplici mentitur specie. (fol. 119r; stanza 29)

> The deacon, who is clothed in the face
> of a human, filled with silent cunning,
> conceals deceits in the form of justice,
> and counterfeits piety in his plain appearance.

Here the traditional interpretation, as proposed by Jerome, is abandoned for a much harsher scheme, wherein the likeness of a man is taken not as indicative of the indwelling of divinity in humanity but as indicative of archetypal malice, the concealment of inhuman agency by means of a human face. The deacon – subject to the pope (the lion), the bishop (the bullcalf), and the archdeacon (the eagle) – must appear to look like a man in order that he can more effectively conceal his malicious designs. The comparison is repeated in stanza 48 ("Humanum menciens humana facie," fol. 119v; "lying to humans with a human face") as part of the dreamer's vision of the specific sins of the clergy.

In the *Apocalypsis goliae*, the deacon sins widely and creatively, but each of his stereotypical transgressions has to do with intentionally misrepresenting his intentions to aid others, as both a spiritual and a social agent of church. Each stanza in the section aligning the deacon's allegorical figuration with his sins further details a way in which his humanity is at stake in his deceit. So, in a series of puns on *canon* (both church law and churchman), *canere* (sing), and *canis* (dog; he is the "dog of the archdeacon"), the deacon barks out the strictures of canon-law, preaches right action for his own benefit, prefers the discord of simony to the harmony of the liturgy (another meaning for *canon*), and so frequently engages in simony. He abuses grammatical learning for similar purposes for his own purse; he raises legal disputes in order to judge them in his own favor, only pretending piety for his own ends and confusing true knowledge with false ("certus in dubiis, in certis dubitat," fol. 119v; stanza

---

[31] All citations of the *Apocalypsis goliae episcopi* are given by stanza number from Wright, *Walter Mapes*. Where necessary, I have silently emended Wright's text to agree with the text present in Bodley 851. All translations are my own.

51); and finally, he promises *quid pro quo* help to others but never returns any favors, since after he has been given aid (usually in the form of money), "he drinks it all away and overindulges in the surplus" ("re*rum* q*ue* bibula... monete crapula," fol. 119v; stanza 52), refusing to return the assistance – as though he suffers from gouty feet ("ibit podagrice ad opem op*eris*," fol. 119v; stanza 53). He is, in short, rather *virus* (sickness) and *virosa* (fetid) than *vir* (man), attacking others while pretending to give them aid (stanza 48). The deacon of the *Apocalypsis goliae* has the likeness of a man in precisely the way Jerome avoids meaning in his discussion of Matthew and Christ, since he pretends to be human but is actually inhuman and so routinely inhumane.

Hunger's refusal to say what he means because he is "not a deacon" signals the ways his character develops according to the same satirical and allegorical structures worked out in the depiction of the deacon provided by the *Apocalypsis goliae*. Many critics have noted how Hunger comes to signify both an internal condition (for each person, the state of being hungry) and an external condition (a general lack of food to go around; famine). This dual-allegory can be understood to reflect specific historical working conditions following the Statute of Laborers of 1349 and further legislation in 1351 and 1376.[32] But the manuscript affiliation between *Piers* and the *Apocalypsis goliae* further points toward a malicious duplicity in the allegorical figure of Hunger that is worked out, loosely, in the narrative of *Piers* passus Z.7 according to terms familiar from the breaking of the third seal in the *Apocalypsis goliae*.

Within passus Z.7, Hunger is transformed from a signifier of insufficiency – both internal and external, signifying both a rumbling stomach and an effect of bad harvest – into a signifier of excess, again both internal and external, signifying individual gluttony (the state of having consumed too much) and a widespread social condition of miserliness (the hoarding of that which should be shared). In fact, the sparse marginal indicators found in Bodley 851 appear to divide the Hunger narrative into two sections that correspond to this transformation: the first section runs from lines Z.7.153–278 and the second from lines Z.7.279–328, where the passus ends.

Since the Z-text lacks many lines familiar from the B- and C-texts of *Piers* and introduces at least one long section of its own, I recount the narrative in broad strokes before more closely analyzing its construction in terms of the

---

[32] Anne Middleton, "Acts of Vagrancy: The C Version 'Autobiography' and the Statute of 1388," in *Written Work: Langland, Labor, and Authorship*, ed. Steven Justice and Kathryn Kerby-Fulton (Philadelphia, PA: University of Pennsylvania Press, 1997), 208–317. See also Emily Steiner, *Reading Piers Plowman* (Cambridge: Cambridge University Press, 2013), 83–92; Aers, "Poverty, Work, and Community," James Simpson, *Piers Plowman: An Introduction to the B-Text* (New York: Longman, 1990), 72ff; and A. C. Spearing, "The Development of a Theme in *Piers Plowman*," *The Review of English Studies* 11.43 (1960): 246ff.

Apocalypsis goliae. In the first section, Hunger acts primarily as an agent of insufficiency. Piers summons Hunger in order to "Awrek me of thys wastores... that this world schenden" (Z.7.155). Hunger follows orders – sometimes gruesomely, "that alle ys gottes swolle / ant bledde into the bodyward a bolle ful of growel" (Z.7.163–4) – until Piers decides only fifty lines later that his ploy has been effective, since Hunger has not only punished the "wastores" physically but enacted in many of them physical transformation by way of labor: "Hungur hem heled myt an ote cake," and so forth (Z7.177ff.; in Bodley 851, "myt" is used regularly for "with"). At this moment, since the ploy appears to have worked splendidly, Piers asks Hunger to head back to his own home ("a preyd Hungur to wende / Hom into ys oune erd ant halde there euer"; Z.7.184–5). Before Hunger can depart, however, Piers raises the tricky, obvious question of what to do about "beggares ant byddares," those who cannot labor effectively for themselves, the ones Piers calls "my blody brethurne" (Z.7.187, 191). This question elicits the response from Hunger discussed above, including the parable of the talents, which insists on what Steiner calls "the fiction that there is a natural relationship between work and food."[33] After Piers, still not satisfied, repeats his question, Hunger declares that such "beggares and byddares" suffer rather from an acute case of laziness and surfeit than from sickness or disability: it is because "They han manged ouer muche – that maketh hem to grone; / Ant eke ydronke to depe – that doth hem harme ofte!" (Z.7.244–5). In a long rant, he insists among other things that what looks like charity is often abetting of gluttony (Z.7.252–5), that health is given rather from heaven than by food no matter what any physician might say (Z.7.268–273), and that Londoners are known abroad for having taken Gluttony as a god (Z.7.274–8). In all of these instances, an apparent lack of sustenance in fact signals overabundance.

In the second section Hunger acts primarily as an agent of excess. Piers, convinced by Hunger's arguments, agrees not only to follow his plan but to give him free reign over society ("Wende now wen thy wille ys, that wyl the bytyde"; Z.7.279–81). Immediately – and it is easy, in every rendition of *Piers*, to miss how quickly this transformation occurs – Hunger declares that he will not leave "Tyl Y haue dyned by thys day ant ydrunke both" (Z.7.283). Adopting a new allegorical position, Hunger no longer operates as a condition that might stir action; rather, as of these lines, Hunger becomes a force of consumption, transforming into that which is fed rather than remaining that which requires feeding. With these lines, too, Piers appears to suffer a change in hierarchical position, since even he "haued... no peny pulletus to bigge, / 'Noythyr ges ne grys, but to grene chesus" (Z.7.284–5).[34] Like those he considered the objects

---

[33] Steiner, *Reading Piers Plowman*, 85.

[34] While *Piers* shows little interest in the aristocracy in this episode or elsewhere, it is not the case here, as Margaret Kim asserts, that "Hunger... is never a threat to

of charity only fifty lines prior, he barely has enough food (and food widely considered disgusting, at that) to survive. Where, in the previous section, Hunger had forced the common folk to acknowledge the necessity of labor for (comestible) reward, in this section Hunger forces the common folk to bring to him any and all food that they possess:

> Alle the pore peple thenne pesecoddus fette;
> Benus ant bake apples they broughten in here lappe,
> Chibolles and chireuilles ant chiries ful ripe,
> Ant profredon thys present to plese myd Hungur.
> Hungur ett this in haste ant axed aftur more.
> Thenne the folk for fere fetten hym monye
> Grene poret ant pesus to peyse hym for euere.
> By that yt neyghled nere heruest that newe corn cam to chepinge;
> Thenne was folk fayn, ant fedde Hungur myt the beste –
> Wyth gode ale ant glotonye gerten hym to slepe. (Z.7.296–305)

Brought any and all kind of food but still not sated, here Hunger assumes the aspect of his own sinful perversion, taking the need for sustenance to gluttonous extremes and consuming any edible thing that comes his way – however delectable or repugnant the food may be, from early spring onions to good ale. Indeed, the gifts to Hunger read initially like an abecedary, as though to suggest by means of linguistic order and gastronomic variety how comprehensive Hunger's consumption has become. With Hunger surfeited unto sleep, Wastor is once again free to wander about (Z.7.306), and even the peasants who once went hungry become picky about the food that they eat (Z.7.307–17). Grumblings from the peasantry cause the king and his counsel to take notice (Z.7.319–21), and the narrating voice warns all readers that famine will return, which means there is no use in becoming accustomed to fine foods, since "Hungur hydurward hasteth hym faste!" (Z.7.324).[35] Where famine once was, famine is predicted: between dearth and dearth only gluttony might thrive.

Like the deacon of the *Apocalypsis goliae* he claims not to be, Hunger only adopts the social semblances necessary to achieve perverse and excessive benefits for himself. As with the pseudo-Mappean figure "disguised in human face," so too with Hunger, who pretends for the first half of the episode to bring aid to Piers and the community of the half-acre – feigning contribution,

---

those better off, such as Piers and his friends" ("Hunger, Need, and the Politics of Poverty in *Piers Plowman*," *YLS* 16 [2002], 156).

[35] Schmidt notes, in the closing lines to Z.7, a possible echo of the Bridlington *Prophecy*, another popular Latin poem of the fourteenth century present in Bodley 851. Resonances between the two texts deserve further critical attention than this chapter can provide.

arguing for specific legal action – and reveals in its second half that his foremost concern was only ever for himself and his own gain. Preaching through Genesis, Wisdom, and Matthew, he abuses his own rhetorical competencies in order that he might eventually gain from them; he engages in legal disputation familiar to fourteenth century readers from the Statute of Laborers, a coercive structure more than hinted at with the king's appearance at the end of the passus; and – most tellingly – he appears to provide aid to Piers while in fact undermining Piers' ambitious social project and receiving aid himself. Hunger argues against charity, brings discomfort upon all of society, and finally transforms a once-grateful workforce into a group of people less content and more hungry than ever – all of this, in spite of their increased food supply and experience as laborers.

Pretending to act as an agent of right action, Hunger is revealed in the end to be a figure of consumption, engaging in precisely the gluttonous behavior for which he criticizes the people of London at the close of the Z-text's first section. Through him, Wastor not only is not chased away but gains in strength, contaminating the upper classes and the peasants alike through Hunger's egregious transformation into Gluttony. Hunger's strange early claim – "for Y am no dekne" – is important and revelatory precisely because, in the allegorical terms established by the *Apocalypsis goliae*, it is not true. He performs in every aspect the part of the deacon in the *Apocalypsis goliae*, perverting human nature where – by way of reference to Christ – it should have been purified.

Moreover, like the deacon of the *Apocalypsis goliae* he claims not to be, Hunger's social deceits have wide-ranging spiritual effects. As Steiner notes, some scribal texts of *Piers* stage a debate between competing authorities on almsgiving in the following passus: citing Cato, the narrating voice warns against giving alms to those who are not truly needy, but citing Gregory the Great (while in fact following St. Jerome), the same voice suggests that one should give freely to any who might ask, since it is impossible to know who is, in fact, truly needy.[36] But the Z-text skips over such quibbling, in the passus that follows the Hunger episode, in order to underscore the eschatological ramifications of having plenty and going without:

> For [a] that begget or byt, but yf he nede haue
> He ys fals wyth the fend ant defraududh the nedy,
> Andt eke gyleth the gyuer ageynes ys wille.
> Thus they leuen nat, ne no lawe kepen:
> Were they haue haly watur or haly bred, habbeth they no ward,
> Ant eke vnshcryuen schrewus thyl Schyr Thorsday at eue.
> (Z.8.71–6)

---

[36] Steiner, *Reading Piers Plowman*, 88–9; see also Mann, "Need Revisited"; Aers, "Poverty, Work, and Community."

Turning the problem of determining who is worthy of aid on its head, the poem reverses perspective from the giver to the receiver. Whereas in passus 7, Piers frets over the relative sinfulness of giving aid to those not in need while withholding aid from those in true need, in passus 8 the suggestion is rather that the beggars themselves know whether or not they truly have need of charitable almsgiving. Those who beg without need – who pretend to be hungry but in fact are in no danger of starvation – not only associate themselves with the devil but prevent those truly in need from receiving aid ("defraudeth the nedy"), so drawing the givers of aid unwillingly into a broader social network of sin and deceit. Like the deacon of the *Apocalypsis goliae*, they pretend spiritual benefit while in fact defrauding the social organism. These deceivers keep no specific law, legal or moral: they care nothing for baptism or communion, and they put off confession until the last possible moment on Holy Thursday.

In this moment, food is no longer understood simply as physical sustenance. Food and drink, in this telling, are and were always holy water and holy bread. The poem's invocation of fraud uncovers an allegorical meaning always present in the Hunger episode as well, wherein any image of food being distributed among a community of persons might also signify the sacrament of the eucharist distributed among a community of believers. As Katherine Trower writes:

> This recapitulation of an earlier action, where Hunger had assailed the folk and forced them to labor for spiritual food (VI.173ff) is intended to re-emphasize the attitudes that Piers and the folk must take toward the production and consumption of physical goods as these are to be used for the attainment of their spiritual goal, the Kingdom of Heaven.[37]

Indeed, in the reading I propose, physical goods form concrete representations of spiritual consumption and attendant participation in heavenly community. It is not the case that "the physical immediacy of this passage does not allow allegorical abstraction" or that "dire material conditions can, and perhaps in this case should, overshadow spiritual 'compulsion.'"[38] Rather, physical immediacy and spiritual significance become, in this moment in *Piers*, indistinguishable from one another. To beg without need is not only to steal away

---

[37] Katherine Trower, "The Figure of Hunger in *Piers Plowman*." *American Benedictine Review* 24 (1973), 253.

[38] Kathleen M. Hewett-Smith, "Allegory on the Half-Acre: The Demands of History," *YLS* 10 (1996), 12. I am not convinced that there is any necessary opposition between the abstract and the concrete, as Hewett-Smith's overall framework assumes. See Nicholas Gaskill, "The Close and the Concrete: Aesthetic Formalism in Context," *New Literary History* 47.4 (2016): 505–24.

sustenance which might rightly benefit another, but to put into jeopardy, for both self and other, participation in heavenly rewards.

So, the Hunger episode not only describes a failed social program but further meditates upon eucharistic economies of grace, and Hunger's perverse transformation into Gluttony signals a social perversion of the act of communion itself. We might recall that all the folk present on Piers's half-acre arrive there seeking Truth (however sincerely or insincerely!), and that the labor in his field also signified "a stay-at-home pilgrimage on the medieval manor."[39] In this suggestive tropological reading, any image of consumption might also be understood as an image of communion, that kind of eating which must always imply individual and communal sustenance simultaneously. Hunger, in his original form, ought to figure as a kind of devotion, and so represent a motivating appetite for the eucharist. He inspires desire of that which should be desired. Hunger's reasoning is therefore acceptable to Piers, with his concern for his "blody brethurne," and more specifically his insistence that "they haue bred and brede" – that is, sustenance and belonging, both material and spiritual (Z.7.191, 199). To cause to eat is to cause to commune, and so to belong to a community oriented toward truth, and so to participate in true (or Truth's) sanctification.

But Hunger's quick transformation into Gluttony refuses the soteriological terms of this image, forcefully insisting that food is food, such than one can delineate its types and qualify its value, consuming all but preferring some. It is, in fact, his insistence upon consumption as a singularly physical appetite that obscures the soteriological significance otherwise available. In a turn reminiscent of the repentance of the seven deadly sins, three passūs prior, Gluttony is what prevents sustenance from signifying properly its divine referent – having no regard for "haly watur or haly bred." The perversion of hunger is not abstinence, as the allegorized sin would have it ("Ar Abstinence myn aunte haue yf me leue"; Z.5.108), but excess. Gluttony is not the likeness of man but the likeness of disease: he is "a fetid thing of blood" (*Apocalypsis goliae*, stanza 48) and "alle ys gottes swolle / Ant bledde into the bodyward a bolle ful of growel" (Z.7.163–4).

Forged by means of a common satirical schema based on a common textual *locus* and resembling in his perversity the deacon of the *Apocalypsis goliae*, Hunger's transformation into gluttony also resonates with the way the *Apocalypsis goliae* describes the sins of abbots and their monks. In the *Apocalypsis goliae*, the sins of the abbot already echo the sins of the deacon; they share gluttonous inclination toward excess in alms-collecting (stanza 100) and deceitful argument (stanza 98), and the abbot himself is called *ingluvies* ("gluttony"; stanza 99). Most importantly, however, he treats the chalice of

---

[39] Steiner, *Reading Piers Plowman*, 83.

communion as a common drinking vessel, mocking the eucharist and the incarnation in one devious gesture:

> Du*m* cena*m* celebrat abbas cu*m* fratribus,
> Torquent*ur* calices a p*r*opinantib*us*,
> Vinu*m* que geminis extollit manib*us*,
> Et sic gra*n*dissonis exclamat vocib*us*,
>
> "O q*u*am glorifica luce*r*na Domini
> Calix inebrians in manu strenui!
> O! he! Bacche! dux sis n*o*stro co*n*uentui,
> Stirpis davitice nos p*r*ole p*r*olui!"
>
> Resume*n*s poculu*m* tractu*m* a cerere,
> Clamat, "Hu*n*c calice*m* in suo g*e*ner*e*
> Que*m* bibiturus sum, potestis bibere?"
> Responde*m*, "possum*us*! ha! sic fac p*r*opere!" (fol. 120r; stanzas 91–93)

> When the abbot celebrates supper with his brothers,
> Chalices are tipped out to the cupbearers,
> And he lifts up the wine with his twin hands,
> And thus exclaims in a booming voice,
>
> 'O how glorious the lamp of the Lord,
> The inebriating chalice in the hand of the bold!
> O! Hey! Bacchus! You should be leader of our gathering,
> We are cleansed by the fruit of David's vine!'
>
> Taking up a draught drawn from grain,
> He shouts, 'Can you all drink this cup,
> of its own kind, which I shall drink?'
> And they respond, 'We are able! Ha! Do it quickly!'

The abbot and his monks here perform the same rejection of eschatological significance as does Hunger in his turn toward gluttony. Where the wine of the chalice is supposed to represent Christ's blood, these "demoniacs" (fol. 120r; stanza 96) instead insist upon the literal matter of the wine as something to be consumed to excess. In doing so, they jest hyperbolically at the expense of the incarnation and the eucharist simultaneously, using the same words to describe wine-guzzling as Christ uses to describe his betrayal at the Last Supper ("Do it quickly!"; John 13:27). The monastic deviants of the *Apocalypsis goliae* insist that wine is wine and cups are cups as Gluttonous Hunger insists that food is food, to be eaten and eaten and eaten. What ought to signify in an economy of salvation is made to signify solely in an economy of production and consumption – and even then, deeply unethically.

But *Piers* and the *Apocalypsis goliae* together might be understood to insist in response that such literal-mindedness can be recovered yet, for spiritual purposes. *Piers* displays its satirical flexibilities most effectively as it traces onto the subject of the poem and its observer (the reader) simultaneously the responsibility for deciding between two visions, the one abject, social, and economical, the other divine, communal, and replete with grace. I have argued elsewhere, in an analysis of the memorial and imaginative psychosomatic constructions of the *Apocalypsis goliae*, that its dreamer's final failure to recount the glories of the third tier of heaven constitutes at once a satirical jab at visionary literature generally and a sincere engagement with the descriptive problem of how to depict a communal, utopic, heavenly state essentially indescribable in earthbound language.[40] There, the dreamer's insistence on consuming the bread of heaven and drinking the waters of Lethe figure both as indicative of the poem's genre – revealing once more that the dreamer is more likely to think with his gut than his intellect – and as indicative of a kind of participation otherwise unavailable to reason. The dreamer takes and eats too much food, but he also takes and eats that which is offered to him by the highest court of heaven. In the *Apocalypsis goliae*, overconsumption is held undecided, balanced precariously between gluttony and devotion.

The Z-text of *Piers* fashions, through similar language and satirical concerns, the same indecisiveness. If, after all, food might always signify communion, would not the only correct response be to consume enthusiastically what is proffered? In this view, Hunger might be better understood as transformed into Devotion than Gluttony: for a comparable figure, we might think of Margery Kempe, whose enthusiasm for communion many found irritating but few would condemn. If this is a vision of pilgrimage, and so of a spiritual journey, then how could one possibly overconsume the material of its sustenance? It is only an insistence, represented definitively in *Piers* by the return of the "kyng ant al the consayl," that Hunger must always stand for a physical appetite that forces the terms of his consumption into those of gluttony rather than piety, of sin rather than sanctity. As with the dreamer of the *Apocalypsis goliae*, so with Hunger and his legions of beggars who might only be pretending to be in need, the reader (whose dilemma is figured by Piers himself) must decide how they should be interpreted. The distance between surfeit and sacrament is measured by religious, social, and political significance – a distance both bridged and made impassable in the act of interpretation.

In positing a close textual relation between the *Apocalypsis goliae* and the Z-text of *Piers*, we gain some insight into what one experience of reading

---

[40] Thomas C. Sawyer, "Bookish Brains and Visionary Learning in the *Apocalypsis goliae episcopi*," *ELH* 89.1 (2022), 1–31.

these two poems together might have been like, around the turn of the fifteenth century. The above reading cannot provide access to any concrete aspect of Scribe X's inner thoughts or motivations. Whether Scribe X associated the *Apocalypsis goliae* with *Piers* on account of the connection traced in this section remains an unanswerable question. It does not follow from the evocative pairing of these two poems that the compiler of Bodley 851 was also responsible for redacting its text of *Piers*. Nor does it follow that the Z-redactor considered the author of the *Apocalypsis goliae* and the author of *Piers* to be the same person (as did Scribe X), much less that he thought both composed by Walter Map. The analysis I have undertaken, however, inquires into the complex and suggestive interrelation of two poems according to their production within a shared manuscript context – which is to say that it has uncovered one compelling aspect of the codicological unconscious of Bodley 851.

By analyzing the Hunger episode in the Z-text as it relates to depictions of deception and consumption in the *Apocalypsis goliae*, modern readers can better approximate a broad literary and cultural field, otherwise obscured in critical practice, as it may have been available to a medieval audience. The field in question is described accurately, and yet falsely, in terms of Walter Map's late-medieval reputation. Of course, technically speaking, manuscript affiliation is not necessary for the analysis undertaken in this section: insofar as the Z-redactor may have borrowed from the *Apocalypsis goliae*, the connection sits in plain sight. The individual manuscript contexts of Bodley 851 nevertheless prompt the modern critic to look for such a connection where no connection has been observed before. By paying attention to how medieval readers read *Piers*, and what they read alongside it, we can come to understand the poem's complexity more fully. Material evidence guides interpretation.

Map's Anti-marital Allegory

Map's reputation as arch-antifeminist serves as an excellent testing ground for a further example of pseudo-Mappean resonance within the Z-text of *Piers* predicated upon generic rather than allegorical likeness. Of the texts Map actually composed, it was his misogamous satire (the *Dissuasio*) that circulated most widely among medieval audiences. Moreover, within the pseudonymous tradition of social, political, and anti-ecclesiastical satire frequently attributed to Map, one of the most widely copied poems that would become attributed to him was the *De coniuge*, discussed at length in Chapter 2 of the present monograph. In Bodley 851, the *De coniuge* is addressed to Walter (e.g., "Guaterus," fol. 80v, pl. 6; final line of column 2), though not explicitly ascribed to Map. The *Dissuasio* and the *De coniuge* establish a potently reductive Mappean field for understanding the Z-text's misogamist commitments.

The *Dissuasio* and the *De coniuge* can be found copied together in at least four manuscripts – three now held in Oxford (including Bodley 851), and one in Munich.[41] The *De coniuge* was commonly attributed to Map in late-medieval English manuscripts (e.g., BodL. MS Additional A.44; BL Cotton MS Vespasian E.12). English manuscripts containing the *De coniuge* frequently share further material with Bodley 851 and with one another – most commonly the *Apocalypsis goliae*, but likewise the *Speculum stultorum*, the Bridlington *Prophecy*, and further goliardic poems. Such manuscripts likely informed the later ascription of the *De coniuge* and the *Apocalypsis goliae*, among twenty-eight poems now mostly considered anonymous, to Map by John Bale.[42] In the *Dissuasio* and the *De coniuge*, we observe two influential representatives of two interlocking literary traditions present throughout *Piers*: antifeminist literature frequently associated with the literate clergy and goliardic literature frequently associated with school and university contexts.

The association between the Z-text and Map's misogamous fame raises the question of how *Piers* might be understood to participate within the tradition of anti-marital writings penned in the late-medieval period. The Z-text does not borrow directly from the *Dissuasio* or the *De coniuge* in its specific language, as we saw it borrow from the *Apocalypsis goliae*. Nor should we expect it to, given that Scribe X compiled but did not personally redact the Z-text. As in the above analysis of the *Apocalypsis goliae* and the Z-text together, however, the co-occurrence of two famous misogamous texts alongside *Piers* within Bodley 851 might prompt a focused consideration of how the Z-text could be received as a misogamous poem, in conversation with a misogamist tradition associated with Walter Map. What is important to the present inquiry within the specific manuscript context of Bodley 851 is rather the significance of compilation than of composition.

To my knowledge, there is no extended discussion of *Piers* in terms of late-medieval misogamy. Of course, scholarship regularly acknowledges misogynous elements within the *Piers* tradition. As several classic studies show, venality satire and estates satire inform the first vision, and both modes of social critique depend upon gendered stereotypes.[43] Moreover, the *Piers*-

---

[41] BodL. MSS Add. A.44, Bodley 851, and Digby 166; Munich, Bayerische Staatsbibliothek, Clm 631.

[42] Bale, *Scriptorum illustrium*, 253–4; see Rigg, "Golias and Other Pseudonyms."

[43] John A. Yunck, *The Lineage of Lady Meed: The Development of Mediaeval Venality Satire* (Notre Dame, IN: University of Notre Dame Press, 1963); and Roberta D. Cornelius, "*Piers Plowman* and the *Roman de Fauvel*," *PMLA* 47.2 (1932): 363–7. See also Andrew Galloway, "Madame Meed: Fauvel, Isabella, and the French Circumstances of *Piers Plowman*," *YLS* 30 (2016): 227–52; and Jamie K. Taylor, "Lies, Puns, Tallies: Marital and Material Deceit in Langland and Chaucer," *Speculum* 93.1 (2018): 111–21.

author's debt to the schools is well documented: it is not surprising to discover traces of that debt, including traces of schoolboy misogyny, in any version of *Piers*.[44] And the first vision's marriage of Meed remains a touchstone for feminist criticism in Middle English, broadly, and for consideration of the poem's allegorical uses of marriage, specifically. Nevertheless, scholars most commonly treat the institution of marriage in *Piers* in historical terms (how does marriage in the poem resemble actual marriages in late-medieval England?) or in theological terms (how does marriage in the poem act as an analogy for a relationship between humans and god?).[45] If, as I argued in Chapter 2, misogamist tendencies can lead to strange and unexpected literary formations, we might ask in topical terms: how do Mappean tirades against marriage inform a reading of the text of *Piers* in the manuscript they share?

The multiple aborted marriages of Lady Meed in the first vision of *Piers* form a pointed example of literary meditation on the harms of matrimony and the fickleness of women, set in contrast to the purity of Holy Church. Through its allegorical depiction of the problems inherent to Meed's marriage, passus Z.2 outlines a bifurcated perspective on the sacrament of marriage comparable to the bifurcated perspective on the Eucharist on display in the Hunger episode in the second vision. As above in regard to consumption, so too in regard to matrimony, *Piers* forces onto the subject of the poem and its observer (the reader) simultaneously the responsibility for deciding between two opposing interpretations.

The first vision of *Piers* provides a richly detailed social infrastructure with multiple shifting vectors of allegorical implication.[46] Applying developments in feminist theory to criticism on *Piers*, recent interpretations of Meed's

---

[44] See Galloway, "Piers Plowman and the Schools"; Alford, "Langland's Learning"; Hanna III, "School and Scorn"; and Christopher Cannon, *From Literacy to Literature: England, 1300–1400* (Oxford: Oxford University Press, 2016).

[45] For historical inquiry, see David Strong, "Mede's Right to Marry: A Consideration of Medieval Natural Law," *Medieval Perspectives* 21 (2005): 156–76; Conor McCarthy, "Marriage and Mede in Passus 2 to 4 of *Piers Plowman*," *Nottingham Medieval Studies* 44 (2000): 154–66; Kimberly Keller, "For Better and Worse: Women and Marriage in *Piers Plowman*," in *Medieval Family Roles: A Book of Essays*, ed. Cathy Jorgensen Itnyre (New York: Garland, 1996), 67–83; Elizabeth Fowler, "Civil Death and the Maiden: Agency and the Conditions of Contract in *Piers Plowman*," *Speculum* 70.4 (1995): 760–92; and M. Teresa Tavormina, "Kindly Similitude: Langland's Matrimonial Trinity," *Modern Philology* 80.2 (1982): 117–28. For theological inquiry, see Mary Clemente Davlin, "Genealogical Terms in *Piers Plowman*," *YLS* 26 (2012): 111–32; and Isabel Davis, "'The Trinite Is Our Everlasting Lover': Marriage and Trinitarian Love in the Later Middle Ages," *Speculum* 86.4 (2011): 914–63.

[46] See M. Teresa Tavormina, *Kindly Similitude: Marriage and Family in Piers Plowman* (Cambridge: D. S. Brewer, 1995); Helen Cooper, "Gender and Personification in *Piers Plowman*," *YLS* 5 (1991): 31–48.

travails at court have tended to diverge from M. Teresa Tavormina's suggestion that *Piers* is "only tangentially" indebted to "the misogynistic... tradition."[47] As scholars have long noted, each of Holy Church and Meed – but Meed especially – can be understood allegorically and historically as representing medieval forms of "traffic in women."[48] Contemporary interpretations of *Piers* tend to assume the pervasiveness of misogyny as a structure of oppression evident in the first vision's depiction of Meed, focusing especially on dismissive treatment of her by Conscience and Reason in the king's court. As Holly Crocker writes, Meed's "eroticized dealing utilizes misogynist stereotypes that associate women's persuasiveness with illicit sexuality."[49] Refreshingly, in her critique of the ideological assumptions made about gendered structures in *Piers*, Crocker further sets aside the poem's allegorical significance in favor of uncovering "another view of the human, one that begins from the standpoint of women's vulnerability."[50] Still, for the majority of readings, from Cooper to Crocker, what is important is not *what* Meed signifies allegorically – as material, fiscal, hierarchical, or spiritual reward with some specific psychosomatic bearing on the construction of the poem's discursive structure – but *how* Meed signifies as a gendered body within an imagined human society. Such readings trace the poem's representation of medieval misogyny without necessarily attending to its concurrent representation of misogamy: Meed gains critical significance as woman, but not as wife.

Taken alongside feminist work on *Piers* in general, inquiry into the misogamy of the Z-text might therefore serve to underscore the surface-level fact that the first part of the first vision is, most basically, a misogamous poem. It takes as its primary subject matter the disadvantages of marriage to any woman (like Meed) for any man (like Will?) who might want to devote himself to conscience, reason, and the church (or: Conscience, Reason, and Holy Church). The influence of competing satirical forms should not prevent us from recognizing that the Meed episode is fundamentally dependent upon

---

[47] Tavormina, *Kindly Similitude*, x.

[48] See Colette Murphy, "Lady Holy Church and Meed the Maid: Re-Envisioning Female Personifications in *Piers Plowman*," in *Feminist Readings in Middle English Literature: The Wife of Bath and All Her Sect*, eds. Ruth Evans and Lesley Johnson (New York: Routledge, 1994), 140–64; Stephanie Trigg, "The Traffic in Medieval Women: Alice Perrers, Feminist Criticism and *Piers Plowman*," *YLS* 12 (1998): 5–29; Fowler, "Civil Death and the Maiden"; and Clare A. Lees, "Gender and Exchange in Piers Plowman," in *Class and Gender in Early English Literature: Intersections*, eds. Britton J. Harwood and Gillian R. Overing (Bloomington, IN: Indiana University Press, 1994), 112–30.

[49] Holly A. Crocker, "Feminism without Gender: *Piers Plowman*, 'Mede the Mayde,' and Late Medieval Literary Studies," *Exemplaria* 31.2 (2019): 97.

[50] Crocker, "Feminism without Gender," 99.

misogamous rhetorics.[51] If, as Masha Raskolnikov writes, "Meed actually *is* Woman as an object of exchange, consolidating or threatening the bonds between men," then it is also true that the first vision shares its most basic rhetorical function (to persuade against marriage) with the *De coniuge* and the *Dissuasio*.[52] Crocker contends, in a positive formulation, that, "Almost to a man, everyone who sees her wants her. Almost without exception, Mede gratifies each petition for reward."[53] Her valorizing phrasing, however, comes unsettlingly near to the primary complaint of the *De coniuge* (following the antifeminist tradition led by Jerome and Map) about wives in general: that they are never satisfied, endlessly desiring and endlessly overwhelming structures of social containment, however carefully selected and constructed. In the *De coniuge*, the *Dissuasio*, and *Piers* together, "it is her corruption [of Meed, of the imagined wife], not theirs [men, husbands], which the poem supposedly discloses."[54] Accordingly, *Piers* suggests that the list of Meed's suitors might be extended almost endlessly, from False to Conscience, lawyers to friars, the peaceful and the warlike, the sinful and the sinned-against.

In fact, the manicule preserved in the Z-text marks Theology's furious misogamous speech against the proposed marriage between Meed and False (Z.2.86; fol. 127v). Often assumed to respond to the wrongheaded pursuit of one particular marriage, Theology's declamation in Bodley 851 denounces any earthly marriage whatsoever:

> Thenne tened hym Theologye wen he thys tale yherde,
> Ant seyde to Cyuy[le], 'Now sorwe on thy bokes,
> Such weddingus to wyrche to wrathen the Trewthe!
> Ant ar thys wedding be wrought, wo the betyde!
> For Mede ys moylere, of Mendes engendret;
> God grawnteth hymsylf to gyue Mede to trewthe,
> Ant thow hast gye here to a gloten – now God gyue the sorwe!
> The tyxtus telleth nat so, Trewthe wot the sothe:
> *Dignus est operarius* hys huyre to haue –
> Ant thow hast faste here wyth False, we! fy on the lawe!
> For al by lesyngus tow lyuest ant lechoures wercus;

---

[51] *Pace* Tavormina, *Kindly Similitude*, 43: "I do not read the Meed episode as being *primarily* about the institution of marriage or about specific literal marriages."

[52] Masha Raskolnikov, *Body against Soul: Gender and Sowlehele in Middle English Allegory* (Columbus, OH: Ohio State University Press, 2009), 174.

[53] Crocker, "Feminism without Gender," 96.

[54] Crocker, 96. I am not as convinced as Crocker that the *Piers*-author intended to reveal "how the structure of medieval gender really works, by blaming women for problems that men perpetuate" (97). Such a revelation seems to me, rather, built into misogamous discourse more generally, however practiced medieval readerships may have been at ignoring the implications of their prejudice (see Chapter 2).

> Thow schalt abygge thys bargayn, by my fadur sowle!
> Sire Symonye ant thysylue schendeth Holy Chirche,
> Wyth notaryes nysotes nuyest the peple,
> And sowsest yow in synne wyth Seynte Marye rentus.'
> (Z.2.86–100)

What are "such weddingus," apart from the marriage match at hand? Observing a scribal alteration in Lincoln's Inn MS Hale 150, wherein a line that describes Meed in most other manuscripts is transposed with no explanation into a description of Holy Church several passūs earlier, Steiner argues that "built into personification is a basic interchangeability" and indeed that "female personification, always sexualized, underlines the interchangeability and relationality of personification allegory."[55] She points to the opposition presumed, in Theology's tirade, between Holy Church and Meed – one granting salvation, the other earthly reward – as insufficient to explain their conflation in Hale 150, which misunderstands their characterizations while revealing their fundamental sameness as objects of exchange. The Z-text in Bodley 851, however, replicates a similar confusion about objects of marriage without replicating the parallel confusion about their significance as personifications. Theology makes an interpretive claim about Meed, arguing that she ought to participate in a system of exchange founded and facilitated by Truth (or truth). Her proposed marriage to False participates in the corruption of her significance and so causes harm where, properly understood, harm should have been remediated ("of Mendes engendret"). Civil Law and Simony "sowsest... in synne" what "God grawnteth hymsylf" and so "schendeth Holy Chirche." The language here mirrors common clerical discourse concerning how marriage, with its thirty-fold rewards, must necessarily corrupt the purer state of virginity, with its hundred-fold rewards.[56] In Theology's understanding, the stakes of Meed's significance are made inextricable from the state of Holy Church, since a mis-valuation of one must cause harm to ("schendeth") the other.

The problem in Bodley 851 is not that Holy Church and Meed are perfectly interchangeable, as allegories or as gendered characters, but that there exists some proportional bond between them that can only be made evident in their social and allegorical responses to marriage. Indeed, Theology's tirade links these female personifications in terms of their significance as marriageable subjects. Whatever action misappropriates Meed must also harm Holy Church, not because Meed marries whomever Holy Church ought properly to marry, but because Meed's improper marriage has the power to shift fundamentally

---

[55] Steiner, *Reading Piers Plowman*, 43.

[56] Dyan Elliott, *The Bride of Christ Goes to Hell: Metaphor and Embodiment in the Lives of Pious Women, 200–1500* (Philadelphia, PA: University of Pennsylvania Press, 2012), 79.

the operations of Truth (or truth) and amends (or Mendes) in the world. This operation otherwise would be made allegorically evident by Holy Church. The two female personifications work in tandem, not in competition or in parallel. As the vision continues, it becomes clear that the terms of improper marriage to Meed are not limited only to a proposed marriage with False but extend further to Conscience, Peace, and all the mass of men seeking self-gain who come to surround Meed, misunderstanding her significance. In Theology's reading, any understanding of Meed wherein she signifies falsely implies "such weddingus" to "a gloton."

So understood as a universal statement predicated upon a single proposed allegorical event, Theology's argument against Meed's marriage to False underscores the vision's polemic against marriage itself as a social institution. For Theology, marriage not only reveals but also generates falsity and instability. Theology makes an absolute and positive statement about Meed's nature. Properly understood, "Mede ys moylere," which is to say legitimate, effective, and uncorrupted. She might signify a quality of mercy that is not strained. Once proposed in marriage, however, Mede becomes a source of corruption and uncertainty, bringing "sorwe" rather than the product of "Mendes."[57] Marriage itself catalyzes Theology's distinction: as for Jerome, "the love of woman in general" might be "listed among the greatest of evils," so "Mede the mayde" becomes a source of corruption precisely because she is understood so generally (and falsely) to be a possible partner in marriage (Z.2.20).[58] It is not Meed herself but the proposition that Meed should be wed that "perverts the ideal of love for all men into an indiscriminate depravity."[59] In fact, the possibility of marriage for Meed to anyone but Truth (on which counterfactual, more below) may be understood to make her partner False – that is, to transform whomever her partner might be into an allegory for falsity.

What distinguishes False from Conscience is most fundamentally his acceptance of marriage to Meed, and it is the acceptance itself that makes their marriage improper. No complex allegorical structure is necessary for understanding the misogamist force of the vision at this critical juncture. Theology suggests as much himself, forecasting the further events of the *visio* and assuring Civil Law and Simony that "yf he [Conscience] fynd yow in defawte and wyt the Fals holde, / Hyt schall besytte youre sowle ful sowre at the laste" (Z.2.113–14). Although Meed and Holy Church share a substantial quantity of structural features that might facilitate their conflation within the poem (as in

---

[57] Readers accustomed to B- or C-texts of *Piers* might note that, in the Z-text, Holy Church makes no claim to marital competition between herself and Meed (B.2.32–5, C.2.34–7).

[58] *Adversus Jovinian*, 1.28, quoted in translation from Hanna and Lawler, eds., *Jankyn's Book*, 1:188.

[59] Tavormina, *Kindly Similitude*, 36.

Steiner's argument from Hale 150), the primary distinguishing feature between the two female figures in Bodley 851 is made most concretely in terms of their stance toward matrimony. When Meed is rightly understood, like Holy Church, to be held apart from earthly marriage, she remains inviolable, virginal, and of right lineage; but when considered marriageable otherwise, she becomes volatile and promiscuous, such that "Wrong ys here syre" (Z.2.23). Meed must be understood as an allegory for wickedness only insofar as she might become a wife.

What remains constant among Meed's suitors is how unsuitable all must be, in the end, not on account of any specific quality in any proposed husband but because Meed by her nature cannot be constrained to one purpose – which is to say, in allegorical terms, one husband. She can no more belong to False than she can to Conscience, not on account of some fundamental opposition between wrong and right action, but on account of their fundamental sameness as potential marriage-matches with Meed. False may be wicked and Conscience may be necessary for right rule, but each emerges as equally insufficient to the demands that Meed would place upon him in matrimony. Framed in terms of the poem's implied subjectivities, it is because Meed would come to occupy the same essential position in relation to any suitor, as an object of marriage-bonds, that the possibility of marriage itself is understood to corrupt her. What corrupts Meed, as significant of an overabundant and excessive economy of giving, is neither overabundance nor excess but the institution of marriage itself. While it is certainly correct to observe misogyny at work in the first vision of *Piers*, it is also necessary to understand the misogamous assumptions that inform that misogyny. In its position against marriage, the Z-text makes an ideological move familiar from Mappean contexts: to be wed is to be corrupted, regardless of whom one weds – and especially if one is a woman.

To be wed, for Meed as a woman and for Meed as an allegory for all women, is in this sense to undertake a categorical moral motion from purity into transgression. If, as Steiner suggests, there is a "basic interchangeability" built into female personification allegory, then one essential aspect of that interchangeability within the context of misogamous satire depends fundamentally upon the relation of each woman, depicted allegorically, to the institution of marriage. As in the *De coniuge* alongside the *Ave virgo* (see Chapter 2), so also in *Piers*, the only marital relationship available to a woman (real, imagined – or allegorical) who would remain pure is marriage to God. If Meed, as Theology claims, had followed God's plan "to gyue Mede to trewthe" (Z.2.91), she might have signified in parallel to Holy Church herself, as an agent of the overabundance of grace rather than an agent of excessive transgression. Instead, Meed is transformed from a potential allegory for the overabundance of heavenly grace (in parallel with Holy Church) into a concrete allegory for the defiling effects of earthly marriage (as in her frequent association, in criticism, with the Whore of Babylon).

Indeed, the opening to passus 2 plays on precisely this slippage between heavenly queen and fallen corruptress. When the dreamer asks "for Marie loue of heune" that Holy Church might teach him "the false for to knowe" (Z.2.5–4), as Andrew Galloway observes, this is the only time in *Piers* that the dreamer directly determines the action of the poem.[60] The dreamer's vision treads the boundary between the heavenly and the infernal. The initial description of Meed as "a wuiman worthily yclothed /... the purest on erthe, / Ycrowned in a crowne, the Kyng hatht no better..." (Z.2.12–14) might suggest, at least to begin with, rather an instantiation of the dreamer's invocation of Mary than of his desire to know the false. Even the "red scarlet" and "rybandes of golde" robing the lady do less to narrow her significance than Holy Church's subsequent identification – which is to say, interpretation – of her appearance: "That ys Mede the mayde... hath nuyed me ful ofte" (Z.2.18–20).

As with the hairsbreadth interpretive difference between Hunger and Gluttony discussed above, Meed is fundamentally transformed by the participatory act of those who misinterpret her significance. What causes harm to ("schendeth") Holy Church is not any action taken by Meed herself but the fact that Civil Law and Simony use the tribute they owe to "Saint Mary" for personal gain ("sowsest yow in synne with Seynte Marye rentus"; Z.2.100–3). That Holy Church herself names not "Mendes" but "Wrong" as Meed's father further complicates any straightforward interchangeability between them (Z.2.23), suggesting in Theology's terms that Holy Church has misjudged Meed's significance and so done herself harm. Allegorically speaking, when the church understands spiritual grace in earthly terms, and when riches are associated inviolably with earthly rather than heavenly amends, both the quality of grace and the condition of the institution suffer. Holy Church might recall the bifurcation of value inherent within her own dictum: "Wan alle tresores ar tried, trewthe ys the beste" (Z.1.30).

As with the distinction between the Virgin Mary in the *Ave virgo* and the adulterous wife of the *De coniuge*, overabundance itself is not a cause of transgression. Rather, the possibility for transgression depends upon an initial act of interpretation, when interchangeability – a commensurate functionality between what is owed to Mary and what can be used for social or political or personal gain – is assumed. If, as James Simpson has influentially argued, "marriage serves Langland's personification allegory by offering a model through which the senses of words could be semantically linked (or not) with the senses of other words," then it is also the case that all improper links between words might be framed within the medieval misogamist tradition as a symptom of a problem inherent within wedlock itself.[61] The moment when divine grace and earthly remuneration are confused is, fundamentally,

---

[60] Galloway, *Penn Commentary*, vol. 1, 225.
[61] Simpson, *Introduction*, 45.

an interpretive moment, one that corrupts the church even as Holy Church misunderstands the source and service of her riches.

The significance of this interpretive moment within Bodley 851 is best exemplified by a consideration of marriage, understood both literally and as carrying tremendous spiritual and social consequences. "The greatest scarcity," pseudo-Map assures the subject of the *De coniuge*, "is of good wives! Among thousands, there will be scarcely a single one."[62] "The best woman," Map's Valerius assures Rufinus in his *Dissuasio*, "who is rarer than the phoenix, cannot be loved without the bitterness of fear and worry and one mishap after another" – and so, of course, she should not be wed.[63] "For Mede ys moylere, of Mendes engendret," Theology exclaims, "Ant Mede ys a mayde, murgust on erthe" – therefore "Yut beth ywar of the wedding!" (Z.2.90, 104, 110). The Z-text confronts the misogamist assumptions embedded within so much medieval literature, enacting in bald allegory the consequences of confusing divine union and human wedlock. Devotion to Holy Church and Mary, in this construct, rather informs than opposes devotion to that which is fickle, false, and misunderstood.

Of course, there are many more misogamous texts than the *De coniuge* and the *Dissuasio* – though few so popular, from the late Middle Ages, as these two. Nor is either text strictly necessary for the analysis undertaken above: as with the borrowing from the *Apocalypsis goliae* in the Hunger episode, so also borrowings from the misogamous tradition in *Piers* sit in plain sight. While *Piers* may not borrow directly from either the *Dissuasio* or the *De coniuge*, their co-presence in Bodley 851 is nevertheless instructive for understanding the poem's misogamous debts. The individual manuscript contexts of Bodley 851, if attended to, reveal affiliations that otherwise would not be manifest – and have not been made manifest previously in critical work on the poem.

---

[62] "Bonarum coniugium est summa raritas / In millenario vix erit vnitas" (fol 81rb; A. G. Rigg, *Gawain on Marriage* [Toronto: Pontifical Institute of Mediaeval Studies, 1986], 88 [stanza J7]).

[63] Hanna and Lawler, eds., *Jankyn's Book*, 1:126. Map proceeds to cite the *Distichs of Cato*, "Be careful to whom you give" (*video cui des*), in order to modify the aphorism: "be careful to whom you give yourself" (*video cui te des*). The same citation has occasioned significant commentary as it is placed in the discussion of charity toward beggars in *Piers Plowman*, as in the Hunger scene above; see John A. Alford, *Piers Plowman: A Guide to the Quotations* (Binghamton, NY: Center for Medieval & Renaissance Texts & Studies, 1992), 54. It is not present in the Z-text, however.

Walter Map's *Piers Plowman*

The resonances this chapter has identified between *Piers Plowman* and its companion texts are by no means sounded uniformly. Whereas the *Apocalypsis goliae* can be understood as a source for the Hunger episode in the Z-text, and so to provide some interpretive precedent for the allegorical transformations within passus 7, the anti-marital tradition represented by the *De coniuge* and the *Dissuasio* informs the first vision at a larger scale. Further shared tendencies between the pseudo-Mappean and the pseudo-Langlandian within Bodley 851 might be observed in their interest in political satire, self-mockery, prophecy, and penitence by way of the Bridlington *Prophecy* or the *Speculum stultorum*. Meed is known, as Michael of Cornwall was known, at St Mary le Bow. The difficulty inherent in seeing and desiring rightly, as a matter of interpretation, forms the pith of Scribe X's other contribution to Part II of Bodley 851, *The debate between heart and eye*. Within the production of a single book, possibilities abound.

It is crucial to observe, therefore, that the hermeneutic possibilities outlined in this chapter are not so unbounded as to upset, rather than inform, further understanding of *Piers* or Bodley 851. Some topics are excluded, on their face, by the material form of the book itself. It would difficult, for example, to construct a compelling argument around *Piers*, Bodley 851, and saints' lives or medical practice, since the manuscript contains little hagiographic or medical material. Neither are the interpretive possibilities outlined in this chapter comprehensive. Much remains to be said, for example, about dimensions of political and ecclesiastical satire central to Bodley 851. Rather, the interpretations offered above are bound by the textual contents of the texts materially affiliated with *Piers* within a singular manuscript context. They are intended to lay the groundwork for further conversation between *Piers* and its many textual companions, particularly its Anglo-Latin companions, in Bodley 851 and in manuscripts further afield.

The state of manuscript scholarship in general, and specifically for *Piers*, precludes a comprehensive discussion of further manuscripts of this poem suitable for the method I have proposed. The majority of *Piers* manuscripts demonstrate, in A. R. Bennett's felicitous phrasing, "high *Piers*-centricity," such that "a solid two-thirds of the corpus consists of manuscripts that are primarily conveyors of the *Piers* text."[64] Moreover, collections as immense as the Vernon manuscript (BodL. MS Eng. Poet.a.1) and Cambridge, University Library MS Dd.1.17 may in fact be too capacious for analysis of the kind I have proposed throughout this study, since the method requires attention not

---

[64] Angela R. Bennett Segler, "Mediation, Meditation, and the Manuscripts of 'Piers Plowman'" (Unpublished dissertation, NYU, 2015), 104; for "*Piers*-centricity," see 100–8.

only to the concurrence of texts in a single manuscript but to the material and agential processes by which those texts were produced. More promising are manuscripts such as Los Angeles, Huntington Library MS Hm 114 (the occasion of Noelle Phillips's excellent study in "Compilational Reading"), Oxford, University College MS 45, BodL. MS Laud misc. 656, or BL Harley MS 3954.[65] To my knowledge, however, no existing scholarly resource details the specific textual companions co-present with *Piers* in each of the collections in which it appears.[66] Even in a study as generous as Bennett's, the specificity of individual texts is easily lost: as with BodL. MS Digby 102, where twenty distinct items in Middle English verse are grouped as a collection of short religious verse (as the author notes) or the present manuscript, Bodley 851, which Bennett lists as having six total texts along with *Piers* (grouping the better part of Part II, including the *Apocalypsis goliae* and the *De coniuge*, under the label of "Latin Satire").[67] Studies in the manuscripts of *Piers* do not regularly provide analytic descriptions of those manuscripts detailed enough to accommodate the method I have adopted here. Much less do editors, whose concern is the production of a text, routinely detail the process of production by which such texts and *Piers* may have come to be collected. For further application of the method I have laid out over the course of this book, which treats the interpretation of texts as inseparable from the production of manuscripts, a full review of manuscript data within the *Piers* tradition may yet be necessary.

As rich and intriguing as *Piers* is within its own textual tradition, the poem gains depth and complexity when read in conversation with its companion texts. David Lawton influentially argued in the inaugural volume of *The Yearbook of Langland Studies* that *Piers* is more concerned with the deployment of shifting and mutable discourses than the preservation of stable genres, persons, or thematic unities. Accordingly, discourse itself constitutes the "myriad contexts and dialogic energy of the poem," such that "it is not the treatment of a persona we see primarily here, but the trying on of the different subjectivities that the different discourses confer – and, finally, the refusal of all."[68] Similarly, in his enduring *Introduction* to *Piers*, James Simpson highlights how "Langland is exploiting or questioning" the authority of a variety of genres and discourses, "and thereby exploiting or questioning the authority of the institution from

---

[65] See Phillips, "Compilational Reading"; along with Simon Horobin, "Harley 3954 and the Audience of Piers *Plowman*," in *Medieval Texts in Context*, ed. Graham D. Caie and Denis Renevey (Abingdon: Routledge, 2008), 68–84.

[66] Apart from Bennett's dissertation, the most relevant resource remains C. David Benson and Lynne S. Blanchfield, eds., *The Manuscripts of Piers Plowman: The B-Version* (Cambridge: D. S. Brewer, 1997).

[67] Bennett, "Mediation, Meditation," 142n3 and 143n6.

[68] David Lawton, "The Subject of *Piers Plowman*," *YLS* 1 (1987), 14.

which" such genres derive.[69] In Lawton's exploratory readings, in Simpson's overview, and in many critical readings to follow, *Piers* becomes an occasion for the broad analysis of subject formation. The poem's generic commitments (not identical with its shifting discursive performances) are at once obvious, complex, and inconsistent precisely because it is interested in exposing the limitations of the discursive fields it adopts, expands, and discards. *Piers* can therefore act as a unifying force without adopting aesthetic unity, taking under its imaginative wing a broad collection of expressions which might otherwise be considered disparate poetic material.

Piers might therefore be uniquely capable of capturing the capaciousness and self-inconsistency evident within Walter Map's false authorial reputation in late-medieval England. Walter Map alone would come to signify the compilation of the goliardic and the authoritative, the trifling and the monumental, in debate, vision, epistle, confession, and prophecy alike (among other literary forms), as composed in prose, rhythm, and meter over the course of several centuries for which Map himself was not factually alive. There would be little reason for a modern reader to consider the *Apocalypsis goliae* and the *De coniuge* together, for example, apart from their joint preservation in so many manuscripts under the auspices of Map's illusory authority, much less the *Apocalypsis goliae* and the *Dissuasio*, or the Bridlington *Prophecy*, or the fantastic tales of the *De nugis*. The Z-text of *Piers* nevertheless captures much of what is incoherent and apparently extraneous about late-medieval projections of Walter Map in much the same way that Map's own reputation captures much of what is incoherent and extraneous about Anglo-Latin literary production more generally. *Piers* like Map – or Map, as we understand *Piers* – weaves together a compilation of generic markers and literary discourses not unified but nevertheless characteristic of its own development, recognizable only as itself by way of that which it fully incorporates, represents, and discards.

In this context, and by way of a closing example, we might consider how the opening lines of the Z-text might signal a commitment to the Mappean for a late-medieval reader like Scribe X:

> In a somer sesoun, wen softe was the sonne,
> Y schope me into schrodus as Y a schep were,
> In abite as an hermite vnholy of wercus,
> Wente wyde in this world wondres to here,
> Ant sey many sellys, Y can nat sey alle.
> Ac in a May morwen vnder Mauerne Hylles
> Me befel a ferly, of fayre me thoughte. (Z.Prol.1–7)

---

[69] Simpson, *Introduction*, 14.

The unique emphasis on the fantastic, wonderful, and difficult to believe that is found in Scribe X's Z-text mimics a thematic focus prominent throughout Walter Map's *De nugis* (see my discussion in Chapter 3). Out of the fifty-plus manuscripts containing some version of the *Piers* Prologue, only Bodley 851 contains the full sequential repetition of "wondres," "sellys," "ferly," and "fayre" in the opening lines. Of course, most of these "unnatural" words can be found scattered in some combination or another throughout other texts of the poem. All copies of the *Piers* Prologue express a desire to hear wonders ("wondres"), the A and B traditions generally include the total reference to the astonishing and the otherly ("ferly" and "fayre"), and the C tradition generally incorporates the reference to the reality-bending ("sellies"). Nor, in any version, does *Piers* restrain its interest in marvels and wonders to the first ten lines of the poem. The dreamer's bewilderment (or bewonderment) forms a motif for the first two visions in Z as in ABC (e.g., "ferly" at A.Prol.62/B.Prol.65/C.Prol.63, "wonder" at A.1.69/B.1.71/C.1.68, and "wonderly" at AB.2.8/C.2.9) and a pursuit of the spectacular underpins much of his quest for Dowel, Dobet, and Dobest.[70] Unique to the Z-text, however, is the narrator's claim that he cannot repeat all of what he has seen ("Y can nat sey alle"; in its parallel line, the C-text expresses a much blander interest in "selkouthe thynges" [C.Prol.5]); and only the Z-text contains the quintessentially Mappean complaint, at this crucial introductory moment, that the narrator is incapable of competently relating his own experience – a complaint that grounds the *Apocalypsis goliae*, the *Dissuasio*, the *De coniuge*, and most of the fantastic tales (*fantasias*) scattered throughout the *De nugis*.[71] Only the Z-text claims each and every one of wonders, the sublime, the fairy, and the surreal as topics of exposition, revelation, and meditation.

As such, the Z-text might be productively understood to announce itself as a *fantasia* in the sense described and enacted in Distinction 2 of Map's *De nugis* (Chapter 3). "It is necessary to hear the works and permissions of the Lord with all patience," Map assures his readers, "because just as he is incomprehensible, so too do his works transcend our own questions and escape our arguments."[72] After all, as Holy Church proclaims, "he ys fader of fayth and formed yow alle / Both wyth fel ant wyth flesch, ant

---

[70] For an extended account of how human agency and the supernatural are represented in *Piers Plowman*, see Rosanne Gasse, "Witchcraft and Sorcery in *Piers Plowman*," *The Chaucer Review* 55.1 (2020): 88–112.

[71] For another perspective on the Z-redactor's tendency towards self-assertion, see Wood, "Monologic Langland."

[72] "Audienda sunt opera et permissiones domini cum omni paciencia, et ipse laudandus in singulis, quia sicut ipse incomprehensibilis est, sic opera sua nostras transcendunt inquisiciones et disputaciones euadunt" (fol. 27vb; James et al., *De nugis* 2.13).

yaf how fiue wyttes" (Z.Prol.105–6). Without insisting on any direct literary influence running between the *De nugis* and *Piers* – that is, without centering the question of their relation on any concern with factual authorship – we can productively interpret the Z-prologue through Scribe X's addition of the Z-text to a pre-existing corpus of Mappean writings whose primary features are narrative ambiguity, flexible wit, and unbridled impulse to follow every pun to the banter end. Though the lens of Scribe X, we might read into *Piers* Z.Prol.1–10 echoes of the *De nugis*. The texts Scribe X collected together under the (false) auspices of Mappean authorship need not be taken as sources or analogues of *Piers* in order to be understood as informing the meaning of *Piers*, either locally, for any attentive readers of MS Bodley 851 (like Scribe X) or broadly, for inquisitive readers of the poem's tradition.

Of course, one need not read Walter Map in order to express readerly uncertainty (or, for that matter, certainty) in response to the opening frame of *Piers*. Many critical analyses of the first lines, passūs, and visions of *Piers* acknowledge their interpretive ambiguities without any reference whatsoever to Map, Mappeana, or Bodley 851. There is no reason to assume that the *Piers*-author had read the *De nugis*, although the fortunes of literary history would suggest he had heard of Walter Map under pseudonymous circumstances. For Scribe X, however, who compiled and decorated the opening lines of the Z-text of *Piers* as a companion to the collection of texts already present within the quires that would become Bodley 851, the co-presence of legitimate Mappean writings and pseudonymous Mappeana takes on further interpretive significance. These opening lines display the same interpretive vagaries as do a great number of Map's stories, as do the closing lines of the *Apocalypsis goliae*, as do the bifurcated figures of Meed and Holy Church, and as does the conclusion to the Hunger episode in Z.7. They are not Map's. They nevertheless fit an authentic Mappean insistence on the kind of duplicitous and obfuscatory style for which he had gained inauthentic fame. In the compilation of *Piers* alongside Walter Map, Scribe X reveals a core affinity between textual likeness and authorial composition dependent upon neither style nor compositional mode.

Through his labor on Bodley 851, Scribe X brought the formal, generic, rhetorical, and discursive breadth of textual material shared by Walter Map and *Piers Plowman* together, enacting through his own comparative practices of compilation one fruitful approach to the imaginative literatures contained within his manuscript. Such breadth of material might be discovered anew in any number of contexts by any number of methods, whether through false expositions of sincere Mappean satire or through scribal modifications to Langlandian allegorical schemas. Through its singular compilation of Walter Map's texts and pseudo-texts and their many companions, Bodley 851 makes evident the many byways of literary history and historical readership only briefly pursued and now too frequently lost to the study of manuscript books, their preserved texts, and the historical readers they represent. The authorial apprehensions of Scribe X may in fact have been authorial misapprehensions. They nevertheless reveal through their material impositions and topical affiliations a strain of received literary interpretation at once inescapable, revealing, informative, and true.

CONCLUSION: MANUSCRIPT MEANING

Any material book is a thing written and a thing made. The argument of *The Making and Meaning of a Medieval Manuscript* has proceeded, throughout, from an examination of making to an examination of writing in critical analysis of the medieval book. In Chapter 1, I described my procedure in its material aspect as *analytical codicology* and in its critical aspect as *recomposition*. These two terms, analytical codicology and recomposition, form two sides of the same methodological coin. Analytical codicology describes processes of observation and inquiry necessary to answer the ostensibly straightforward book-historical question: "How did this book come to be?"[1] Recomposition describes processes of analysis and interpretation necessary to answer a separate hermeneutic question: "How does this book come to mean?" Between these two terms lies the simple fact that material composition and lexical composition are non-identical, and so, in turn, that any recovery of meaning from a manufactured *book*, and not solely some authorial or scribal *text*, depends upon the close examination of non-identical forms of evidence. When we ask, "how do you read a medieval book?" the answer must account for material things and material words together, in inextricable relation to one another, without collapsing the features of codices and the features of texts into a single indistinct evidentiary category. The fundamental contribution of *The Making and Meaning of a Medieval Manuscript* to literary study is a flexible method for moving between categorically distinct types of evidence in consideration of the significance of manuscript books.

Underpinning the method employed throughout this study is a theorization of the *codicological unconscious*, a mode of critical attention to the medieval book that places material production and lexical meaning in conversation in order to recover what these together might leave unsaid, or only implied, about the conditions of their production and the agents who played a primary role in that production. Crucially, this critical mode does not attempt to recover private motives, opinions, or mental states. The question is not, "what exactly was some historical agent thinking in producing this book in this way?" Rather,

---

[1] Michael F. Suarez, "Hard Cases: Confronting Bibliographical Difficulty in Eighteenth-Century Texts," *The Papers of the Bibliographical Society of America* 111.1 (2017), 3.

the codicological unconscious attempts to uncover the conditions of thought, however intentional or unexamined, that informed the making of a given codicological object. The question is, instead: "what does the production of this book in this way, with these contents, in these configurations, reveal about the prevailing conditions of thought that informed its making?"[2] By attending to material evidence, we discover historically grounded opportunities for critical analysis. Such opportunities may lead to synthesis (as in Chapter 3), but they need not (as in Chapter 2); and on occasion, they may lead to interpretations that are themselves counterfactual to literary history conducted elsewhere (as in Chapter 4). Of course, the act of interpretation belongs to the interpreter: it has never been otherwise. Arthur Bahr has written powerfully, working within a separate theoretical framework, that "each reader must determine whether the particular constellation of formal and historical vectors offered by a given object makes such compilational interpretation illuminating," on account of unavoidable reasons "both historical and formal."[3] We can no more recreate the past than any experience of it. The interpretive act nevertheless has the potential to reveal and comprehend patterns of historical thought otherwise strange or unexpected captured within material media. *The Making and Meaning of a Medieval Manuscript* offers one theorized hermeneutic method for discovering, in the oscillation between material and lexical evidence, the literary potential of manufactured books.

Engagement with the codicological unconscious depends upon analytical codicology and recomposition jointly. In order to understand what the production of a book reveals, we must first come to understand how that book was produced – in what stages, by which agents, according to what observable expectations, and with what implicit relation to the resulting artifact we possess today. Moreover, since description necessarily entails selectivity, any understanding of book production will imply the availability of some forms of further interpretation and not others. No single description can fully capture every aspect of a material text, whether singular or composite. Thus, to undertake analytical codicology within any single expository context is to open up some critical possibilities while foreclosing on other possibilities; and to undertake the task of recomposition is to take interest in the significance of a material text as a thing produced by historical agents in relation to one another, rather than as a thing understood within some other interpretive framework: "If a history of readings is made possible only by a comparative history of books, it is equally true that a history of books will have no point if it fails to

---

[2] Compare Christopher Cannon's tantalizing definition of "form" as "*that which thought and things have in common*" (*The Grounds of English Literature* [Oxford: Oxford University Press, 2004], 5; emphasis original).

[3] Arthur Bahr, *Fragments and Assemblages: Forming Compilations of Medieval London* (Chicago, IL: University of Chicago Press, 2013), 255.

account for the meanings they later come to make."[4] Throughout *The Making and Meaning of a Medieval Manuscript*, I have attended especially closely to how scribal agents who contributed to the fashioning of one exemplary manuscript brought some altered implications (or sets of altered implications) to the overall significance of the work. The types of significance implicated by historical action result from but do not recover intentional activity by codicological agents. The codicological unconscious fulfills the analytic promise of recomposition without presuming descriptive totality and avoids the impossibility of recreating private, historical experience.

The Making and Meaning of a Medieval Manuscript uncovers three expressions of the codicological unconscious in a single late-medieval English multi-text manuscript: BodL. MS Bodley 851. As shown earlier, this manuscript is known by scholars of Walter Map, because it contains the sole surviving medieval witness to Map's only surviving written work, the *De nugis curialium*, and it is known by scholars of *Piers Plowman*, because it contains the so-called "Z-text," a scribal rendition of that highly variant poem that does not correspond to any of the main edited versions. The presence of either one of these two textual witnesses would make Bodley 851 remarkable. The presence of both makes Bodley 851 exceptional. Yet these two canonical texts bookend an even more substantial collection of Latin poetic materials representative of an Anglo-Latin tradition commonly witnessed in English manuscripts of the late-fourteenth and fifteenth centuries. For example, the *Apocalypsis goliae episcopi*, the *Speculum stultorum*, and the *Prophecy* attributed to John of Bridlington were each notably popular – in some cases, astonishingly popular – with audiences in England and on the continent between roughly 1350 and 1500. In undertaking to copy these and other texts alongside one another, the scribes of Bodley 851 employed techniques in production common to practitioners of their era in order to create a collection of recognizable literary and cultural value. Alongside its unique texts, then, Bodley 851 also represents how multi-text manuscripts came to be produced, modified, and re-imagined by scribal contributors working in sequence, however collaboratively or disjunctively. In this view, the value of Bodley 851 as an exemplary object of study has as much to do with what makes it commonplace as what makes it unique.

It must be emphasized, however, that *The Making and Meaning of a Medieval Manuscript* is not comprehensive with respect to textual content. In this study, I have not aimed to interpret every possible textual relationship preserved within Bodley 851. Nor have I undertaken to query every textual relationship that emerges from recomposition. Because totality of description is impossible, so too is totality of interpretation. A book titled *The Making*

---

[4] D. F. McKenzie, *Bibliography and the Sociology of Texts* (Cambridge: Cambridge University Press, 1999), 23.

and Meaning of Bodley 851 might quickly come to resemble Borges's Library of Babel, an "indefinite, perhaps infinite" labyrinthian assortment of shifting iterations on the expansive evidence on display in the manuscript under consideration.[5] Even if infinitude ("perhaps") exaggerates the situation, practical considerations nevertheless prohibit any pretensions surrounding interpretive totality: the many strains of material association between manuscript texts offered by so capacious a book as Bodley 851 soon exceed the constraints of academic publishing apparatuses.

This specific manuscript is rich with further possibility, then, both in terms of the scribes I discuss in Chapters 2 through 4 and in terms of later contributors. Additional textual relationships contained within Bodley 851 would repay close attention in terms of their material relationships, particularly those texts copied into Part II by Scribe A and, to a lesser extent, Scribe X. Postmedieval reception of the manuscript forms a tantalizing invitation to interpretation, given the quantity of corrected text and marginal annotations throughout Part I and Part II. Texts added to the flyleaves, too, are of substantial interest for the later trajectory of this book's circulation. The production of Part III is ripe for exploration within the transmission of *Piers Plowman*. Moreover, stepping away from Bodley 851 specifically, there are many similar manuscripts collecting myriad understudied texts – in English, in Latin, and in continental vernaculars – which, too, would repay close attention using the method elucidated throughout this study. A focus on method opens further opportunities for critical inquiry.

Focus on method also serves to differentiate materially plausible patterns of thought from the modern researcher's more imaginative formal constructs. Not every single textual relationship is made equally plausible by collocation within a single manuscript, and analytical codicology should not be confused with any creative reading of a catalogue entry. The researcher might be hard pressed to argue, for example, for a critical connection between *Convocatio sacerdotum* (imposed by Dodsthorpe late in the production of Bodley 851) and the *Ave virgo mater christi* (the earliest material component remaining in the book, imposed by Scribe B). These texts share neither scribe nor hand, neither decorative scheme nor layout, and I am aware of no concrete material indication that Dodsthorpe engaged with Scribe B's labor. If there are abstract conceptual opportunities to read these texts in conversation, those opportunities are not warranted by an examination of the production of Bodley 851. Attention to the codicological unconscious does not license any critical grouping of texts according to modern research interests otherwise fashioned.

In the framework I present within *The Making and Meaning of a Medieval Manuscript*, codicological grounds for examining texts together must be

---

[5] Jorge Luis Borges, "The Library of Babel", in *Collected Fictions*, trans. Andrew Hurley (New York: Viking, 1998), 112.

established prior to the recovery of critical significance from discourse between those texts. More pointedly, by requiring codicological grounds for critical analysis, attention to the codicological unconscious remains agnostic concerning categories of critical interest often taken for granted by modern researchers – including genre, topic, and theme – generated outside of the context of manuscript production. Such categories only emerge as critically relevant according to their own codicological situation. What kind of text a text is, and how it might mean, can only be known through material inquiry.

BIBLIOGRAPHY

Manuscripts

Cambridge

Cambridge University Library
   MS Dd.1.17
   MS Gg.4.27
   MS Gg.5.35
Gonville and Caius College
   MS 385
Trinity College
   MS O.9.38
   MS R.3.20

Edinburgh

National Library of Scotland
   MS Advocates 19.2.1

Harvard

Houghton Library
   Lat. 300

Lincoln

Lincoln Cathedral Library
   MS 91
   MS 105

London

British Library
   Add. MS 22283
   Arundel MS 292
   Cotton MS Nero A.10
   Cotton MS Titus A.20

Cotton MS Vespasian E.12
Harley MS 913
Harley MS 978
Harley MS 2253
Harley MS 3954
Lambeth Palace Library
  MS 357
Lincoln's Inn
  MS Hale 150

Munich

Bayerische Staatsbibliothek
  MS Clm 631

Oxford

Bodleian Library
  MS Add. A.44
  MS Arch. Selden B.24
  MS Ashmole 61
  MS Bodley 603
  MS Bodley 761
  MS Digby 19
  MS Digby 86
  MS Digby 102
  MS Digby 166
  MS Eng. poet. a.1
  MS Fairfax 16
  MS Lat. misc. c.75
  MS Laud misc. 108
  MS Laud mis. 656
  MS Rawl. B.214
  MS Rawl. G.109
Corpus Christi College
  MS 232
University College
  MS 45

San Marino, CA

Huntington Library
  MS Hm 114

Vatican City

Vatican Library
  MS Lat. 3207

Editions

Anonymous. *Expositio Super Apocalypsim*. Accessed July 13, 2023. www.corpusthomisticum.org/x2a08.html.

Augustine. *Of Holy Virginity*. Translated by C. L. Cornish. In Schaff, ed., *A Select Library of the Nicene and PostNicene Fathers of the Christian Church*. Series 1, Vol. 3. 1887, repr., Peabody, MA: Hendrickson, 2004.

—. *On the Good of Marriage*. Translated by C. L. Cornish. In Schaff, ed., *A Select Library of the Nicene and PostNicene Fathers of the Christian Church*. Series 1, Vol. 3. 1887, repr., Peabody, MA: Hendrickson, 2004.

Bede. *In Proverbia Salomonis Libri III*. Edited by D. Hurst. CCSL 119B. Turnhout: Brepols, 1983.

—. *Super Epistulas Catholicas Expositio*. Edited by D. Hurst. CCSL 121. Turnhout: Brepols, 1983.

Bernard of Clairvaux. *Opera*. Edited by Jean Leclercq, C. H. Talbot, and Henri Rochais. 9 vols. Rome: Editiones Cistercienses, 1957–98.

Bonaventure. *The Journey of the Mind to God*. Edited by Stephen F. Brown and translated by Philotheus Boehner. Indianapolis, IN: Hackett, 1993.

Chaucer, Geoffrey. *The Riverside Chaucer*. Edited by Larry Benson *et al*. 3rd ed. Boston, MA: Houghton Mifflin, 1987.

—. *Troilus and Criseyde*. Edited by Stephen Barney. 1st edition. New York: W. W. Norton, 2006.

Christine de Pizan. *The Book of the City of Ladies*. Translated by Earl Jeffrey Richards. Revised edition. New York: Persea Books, 1998.

Curley, Michael J., ed. "The Prophecy of John of Bridlington: An Edition." Ph.D. dissertation, The University of Chicago, 1973.

Hanna, Ralph, and Traugott Lawler. *Jankyn's Book of Wikked Wyves*. 2 vols. Athens, GA: University of Georgia Press, 1997–2014.

Hilka, Alfons. "Eine Mittellateinische DichterFehde: Versus Michaelis Cornubiensis Contra Henricum Abrincensem." In *Mittelalterliche Handschriften: paläographische, kunsthistorische, literarische und bibliotheksgeschichtliche Untersuchungen*, ed. Alois Bömer und Joachim Kirchner Köhler, Leipzig: Karl W. Hiersemann, 1926, 123–54.

Hult, David F., ed. *Debate of the Romance of the Rose*. Chicago, IL: University of Chicago Press, 2010.

Isidore of Seville. *The Etymologies of Isidore of Seville*. Edited and translated by Stephen A. Barney. Cambridge: Cambridge University Press, 2006.

Jerome. *Commentary on Matthew*. Translated by Thomas P. Scheck. Washington, DC: Catholic University of America Press, 2008.

Kirk, G. S., J. E. Raven, and Malcolm Schofield, eds. *The Presocratic Philosophers: A Critical History with a Selection of Texts*. 2nd ed. Cambridge: Cambridge University Press, 1983.

Langland, William. *Piers Plowman: A Parallel-Text Edition of the A, B, C and Z Versions*. Edited by A. V. C. Schmidt. New York: Longman, 1995.

—. *Piers Plowman: The Z Version*. Edited by Charlotte Brewer and A. G. Rigg. Toronto: Pontifical Institute of Mediaeval Studies, 1983.

Lydgate, John. *The Minor Poems of John Lydgate, Part II*. Edited by Henry Noble MacCracken and Merriam Sherwood. EETS o.s. 192. London: Oxford University Press, 1934.

Map, Walter. *De Nugis Curialium*. Edited by Thomas Wright. London: Camden Society, 1850.
—. *De Nugis Curialium: Courtiers' Trifles*. Edited by M. R. James, Christopher Brooke, and R. A. B. Mynors. Oxford: Clarendon Press, 1983.
—. *Master Walter Map's Book, De Nugis Curialium*. Translated by Frederick Tupper and Marbury Bladen Ogle. London: Chatto & Windus, 1924.
—. *De nugis curialium*. Edited by M. R. James. Oxford: Clarendon Press, 1914.
Neckam, Alexander. *Sacerdos ad altare*. Edited by C. McDonough. CCCM 227. Turnhout: Brepols, 2010.
Nigel of Longchamp. *Speculum Stultorum*. Edited and translated by Jill Mann. Oxford: Oxford University Press, 2023.
Peter de Celle. *Commentaria in Ruth*. Edited by G. de Martel. CCCM 54. Turnhout: Brepols, 1983.
Richard of St. Victor. "In Apocalypsim Joannis," In *Richardus S. Victoris*. Edited by J. P. Migne. PL 196. Paris: 1855.
Rigg, A. G, ed. *Gawain on Marriage: The Textual Tradition of the De Coniuge Non Ducenda with Critical Edition and Translation*. Toronto: Pontifical Institute of Mediaeval Studies, 1986.
—. *The Poems of Walter of Wimborne*. Toronto: Pontifical Institute of Mediaeval Studies, 1978.
—. "Propaganda of the Hundred Years War: Poems on the Battles of Crecy and Durham (1346): A Critical Edition." *Traditio* 54 (1999): 169–211.
Roberts, Alexander, A. Cleveland Coxe and James Donaldson, eds. *The Ante-Nicene Fathers: Translations of the Writings of the Fathers down to A.D. 325*. 10 vols. Grand Rapids, MI: Eerdmans, 1965–70.
Strecker, Karl, ed. *Die Apokalypse Des Golias*. Rome: W. Regenberg, 1928.
Walfridus Strabo. *Liber Proverbiorum*. Edited by J. P. Migne. PL 113. Paris, 1852.
Weber, Robert, ed. *Biblia Sacra*. 2 vols. 4th edition. Stuttgart: Württembergische Bibelanstalt, 1969.
Wright, J. Robert, ed. *Proverbs, Ecclesiastes, Song of Solomon*. Ancient Christian Commentary on Scripture, vol. 9. Downers Grove, IL: InterVarsity Press, 2005.
Wright, Thomas. *The Latin Poems: Commonly Attributed to Walter Mapes*. London: Camden Society, 1841.
Ziolkowski, Jan M. and Bridget K. Balint, eds. *A Garland of Satire, Wisdom, and History: Latin Verse from Twelfth-Century France (Carmina Houghtoniensia)*. Cambridge, MA: Houghton Library of the Harvard College Library, distributed by Harvard University Press, 2007.

Secondary Materials

Aers, David. *Community, Gender, and Individual Identity: English Writing, 1360–1430*. New York: Routledge, 1988.
Alford, John A. "Langland's Learning." *YLS* 9 (1995): 1–17.
—. *Piers Plowman: A Guide to the Quotations*. Binghamton, NY: Center for Medieval & Renaissance Texts & Studies, 1992.
Astell, Ann W. *The Song of Songs in the Middle Ages*. Ithaca, NY: Cornell University Press, 1990.

Bahr, Arthur. "Celebrate Fragments." *New Chaucer Society Blog* (blog), December 5, 2013; last accessed 23 January 2025, https://newchaucersociety.org/blogpost/2106274/496971/Celebrate-Fragments-December-5-2013
—. *Fragments and Assemblages: Forming Compilations of Medieval London.* Chicago, IL: University of Chicago Press, 2013.
—. "Miscellaneity and Variance in the Medieval Book." In Johnston and Van Dussen, eds., *The Medieval Manuscript Book*, 181–98.
Bahr, Arthur, and Alexandra Gillespie. "Medieval English Manuscripts: Form, Aesthetics, and the Literary Text." *Chaucer Review* 47.4 (2013): 346–60.
Bale, John. *Scriptorum Illustrium Maioris Brytannie.* Basil, 1557.
Bardsley, Sandy. *Women's Roles in the Middle Ages.* Westport, CT: Greenwood Press, 2007.
Bartlett, Robert. *The Natural and the Supernatural in the Middle Ages.* Cambridge: Cambridge University Press, 2008.
Beadle, Richard, and Colin Burrow, eds. *Manuscript Miscellanies, c. 1450–1700.* London: British Library, 2011.
Beavis, Ian C. "Worms, Leeches, Centipedes, Woodlice, Etc." In *Insects and Other Invertebrates in Classical Antiquity*, 1–20. Liverpool: Liverpool University Press, 1988.
Bell, Kimberly K., and Julie Nelson Couch, eds. *The Texts and Contexts of Oxford, Bodleian Library, Ms. Laud Misc. 108: The Shaping of English Vernacular Narrative.* Boston, MA: Brill, 2011.
Bennett Segler, Angela R. "Mediation, Meditation, and the Manuscripts of 'Piers Plowman.'" Unpublished dissertation, New York University, 2015.
Benson, C. David. *Public Piers Plowman: Modern Scholarship and Late Medieval English Culture.* University Park, PA: Pennsylvania State University Press, 2004.
Benson, C. David, and Lynne S. Blanchfield, eds. *The Manuscripts of Piers Plowman: The B-Version.* Cambridge: D. S. Brewer, 1997.
Binkley, Peter. "Medieval Latin Poetic Anthologies (VI): The Cotton Anthology of Henry of Avranches." *Mediaeval Studies* 52 (1990): 221–54.
Birkholz, Daniel. *Harley Manuscript Geographies: Literary History and the Medieval Miscellany.* Manchester: Manchester University Press, 2020.
Blamires, Alcuin. *The Case for Women in Medieval Culture.* Oxford: Oxford University Press, 1997.
Blamires, Alcuin, Karen Pratt, and C. William Marx, eds. *Woman Defamed and Woman Defended: An Anthology of Medieval Texts.* Oxford: Clarendon Press, 1992.
Bloch, R. Howard. *Medieval Misogyny and the Invention of Western Romantic Love.* Chicago, IL: University of Chicago Press, 1991.
Bloomfield, Morton W. *Piers Plowman as a Fourteenth-Century Apocalypse.* New Brunswick, NJ: Rutgers University Press, 1962.
Blumenfeld-Kosinski, Renate. "Christine De Pizan and the Misogynistic Tradition." *Romanic Review* 81.3 (1990): 279–92.
Boffey, Julia. *Manuscript and Print in London c.1475–1530.* London: British Library, 2012.
—. "Short Texts in Manuscript Anthologies: The Minor Poems of John Lydgate in Two Fifteenth-Century Collections." In Nichols and Wenzel, eds., *The Whole Book*, 69–82.

Boffey, Julia, and John J. Thompson. "Anthologies and Miscellanies: Production and Choice of Texts." In Griffiths and Pearsall, eds., *Book Production and Publishing*, 279–315.

Borges, Jorge Luis. *Collected Fictions*. Translated by Andrew Hurley. New York: Viking, 1998.

Boss, Sarah Jane. *Empress and Handmaid: On Nature and Gender in the Cult of the Virgin Mary*. London: Cassell, 2000.

Brady, Lindy. *Writing the Welsh Borderlands in Anglo-Saxon England*. Manchester: Manchester University Press, 2017.

Brantley, Jessica. *Reading in the Wilderness: Private Devotion and Public Performance in Late Medieval England*. Chicago, IL: University of Chicago Press, 2007.

Breen, Katharine. *Imagining an English Reading Public, 1150–1400*. Cambridge: Cambridge University Press, 2010.

Brewer, Charlotte. *Editing Piers Plowman: The Evolution of the Text*. Cambridge: Cambridge University Press, 1996.

Brewer, Charlotte, and A. G. Rigg, eds. *Piers Plowman: A Facsimile of the Z-Text in Bodleian Library, Oxford, MS Bodley 851*. Cambridge: D. S. Brewer, 1994.

Burger, Glenn. *Conduct Becoming: Good Wives and Husbands in the Later Middle Ages*. Philadelphia, PA: University of Pennsylvania Press, 2018.

Busby, Keith. *Codex and Context: Reading Old French Verse Narrative in Manuscript*. New York: Rodopi, 2002.

Bynum, Caroline Walker. *Holy Feast and Holy Fast: The Religious Significance of Food to Medieval Women*. Berkeley, CA: University of California Press, 1987.

—. *Metamorphosis and Identity*. New York: Zone Books, 2001.

—. "Miracles and Marvels: The Limits of Alterity." In *Vita Religiosa Im Mittelalter*, edited by Franz Felten and Nikolas Jaspert, 799–817. Berlin: Duncker and Humblot, 1999.

Cannon, Christopher. "Form." In *Middle English*, edited by Paul Strohm, 177–90. Oxford: Oxford University Press, 2007.

—. *From Literacy to Literature: England, 1300–1400*. Oxford: Oxford University Press, 2016.

—. "Vernacular Latin." *Speculum* 90.3 (2015): 641–53.

—. *The Grounds of English Literature*. Oxford: Oxford University Press, 2004.

Carruthers, Mary J. *The Book of Memory: A Study of Memory in Medieval Culture*. 2nd ed. Cambridge: Cambridge University Press, 2008.

—. *The Craft of Thought: Meditation, Rhetoric, and the Making of Images, 400–1200*. Cambridge: Cambridge University Press, 1998.

Cartlidge, Neil. "Masters in the Art of Lying? The Literary Relationship between Hugh of Rhuddlan and Walter Map." *The Modern Language Review* 106.1 (2011): 1–16.

—. "'Vinegar upon Nitre'? Walter Map's Romance of Sadius and Galo." In *Cultural Translations in Medieval Romance*, edited by Victoria Flood and Megan G. Leitch, 117–34. Cambridge: D. S. Brewer, 2022.

—. "Walter Map and the Matter of Britain by Joshua Byron Smith (Review)." *Digital Philology: A Journal of Medieval Cultures* 8, no. 1 (2019): 145–8.

Chartier, Roger. *The Order of Books: Readers, Authors, and Libraries in Europe between the Fourteenth and Eighteenth Centuries*. Stanford, CA: Stanford University Press, 1994.

Clanchy, M. T. *From Memory to Written Record: England, 1066–1307*. 3rd edition. Malden, MA: Wiley-Blackwell, 2013.

Clemens, Raymond, and Timothy Graham. *Introduction to Manuscript Studies*. Ithaca, NY: Cornell University Press, 2007.

Connolly, Margaret. "The Whole Book and the Whole Picture: Editions and Facsimiles of Medieval Miscellanies and Their Influence." In Connolly and Radulescu, eds., *Insular Books*, 281–99.

Connolly, Margaret, and Linne R. Mooney, eds. *Design and Distribution of Late Medieval Manuscripts in England*. York: York Medieval Press, 2008.

Connolly, Margaret, and Raluca L. Radulescu, eds. *Insular Books: Vernacular Manuscript Miscellanies in Late Medieval Britain*. Oxford: Oxford University Press, 2015.

Cooper, Helen. "Gender and Personification in *Piers Plowman*." *YLS* 5 (1991): 31–48.

Cornelius, Roberta D. "*Piers Plowman* and the *Roman de Fauvel*." *PMLA* 47.2 (1932): 363–67.

Coxon, Sebastian. "Wit, Laughter, and Authority in Walter Map's De Nugis Curialium." In *Author, Reader, Book: Medieval Authorship in Theory and Practice*, edited by Stephen Partridge and Erik Kwakkel, 38–55. Toronto: University of Toronto Press, 2012.

Crocker, Holly A. "Feminism without Gender: Piers Plowman, 'Mede the Mayde,' and Late Medieval Literary Studies." *Exemplaria* 31.2 (2019): 93–104.

—. *The Matter of Virtue: Women's Ethical Action from Chaucer to Shakespeare*. Philadelphia, PA: University of Pennsylvania Press, 2019.

Da Rold, Orietta, and Elaine M. Treharne, eds. *The Cambridge Companion to Medieval British Manuscripts*. Cambridge: Cambridge University Press, 2020.

Davies, Daniel, and R. D. Perry, eds. *Literatures of the Hundred Years War*. Manchester: Manchester University Press, 2024.

Davis, Isabel. "'The Trinite Is Our Everlasting Lover': Marriage and Trinitarian Love in the Later Middle Ages." *Speculum* 86.4 (2011): 914–63.

Davlin, Mary Clemente. "Genealogical Terms in *Piers Plowman*." *YLS* 26 (2012): 111–32.

D'Avray, D. L. *Medieval Marriage Sermons: Mass Communication in a Culture without Print*. Oxford: Oxford University Press, 2001.

De Hamel, Christopher. *Glossed Books of the Bible and the Origins of the Paris Booktrade*. Cambridge: D. S. Brewer, 1984.

—. *Scribes and Illuminators*. Toronto: University of Toronto Press, 1992.

Derolez, Albert. *The Palaeography of Gothic Manuscript Books: From the Twelfth to the Early Sixteenth Century*. Cambridge: Cambridge University Press, 2003.

Derrida, Jacques. "Archive Fever: A Freudian Impression." *Diacritics: A Review of Contemporary Criticism* 25.2 (1995): 9–63.

Dinkova-Bruun, Greti. "Medieval Latin Poetic Anthologies (VII): The Biblical Anthology from York Minster Library (MS. XVI Q 14)." *Mediaeval Studies* 64 (2002): 61–109.

Dinshaw, Carolyn. *Chaucer's Sexual Poetics*. Madison, WI: University of Wisconsin Press, 1989.

Dinshaw, Carolyn, and David Wallace, eds. *The Cambridge Companion to Medieval Women's Writing*. Cambridge: Cambridge University Press, 2003.

Donavin, Georgiana. *Scribit Mater: Mary and the Language Arts in the Literature of Medieval England*. Washington, DC: Catholic University of America Press, 2012.

Drimmer, Sonja. "Connoisseurship, Art History, and the Paleographical Impasse in Middle English Studies." *Speculum* 97.2 (2022): 415–68.

Driver, Martha, and Michael Orr. "Decorating and Illustrating the Page." In Gillespie and Wakelin, eds., *The Production of Books*, 104–28.

Dronke, Peter. "The Lyrical Compositions of Philip the Chancellor." *Studi Medievali* 28 (1987): 563–92.

Duggan, Hoyt N. "The Authenticity of the Z Text of 'Piers Plowman': Further Notes on Metrical Evidence." *Medium Ævum* 56.1 (1987): 25–45.

Echard, Siân. "Clothes Make the Man: The Importance of Appearance in Walter Map's De Gadone Milite Strenuissimo." In *Anglo-Latin and Its Heritage*, 93–108. Turnhout: Brepols, 2010.

—. "Map's Metafiction: Author, Narrator and Reader in De Nugis Curialum." *Exemplaria* 8.2 (1996): 287–314.

Edwards, A. S. G., Vincent Gillespie, and Ralph Hanna, eds. *The English Medieval Book: Studies in Memory of Jeremy Griffiths*. London: British Library, 2000.

Edwards, Robert. "Walter Map: Authorship and the Space of Writing." *New Literary History* 38.2 (2007): 273–92.

Elliott, Dyan. "Marriage." In Dinshaw and Wallace, eds., *The Cambridge Companion to Medieval Women's Writing*, 40–57.

—. *Spiritual Marriage: Sexual Abstinence in Medieval Wedlock*. Princeton, NJ: Princeton University Press, 1993.

—. *The Bride of Christ Goes to Hell: Metaphor and Embodiment in the Lives of Pious Women, 200–1500*. Philadelphia, PA: University of Pennsylvania Press, 2012.

Emden, A. B. *A Biographical Register of the University of Oxford to A. D. 1500*. 3 vols. Oxford: Clarendon Press, 1957–59.

Evans, Ruth. "Virginities." In Dinshaw and Wallace, eds., *The Cambridge Companion to Medieval Women's Writing*, 21–39.

Fein, Susanna, ed. *Interpreting MS Digby 86: A Trilingual Book from Thirteenth-Century Worcestershire*. York: York Medieval Press, 2019.

—, ed. *Studies in the Harley Manuscript: The Scribes, Contents, and Social Contexts of British Library MS Harley 2253*. Kalamazoo, MI: Medieval Institute Publications, 2000.

—, ed. *The Auchinleck Manuscript: New Perspectives*. York: York Medieval Press, 2016.

Fein, Susanna, and Michael Johnston, eds. *Robert Thornton and His Books: Essays on the Lincoln and London Thornton Manuscripts*. York: York Medieval Press, 2014.

Fisher, Matthew. *Scribal Authorship and the Writing of History in Medieval England*. Columbus, OH: Ohio State University Press, 2012.

Flood, Victoria. "Political Prodigies: Incubi Succubi In Walter Map's *De Nugis Curialium* and Gerald Of Wales's *Itinerarium Cambriae*." *Nottingham Medieval Studies* 57 (2013): 21–46.

Fowler, Elizabeth. "Civil Death and the Maiden: Agency and the Conditions of Contract in *Piers Plowman*." *Speculum* 70.4 (1995): 760–92.

Fuller, Karrie. "The Craft of the 'Z-Maker': Reading the Z Text's Unique Lines in Context." *YLS* 27 (2013): 15–43.

Fumo, Jamie C. "Argus' Eyes, Midas' Ears, and the Wife of Bath as Storyteller." In *Metamorphosis: The Changing Face of Ovid in Medieval and Early Modern Europe*, edited by Steven Rupp, 129–50. Toronto: Centre for Reformation and Renaissance Studies, 2007.

Galloway, Andrew. "Madame Meed: Fauvel, Isabella, and the French Circumstances *of Piers Plowman*." *YLS* 30 (2016): 227–52.

—. "*Piers Plowman* and the Schools." *YLS* 6 (1992): 89–107.

—. *The Penn Commentary on Piers Plowman*. Vol. 1. Philadelphia, PA: University of Pennsylvania Press, 2006.

Gameson, Richard, ed. *The Cambridge History of the Book in Britain. Volume 1: c. 400–1100*. Cambridge: Cambridge University Press, 2012.

Gaskell, Philip. *A New Introduction to Bibliography*. New Castle, DE: Oak Knoll Press, 1995.

Gaskill, Nicholas. "The Close and the Concrete: Aesthetic Formalism in Context." *New Literary History* 47.4 (2016): 505–24.

Gasse, Rosanne. "Witchcraft and Sorcery in *Piers Plowman*." *The Chaucer Review* 55.1 (2020): 88–112.

Gilbert, Jane, and Sara Harris. "The Written Word: Literacy across Languages." In Da Rold and Treharne, eds., *The Cambridge Companion to Medieval British Manuscripts*, 149–78.

Gillespie, Alexandra. "Are The Canterbury Tales a Book?" *Exemplaria* 30.1 (2018): 66–83.

—. "Medieval Books, Their Booklets, and Booklet Theory." In Beadle and Burrow, eds., *Manuscript Miscellanies c. 1450–1700*, 1–29.

Gillespie, Alexandra, and Daniel Wakelin, eds. *The Production of Books in England 1350–1500*. Cambridge: Cambridge University Press, 2011.

Gordon, Stephen. "Monstrous Words, Monstrous Bodies: Irony and the Walking Dead in Walter Map's De Nugis Curialium." *English Studies* 96.4 (2015): 379–402.

—. "Parody, Sarcasm, and Invective in the Nugae of Walter Map." *The Journal of English and Germanic Philology* 116.1 (2017): 82–107.

Green, Richard Firth. *Elf Queens and Holy Friars: Fairy Beliefs and the Medieval Church*. Philadelphia, PA: University of Pennsylvania Press, 2016.

—. "The Lost Exemplar of the Z-Text of *Piers Plowman* and Its 20-Line Pages." *Medium Aevum* 56.2 (1987): 307–10.

Griffiths, Jeremy, and Derek Pearsall, eds. *Book Production and Publishing in Britain, 1375–1475*. Cambridge: Cambridge University Press, 1989.

Gruenler, Curtis A. *Piers Plowman and the Poetics of Enigma: Riddles, Rhetoric, and Theology*. Notre Dame, IN: University of Notre Dame Press, 2017.

Gruys, A., and J. P. Gumbert, eds. *Codicologica: Towards a Science of Handwritten Books.* 5 vols. Leiden: E. J. Brill, 1976–1980.

Gumbert, Johann Peter. "Codicological Units: Towards a Terminology for the Stratigraphy of the Non-Homogeneous Codex." *Segno e Testo: International Journal of Manuscripts and Text Transmission* 2 (2004): 17–42.

Hanna, Ralph. "Booklets in Medieval Manuscripts: Further Considerations." In *Pursuing History*, 23–34. Stanford, CA: Stanford University Press, 1996.

—. "Booklets in Medieval Manuscripts: Further Considerations." *Studies in Bibliography* 39 (1986): 100–111.

—. *Introducing English Medieval Book History: Manuscripts, Their Producers and Their Readers.* Liverpool: Liverpool University Press, 2013.

—. "Miscellaneity and Vernacularity: Conditions of Literary Production in Late Medieval England." In Nichols and Wenzel, eds., *The Whole Book*, 37–51.

—. "MS Bodley 851 and the Dissemination of *Piers Plowman*," in *Pursuing History*, 195–202.

—. *Pursuing History: Middle English Manuscripts and Their Texts.* Stanford, CA: Stanford University Press, 1996.

—. "School and Scorn: Gender in *Piers Plowman*." In *New Medieval Literatures III*, edited by David Lawton, Wendy Scase, and Rita Copeland, 213–27. Oxford: Oxford University Press, 1999.

—. "Studies in the Manuscripts of *Piers Plowman*." *YLS* 7 (1993): 1–25.

—. "The Matter of Fulk: Romance and History in the Marches." *The Journal of English and Germanic Philology* 110.3 (2011): 337–58.

—, ed. *The Penn Commentary on Piers Plowman.* Vol. 2. Philadelphia, PA: University of Pennsylvania Press, 2017.

Hansen, Elaine Tuttle. *Chaucer and the Fictions of Gender.* Berkeley, CA: University of California Press, 1992.

Harris, Carissa M. "'All the Strete My Voyce Shall Heare': Gender, Voice, and Desire in the Lyrics of Bodleian MS Ashmole 176." *Journal of the Early Book Society* 20 (2017): 29–58.

Harris, Carissa M. and Fiona Somerset, eds. "Historicizing Consent." Special issue. *SAC* (2022), 268–367.

Hewett-Smith, Kathleen M. "Allegory on the Half-Acre: The Demands of History." *YLS* 10 (1996): 1–22.

Hicks, Andrew. "Pythagoras and Pythagoreanism in Late Antiquity and the Middle Ages." In *A History of Pythagoreanism*, edited by Carl A. Huffman, 416–34. Cambridge: Cambridge University Press, 2014.

Hinton, James. "Walter Map's *De Nugis Curialium*: Its Plan and Composition." *PMLA* 32.1 (1917): 81–132.

Hollywood, Amy M. *The Soul as Virgin Wife: Mechthild of Magdeburg, Marguerite Porete, and Meister Eckhart.* Notre Dame, IN: University of Notre Dame Press, 1995.

Holsinger, Bruce W. *On Parchment: Animals, Archives, and the Making of Culture from Herodotus to the Digital Age.* New Haven, CT: Yale University Press, 2022.

Horobin, Simon. "Harley 3954 and the Audience of *Piers Plowman*." In *Medieval Texts in Context*, edited by Graham D. Caie and Denis Renevey, 68–84. Abingdon: Routledge, 2008.

Hunt, Tony. *Teaching and Learning Latin in Thirteenth-Century England*. 3 vols. Cambridge: D. S. Brewer, 1991.

Jaeger, C. Stephen. *Ennobling Love: In Search of a Lost Sensibility*. Philadelphia, PA: University of Pennsylvania Press, 1999.

—. "Pessimism in the Twelfth-Century 'Renaissance.'" *Speculum* 78.4 (2003): 1151–83.

Jameson, Fredric. *The Political Unconscious: Narrative as a Socially Symbolic Act*. 7th printing edition. Ithaca, NY: Cornell University Press, 1982.

Johns, Adrian. *The Nature of the Book: Print and Knowledge in the Making*. Chicago, IL: University of Chicago Press, 1998.

Johnson, Eleanor. *Practicing Literary Theory in the Middle Ages: Ethics and the Mixed Form in Chaucer, Gower, Usk, and Hoccleve*. Chicago, IL: University of Chicago Press, 2013.

Johnston, Michael. *The Middle English Book: Scribes and Readers, 1350–1500*. Oxford: Oxford University Press, 2023.

Johnston, Michael, and Michael Van Dussen, eds. *The Medieval Manuscript Book: Cultural Approaches*. Cambridge: Cambridge University Press, 2015.

Justice, Steven. "Did the Middle Ages Believe in Their Miracles?" *Representations* 103.1 (2008): 1–29.

—. "Eucharistic Miracle and Eucharistic Doubt." *Journal of Medieval and Early Modern Studies* 42.2 (2012): 307–32.

Kamali, Elizabeth Papp. "Tales of the Living Dead: Dealing with Doubt in Medieval English Law." *Speculum* 96.2 (2021): 367–417.

Kane, George. *Piers Plowman: The Evidence for Authorship*. London: Athlone Press, 1965.

—. "The 'Z Version' of *Piers Plowman*." *Speculum* 60.4 (1985): 910–30.

Karnes, Michelle. *Imagination, Meditation, and Cognition in the Middle Ages*. Chicago, IL: University of Chicago Press, 2011.

—. "The Possibilities of Medieval Fiction." *New Literary History* 51.1 (2020): 209–28.

Kay, Sarah. *Animal Skins and the Reading Self in Medieval Latin and French Bestiaries*. Chicago, IL: University of Chicago Press, 2017.

Keller, Kimberly. "For Better and Worse: Women and Marriage in *Piers Plowman*." In *Medieval Family Roles: A Book of Essays*, edited by Cathy Jorgensen Itnyre, 67–83. New York: Garland, 1996.

Kelly, Henry Ansgar. *Love and Marriage in the Age of Chaucer*. Ithaca, NY: Cornell University Press, 1975.

Kelly, Stephen, and John J. Thompson, eds. *Imagining the Book*. Turnhout: Brepols, 2005.

Kerby-Fulton, Kathryn. "Confronting the Scribe-Poet Binary: The Z Text, Writing Office Redaction, and the Oxford Reading Circles." In Kerby-Fulton *et al.*, eds., *New Directions in Medieval Manuscript Studies and Reading Practices*, 489–515.

—. "Oxford." In *Europe: A Literary History, 1348–1418*, edited by David Wallace, 208–26. Oxford: Oxford University Press, 2016.

—. "Professional Readers of Langland at Home and Abroad: New Directions in the Political and Bureaucratic Codicology of *Piers Plowman*." In Pearsall, ed., *New Directions in Later Medieval Manuscript Studies*, 103–29.

Kerby-Fulton, Kathryn, Linda Olson, and Maidie Hilmo. *Opening up Middle English Manuscripts: Literary and Visual Approaches*. Ithaca, NY: Cornell University Press, 2012.

Kerby-Fulton, Kathryn, John J. Thompson, Sarah Baechle, and Derek Pearsall, eds. *New Directions in Medieval Manuscript Studies and Reading Practices: Essays in Honor of Derek Pearsall*. Notre Dame, IN: University of Notre Dame Press, 2014.

Kim, Margaret. "Hunger, Need, and the Politics of Poverty in *Piers Plowman*." *YLS* 16 (2002): 131–68.

Knight, Jeffrey Todd. *Bound to Read: Compilations, Collections, and the Making of Renaissance Literature*. Philadelphia, PA: University of Pennsylvania Press, 2013.

Krochalis, Jeanne, and Edward H. Peters, eds. *The world of Piers Plowman*. The Middle Ages. Philadelphia, PA: University of Pennsylvania Press, 1975.

Kwakkel, Erik. "Towards a Terminology for the Analysis of Composite Manuscripts." *Gazette Du Livre Médiéval* 41.1 (2002): 12–19.

Lalou, Elisabeth. *Les Tablettes à écrire de l'Antiquité à l'époque moderne*. Turnhout: Brepols, 1992.

Lawler, Traugott. "Langland Versificator." *YLS* 25 (2011): 37–76.

Lawton, David. "The Subject of Piers Plowman." *YLS* 1 (1987): 1–30.

—. *Voice in Later Medieval English Literature: Public Interiorities*. Oxford: Oxford University Press, 2017.

Le Goff, Jacques. *The Medieval Imagination*. Translated by Arthur Goldhammer. Chicago, IL: University of Chicago Press, 1988.

Lees, Clare A. "Gender and Exchange in *Piers Plowman*." In *Class and Gender in Early English Literature*, edited by Britton J. Harwood and Gillian R. Overing, 112–30. Bloomington, IN: Indiana University Press, 1994.

Levinson, Marjorie. "What Is New Formalism?" *PMLA* 122.2 (2007): 558–69.

Lipton, Emma. *Affections of the Mind: The Politics of Sacramental Marriage in Late Medieval English Literature*. Notre Dame, IN: University of Notre Dame Press, 2011.

Luscombe, David. "Masters and Their Books in the Schools of the Twelfth Century." *Proceedings of the PMR Conference: Annual Publication of the International Patristic, Mediaeval and Renaissance Conference* 9 (1984): 17–33.

Macherey, Pierre. *A Theory of Literary Production*. Translated by Geoffrey Wall. New York: Routledge, 2006.

Madan, Falconer, and H. H. E. Craster. *A Summary Catalogue of Western Manuscripts in the Bodleian Library at Oxford*. Vol. 2.1. Oxford: Clarendon Press, 1922.

Maniaci, Marilena. *Terminologia del libro manoscritto*. Roma: Istituto centrale per la patologia del libro, 1996.

Mann, Jill. *Chaucer and Medieval Estates Satire*. Cambridge: Cambridge University Press, 1973.

—. "Satiric Subject and Satiric Object in Goliardic Literature." *Mittellateinisches Jahrbuch* 15 (1980): 63–86.

—. "The Nature of Need Revisited." *YLS* 18 (2004): 3–29.

Manne, Kate. *Down Girl: The Logic of Misogyny*. Oxford: Oxford University Press, 2018.

Matter, E. Ann. *The Voice of My Beloved: The Song of Songs in Western Medieval Christianity*. Philadelphia, PA: University of Pennsylvania Press, 1990.

McCarthy, Conor, ed. *Love, Sex and Marriage in the Middle Ages: A Sourcebook*. New York: Routledge, 2004.

—. "Marriage and Mede in Passus 2 to 4 of *Piers Plowman*." *Nottingham Medieval Studies* 44 (2000): 154–66.

McDermott, Ryan. *Tropologies: Ethics and Invention in England, c. 1350–1600*. Notre Dame, IN: University of Notre Dame Press, 2016.

McKenzie, D. F. *Bibliography and the Sociology of Texts*. Cambridge: Cambridge University Press, 1999.

McKitterick, David. *Print, Manuscript and the Search for Order, 1450–1830*. Cambridge: Cambridge University Press, 2003.

Meale, Carol M., and Derek Pearsall, eds. *Makers and Users of Medieval Books: Essays in Honour of A. S. G. Edwards*. Cambridge: D. S. Brewer, 2014.

Mews, Constant J. "Orality, Literacy, and Authority in the Twelfth-Century Schools." *Exemplaria* 2.2 (1990): 475–500.

Meyer-Lee, Robert J. "Abandon the Fragments." *SAC* 35 (2013): 47–83.

Middleton, Anne. "Acts of Vagrancy: The C Version 'Autobiography' and the Statute of 1388." In *Written Work: Langland, Labor, and Authorship*, edited by Steven Justice and Kathryn Kerby-Fulton, 208–317. Philadelphia, PA: University of Pennsylvania Press, 1997.

—. "Editing Terminable and Interminable." *Huntington Library Quarterly* 64.1/2 (2001): 161–86.

—. "Piers Plowman." In *A Manual of the Writings in Middle English, 1050–1500, VII*, edited by Albert E. Hartung. Hamden, CT: Archon Books, 1986.

—. "The Audience and Public of *Piers Plowman*." In *Middle English Alliterative Poetry and Its Literary Background: Seven Essays*, edited by David Lawton, 101–23. Cambridge: D. S. Brewer, 1982.

Minnis, Alastair. *Fallible Authors: Chaucer's Pardoner and Wife of Bath*. Philadelphia, PA: University of Pennsylvania Press, 2008.

—. *Medieval Theory of Authorship: Scholastic Literary Attitudes in the Later Middle Ages*. 2nd edition. Philadelphia, PA: University of Pennsylvania Press, 2010.

Mormando, Franco. "Bernardino of Siena, Popular Preacher and Witch-Hunter: A 1426 Witch Trial in Rome." *Fifteenth Century Studies* 24 (1998): 84–118.

Murphy, Colette. "Lady Holy Church and Meed the Maid: Re-Envisioning Female Personifications in *Piers Plowman*." In *Feminist Readings in Middle English Literature: The Wife of Bath and All Her Sect*, edited by Ruth Evans and Lesley Johnson, 140–64. New York: Routledge, 1994.

Muzerelle, Denis. *Vocabulaire Codicologique: Répertoire Méthodique Des Termes Français Relatifs Aux Manuscrits*. Paris: CEMI, 1985.

Nederman, Cary J. "The Meaning of 'Aristotelianism' in Medieval Moral and Political Thought." *Journal of the History of Ideas* 57.4 (1996): 563–85.

Newhauser, Richard, Vincent Gillespie, Jessica Rosenfeld, and Katie I. Walter, eds. *Chaucer Encyclopedia*. Hoboken, NJ: John Wiley & Sons, 2022.

Newman, Barbara. *God and the Goddesses: Vision, Poetry, and Belief in the Middle Ages*. Philadelphia, PA: University of Pennsylvania Press, 2005.

—. "What Did It Mean to Say 'I Saw'? The Clash between Theory and Practice in Medieval Visionary Culture." *Speculum* 80.1 (2005): 1–43.

Newman, F. X. "The Structure of Vision in Apocalypsis Goliae." *Mediaeval Studies* 29 (1967): 113–23.

Nichols, Stephen G. "Introduction: Philology in a Manuscript Culture." *Speculum* 65.1 (1990): 1–10.

Nichols, Stephen G., and Siegfried Wenzel, eds. *The Whole Book: Cultural Perspectives on the Medieval Miscellany*. Ann Arbor, MI: University of Michigan Press, 1996.

Nolan, Barbara. "Anthologizing Ribaldry: Five Anglo-Norman Fabliaux." In Fein, ed., *Studies in the Harley Manuscript*, 289–327.

Orme, Nicholas. *Medieval Schools: From Roman Britain to Renaissance England*. New Haven, CT: Yale University Press, 2006.

Otter, Monika. *Inventiones: Fiction and Referentiality in Twelfth-Century English Historical Writing*. Chapel Hill, NC: University of North Carolina Press, 1996.

Parkes, M. B. *English Cursive Book Hands, 1250–1500*. Oxford: Clarendon Press, 1969.

—. *Their Hands before Our Eyes: A Closer Look at Scribes: The Lyell Lectures Delivered in the University of Oxford, 1999*. Burlington, VT: Ashgate, 2008.

Parsons, Ben. "An Unrecognized Reference to a Latin Satire in Langland's *Piers Plowman*." *Notes and Queries* 57.1 (2010): 27–29.

Partridge, Stephen. "Designing the Page." In Gillespie and Wakelin, eds., *The Production of Books*, 79–103.

Pearsall, Derek, ed. *New Directions in Later Medieval Manuscript Studies: Essays from the 1998 Harvard Conference*. York: York Medieval Press, 2000.

—. *Old English and Middle English Poetry*. London: Routledge, 1977.

—, ed. *Studies in the Vernon Manuscript*. Cambridge: D. S. Brewer, 1990.

—. "The Whole Book: Late Medieval English Manuscript Miscellanies and Their Modern Interpreters." In Kelly and Thompson, eds., *Imagining the Book*, 17–29.

Phillips, Noelle. "Compilational Reading: Richard Osbarn and Huntington Library MS HM 114." *YLS* 28 (2014): 65–104.

Philpott, Mark. "Haunting the Middle Ages." In *Writing and Fantasy*, edited by Ceri Sullivan and Barbara White, 48–61. New York: Longman, 1999.

Poe, Elizabeth Wilson. *Compilatio: Lyric Texts and Prose Commentaries in Troubadour Manuscript H (Vat. Lat. 3207)*. Lexington, KY: French Forum, 2000.

Pratt, Robert A. "Chaucer and the Hand That Fed Him." *Speculum* 41.4 (1966): 619–42.

—. "Jankyn's Book of Wikked Wyves: Medieval Antimatrimonial Propaganda in the Universities." *Annuale Mediaevale* 3 (1962): 5–27.

—. "Saint Jerome in Jankyn's Book of Wikked Wyves." *Criticism* 5 (1963): 316–22.

—. "The Development of the Wife of Bath." In *Studies in Medieval Literature: In Honor of Professor Albert Croll Baugh*, edited by MacEdward Leach, 45–79, 1961.

Raby, F. J. E. *A History of Secular Latin Poetry in the Middle Ages*. 2 vols. Oxford: Clarendon Press, 1934.

Raskolnikov, Masha. *Body against Soul: Gender and Sowlehele in Middle English Allegory*. Columbus, OH: Ohio State University Press, 2009.

Revard, Carter. "Scribe and Provenance." In *Studies in the Harley Manuscript*, ed. Fein, 21–109.

Reynolds, Brian K. *Gateway to Heaven: Marian Doctrine and Devotion: Image and Typology in the Patristic and Medieval Periods*. Hyde Park. NY: New City Press, 2012.

Reynolds, Susan. "Eadric Silvaticus and the English Resistance." *Historical Research* 54.129 (1981): 102–5.

Reynolds, Suzanne. *Medieval Reading: Grammar, Rhetoric, and the Classical Text*. Cambridge: Cambridge University Press, 1996.

Rigg, A. G. *A Glastonbury Miscellany of the Fifteenth Century: A Descriptive Index of Trinity College, Cambridge, MS.O.9.38*. London: Oxford University Press, 1968.

—. *A History of Anglo-Latin Literature, 1066–1422*. Cambridge: Cambridge University Press, 1992.

—. "Golias and Other Pseudonyms." *Studi Medievali* 18.1 (1977): 65–109.

—. "Medieval Latin Poetic Anthologies (I)." *Mediaeval Studies* 39 (1977): 281–330.

—. "Medieval Latin Poetic Anthologies (II)." *Mediaeval Studies* 40 (1978): 387–407.

—. "Medieval Latin Poetic Anthologies (III)." *Mediaeval Studies* 41 (1979): 468–505.

—. "Medieval Latin Poetic Anthologies (IV)." *Mediaeval Studies* 43 (1981): 472–97.

—. "Walter Map, the Shaggy Dog Story, and the Quaestio Disputata." In *Roma, Magistra Mundi: Itineraria Culturae Medievalis. Mélanges Offerts à Père L.E. Boyle à l'occasion de Son 75e Anniversaire*, 2:723–735. Louvain-la-Neuve: Fédération Internationale des Instituts d'Etudes Médiévales, 1998.

—. "Walter of Wimborne, O.F.M.: An Anglo-Latin Poet of the Thirteenth Century." *Mediaeval Studies* 33 (1971): 371–78.

Robertson, D. W., Jr. "The Wife of Bath and Midas." *SAC* 6 (1984): 1–20.

Robinson, Pamela. "The 'Booklet': A Self-Contained Unit in Composite Manuscripts." In Gruys and Gumbert, eds., *Codicologica* 3:46–69.

Rothenberg, David J. *The Flower of Paradise : Marian Devotion and Secular Song in Medieval and Renaissance Music*. Oxford: Oxford University Press, 2011.

Rouse, Mary A., and Richard H. Rouse. *Authentic Witnesses: Approaches to Medieval Texts and Manuscripts*. Notre Dame, IN: University of Notre Dame Press, 1991.

—. *Bound Fast with Letters: Medieval Writers, Readers, and Texts*. Notre Dame, IN: University of Notre Dame Press, 2013.

—. *Preachers, Florilegia and Sermons: Studies on the Manipulus Florum of Thomas of Ireland*. Toronto: Pontifical Institute of Mediaeval Studies, 1979.

Rubin, Miri. *Mother of God: A History of the Virgin Mary*. New Haven, CT: Yale University Press, 2009.

Russakoff, Anna D. *Imagining the Miraculous: Miraculous Images of the Virgin Mary in French Illuminated Manuscripts, ca. 1250–ca. 1450*. Toronto: Pontifical Institute of Mediaeval Studies, 2019.

Ryley, Hannah. *Re-Using Manuscripts in Late Medieval England: Repairing, Recycling, Sharing*. York: York Medieval Press, 2022.

Rust, Martha Dana. *Imaginary Worlds in Medieval Books: Exploring the Manuscript Matrix*. Basingstoke: Palgrave Macmillan, 2007.

Sawyer, Daniel. *Reading English Verse in Manuscript c.1350–c.1500*. Oxford: Oxford University Press, 2020.

Sawyer, Thomas C. "Bookish Brains and Visionary Learning in the Apocalypsis Goliae Episcopi." *ELH* 89.1 (2022): 1–31.

—. "Book Work: Towards an Extended Codicological Intentionalism." *JMEMS* 55.2 (2025): 159–84.

Sawyer, Thomas C., and Paul Vinhage. "Michael of Cornwall's *First Invective* against Henry of Avranches." *JMLat* 33 (2023): 17–56.

—. "Michael of Cornwall's *Second Invective* against Henry of Avranches." *JMLat* 34 (2024): 153–87.

Scase, Wendy, ed. *The Making of the Vernon Manuscript: The Production and Contexts of Oxford, Bodleian Library, MS Eng. Poet. a. 1*. Turnhout: Brepols, 2013.

Schiller, Gertrud. *Iconography of Christian Art*. 2 vols. Greenwich, CT: New York Graphic Society, 1971.

Schmidt, A. V. C. "The Authenticity of the Z Text of *Piers Plowman*: A Metrical Examination." *Medium Aevum* 53.2 (1984): 295.

Seal, Graham. *Outlaw Heroes in Myth and History*. New York: Anthem Press, 2011.

Seal, Samantha Katz. *Father Chaucer: Generating Authority in The Canterbury Tales*. Oxford: Oxford University Press, 2019.

Seaman, Myra. *Objects of Affection: The Book and the Household in Late Medieval England*. Manchester: Manchester University Press, 2021.

Shillingsburg, Peter L. *Textuality and Knowledge: Essays*. University Park, PA: The Pennsylvania State University Press, 2017.

Shuffelton, George, ed. *Codex Ashmole 61: A Compilation of Popular Middle English Verse*. Kalamazoo, MI: Medieval Institute Publications, 2008.

Sidhu, Nicole Nolan. *Indecent Exposure: Gender, Politics, and Obscene Comedy in Middle English Literature*. Philadelphia, PA: University of Pennsylvania Press, 2016.

Simpson, James. *Piers Plowman: An Introduction to the B-Text*. New York: Longman, 1990.

Sinex, Margaret. "Echoic Irony in Walter Map's Satire against the Cistercians." *Comparative Literature* 54.4 (2002): 275–90.

Smalley, Beryl. *English Friars and Antiquity in the Early Fourteenth Century*. Oxford: Blackwell, 1960.

Smith, Joshua Byron. "Gerald of Wales, Walter Map and the Anglo-Saxon History of Lydbury North." In *Gerald of Wales: New Perspectives on a Medieval Writer and Critic*, edited by Georgia Henley and A. Joseph McMullen, 63–78. Cardiff: University of Wales Press, 2018.

—. *Walter Map and the Matter of Britain*. Philadelphia, PA: University of Pennsylvania Press, 2017.

Smith, Warren S. *Satiric Advice on Women and Marriage: From Plautus to Chaucer*. Ann Arbor, MI: University of Michigan Press, 2010.

Solberg, Emma Maggie. *Virgin Whore*. Ithaca, NY: Cornell University Press, 2018.
Spearing, A. C. "The Development of a Theme in *Piers Plowman*." *The Review of English Studies* 11.43 (1960): 241–53.
Steiner, Emily. *Reading Piers Plowman*. Cambridge: Cambridge University Press, 2013.
Stemmler, Theo. "Miscellany or Anthology? The Structure of Medieval Manuscripts: MS Harley 2253, for Example." In *Studies in the Harley Manuscript*, ed. Fein, 111–21.
Stokes, Roy. *The Function of Bibliography*. 2nd ed. Aldershot: Gower, 1982.
Strakhov, Elizaveta. "Opening Pandora's Box: Charles d'Orléans's Reception and the Work of Critical Bibliography." *The Papers of the Bibliographical Society of America* 116.4 (2022): 499–535.
Strohm, Paul. *Theory and the Premodern Text*. Minneapolis, MN: University of Minnesota Press, 2000.
Strong, David. "Mede's Right to Marry: A Consideration of Medieval Natural Law." *Medieval Perspectives* 21 (2005): 156–76.
Suarez, Michael F. "Hard Cases: Confronting Bibliographical Difficulty in Eighteenth-Century Texts." *The Papers of the Bibliographical Society of America* 111.1 (2017): 1–30.
Suarez, Michael F., and H. R. Woudhuysen, eds. *The Oxford Companion to the Book*. 2 vols. Oxford: Oxford University Press, 2010.
Swanson, Jenny. *John of Wales: A Study of the Works and Ideas of a Thirteenth-Century Friar*. Cambridge: Cambridge University Press, 1989.
Swift, Helen J. *Gender, Writing, and Performance: Men Defending Women in Late Medieval France, 1440–1538*. Oxford: Oxford University Press, 2008.
Tanselle, G. Thomas. *Bibliographical Analysis: A Historical Introduction*. Cambridge: Cambridge University Press, 2009.
Tavormina, M. Teresa. "Kindly Similitude: Langland's Matrimonial Trinity." *Modern Philology* 80.2 (1982): 117–28.
—. *Kindly Similitude: Marriage and Family in Piers Plowman*. Cambridge: D. S. Brewer, 1995.
Taylor, Andrew. *Textual Situations: Three Medieval Manuscripts and Their Readers*. Philadelphia, PA: University of Pennsylvania Press, 2002.
Taylor, Jamie K. "Lies, Puns, Tallies: Marital and Material Deceit in Langland and Chaucer." *Speculum* 93.1 (2018): 111–21.
Thomson, Rodney M. *A Descriptive Catalogue of the Medieval Manuscripts of Corpus Christi College, Oxford*. Cambridge: D. S. Brewer, 2011.
Thomson, Rodney M., and Nigel J. Morgan, eds. *The Cambridge History of the Book in Britain. Volume 2, c. 1100–1400*. Cambridge: Cambridge University Press, 2007.
Townsend, David. "Robert Grosseteste and Walter of Wimborne." *Medium Aevum* 55.1 (1986): 113–17.
Townsend, David, and A. G. Rigg. "Medieval Latin Poetic Anthologies (V): Matthew Paris' Anthology of Henry of Avranches." *Mediaeval Studies* 49 (1987): 352–90.

Trigg, Stephanie. "The Traffic in Medieval Women: Alice Perrers, Feminist Criticism and *Piers Plowman*." *YLS* 12 (1998): 5–29.
Trower, Katherine B. "The Figure of Hunger in *Piers Plowman*." *American Benedictine Review* 24 (1973): 238–60.
Wakelin, Daniel. *Designing English: Early Literature on the Page*. Oxford: Bodleian Library, University of Oxford, 2018.
—. *Immaterial Texts in Late Medieval England: Making English Literary Manuscripts, 1400–1500*. Cambridge: Cambridge University Press, 2022.
—. "Not Diane: The Risk of Error in Chaucerian Classicism." *Exemplaria* 29.4 (2017): 331–48.
—. *Scribal Correction and Literary Craft: English Manuscripts 1375–1510*. Cambridge: Cambridge University Press, 2014.
—. "'Thys Ys My Boke': Imagining the Owner in the Book." In *Spaces for Reading in Later Medieval England*, edited by Mary C. Flannery and Carrie Griffin, 13–33. New York: Palgrave Macmillan, 2016.
Walsh, P. G. "Antifeminism in the High Middle Ages." In Smith, ed., *Satiric Advice on Women and Marriage*, 222–42. Ann Arbor, MI: University of Michigan Press, 2010.
Walther, Hans, and Alfons Hilka. *Initia Carminum Ac Versuum Medii Aevi Posterioris Latinorum: Alphabetisches Verzeichnis Der Versanfänge Mittellateinischer Dichtungen*. Göttingen: Vandenhoeck & Ruprecht, 1959.
Ward, Benedicta. *Miracles and the Medieval Mind: Theory, Record, and Event, 1000–1215*. Philadelphia, PA: University of Pennsylvania Press, 1982.
Warner, Lawrence. "Scribes, Misattributed: Hoccleve and Pinkhurst." *SAC* 37 (2015): 55–100.
Warner, Marina. *Alone of All Her Sex: The Myth and the Cult of the Virgin Mary*. New York: Vintage Books, 1983.
Watson, Nicholas. "The Idea of Latinity." In *The Oxford Handbook of Medieval Latin Literature*, edited by Ralph H. Hexter and David Townsend, 124–48. Oxford: Oxford University Press, 2012.
Wood, Sarah. "Monologic Langland: Contentiousness and the 'Z Version' of *Piers Plowman*." *The Review of English Studies* 68.284 (2017): 224–43.
—. *Piers Plowman and Its Manuscript Tradition*. York: York Medieval Press, 2022.
Woods, Marjorie Curry. *Weeping for Dido: The Classics in the Medieval Classroom*. Princeton, NJ: Princeton University Press, 2019.
Yunck, John A. *The Lineage of Lady Meed: The Development of Mediaeval Venality Satire*. Notre Dame, IN: University of Notre Dame Press, 1963.

INDEX OF MANUSCRIPTS

Cambridge
  Cambridge University Library
    MS Dd.1.17 190–91
    MS Gg.4.27 22
    MS Gg.5.35 (Cambridge
      Songs) 89
  Corpus Christi College
    MS 450 68
  Gonville and Caius College
    MS 385 10
  Trinity College
    MS O.9.38 9 n.8, 92 n.20, 94 n.27
    MS R.3.20 22

Edinburgh
  National Library of Scotland
    MS Advocates 19.2.1
      (Auchinleck) 22, 24–5,
      89, 92

Harvard
  Houghton Library
    Lat. 300 11, 12

Lincoln
  Lincoln Cathedral Library
    MS 91 (Lincoln Thornton) 21, 89
    MS 105 10

London
  British Library
    Add. MS 22283 (Simeon) 89
    Arundel MS 292 89
    Cotton MS Nero A.10 (*Pearl*) 12, 22
    Cotton MS Titus A.20 9 n.8, 11, 42, 68, 92, 95 n.27
    Cotton MS Vespasian E.12 9 n.8, 92, 92 n.20, 95 n.27, 181
    Harley MS 913 (Kildare) 89
    Harley MS 978 12, 68
    Harley MS 2253 (Harley) 12, 89, 92 n.19, 95

    Harley MS 3954 191
  Lambeth Palace Library
    MS 357 49–50
  Lincoln's Inn
    MS Hale 150 185, 187

Munich
  Bayerische Staatsbibliothek
    MS Clm 631 181 n.41

Oxford
  Bodleian Library
    MS Add. A.44 (Bekynton) 10, 68, 92, 181
    MS Arch. Selden B.24 22
    MS Ashmole 61 22, 35
    MS Bodley 603 9 n.8
    MS Bodley 761 50
    MS Digby 19 94
    MS Digby 86 39 n.26
    MS Digby 102 191
    MS Digby 166 9 n.8, 68, 95 n.27, 181 n.41
    MS Eng. poet. a.1 (Vernon) 21, 89, 92, 190
    MS Fairfax 16 (Fairfax) 22
    MS Lat. misc. c.75 10, 68
    MS Laud misc. 108 12
    MS Laud mis. 656 191
    MS Rawl. B.214 9 n.8, 42, 95 n.27
    MS Rawl. G.109 9 n.8, 11, 95 n.27
  Corpus Christi College
    MS 232 43, 94
  University College
    MS 45 191

San Marino
  Huntington Library
    MS Hm 114 160 n.6, 191

Vatican City
  Vatican Library
    MS Lat. 3207 89

GENERAL INDEX

Alnoth the Pious *see* chapter 2.12, chapter 4.10 *under De nugis curialium*
analytical codicology *see under* book history
Anglo-Latin 8–13, 22, 93–5, 123–4, 157
antifeminism 85–90, 110–11, 116–17, 180–4
  see also misogyny, misogamy
Apocalypsis goliae episcopi 8 (Table 1), 28, 47 n.38, 64, 65 (Table 2), 67–8, 80 (Plate 11), 181, 191, 198
  influence on *Piers Plowman* 166–80
  in goliardic "Oxford Group" 95
  as Mappeana 192–4
  in satirical collections 9–10
  for Scribe X 55–61, 165–6
  for Z–redactor 162–4
Augustine, St 96–7, 99–100, 110, 116, 152
authorship 5, 28, 95, 120–1, 123, 157–64, 190–5
  scribal 23, 128, 133, 161–2, 164–5
  see also scribes *under* Bodley 851
Ave virgo mater christi 7 (Table 1), 27, 39, 43–4, 46, 53–4, 64, 65 (Table 2), 68, 84–5, 91, 109–10, 165, 199
  authorship and circulation 93–4
  decoration of 60–1
  embodiment 113–17
  influence on *Piers Plowman* 187–8
  insatiability 103–7
  reception 96–8
  for Scribe B 41–2

Babio 7 (Table 1), 9, 10, 47, 49–50, 59, 64, 65 (Table 2), 78 (Plate 9)
Bale, John 10, 34, 165 n.17, 181
Battle of Crécy (poem) 7 (Table 1), 41–2, 66 (Table 2)
Battle of Neville's Cross (poem) 7 (Table 1), 41–2, 56–57, 65 (Table 2), 79 (Plate 10)

bibliography *see under* book history
Bodley 851
  components
    chapter headings 47, 50–2, 55, 58–61, 62, 71–74 (Plates 2–5), 77–78 (Plates 8–9), 79 (Plate 11), 82 (Plate 13), 125–8, 129–132
    decoration 39
      paraphs 43, 48–9, 52–3, 54, 60–1, 74–77 (Plates 5–8), 159–64
      penwork initials 43, 48–9, 52, 55, 59–60, 72–3 (Plates 3–4), 75 (Plate 6), 78 (Plate 9), 81 (Plate 11)
      puzzle initials 59, 71 (Plate 2), 81 (Plate 12), 165–66
      red–touched initial letters 45–6, 48–50, 52–3, 75–78 (Plates 6–9)
      rubrication 37, 47, 50–2, 57–62, 66–7, 71–78 (Plates 2–9), 81 (Plate 11), 82–3 (Plates 13–14), 129–31, 166
    ex libris 34–6, 37, 39–41, 55, 62–4, 67, 70 (Plate 1)
    flyleaves 11, 38, 68, 199
    Part I 6 (Table 1), 39, 41, 47, 118–21, 199
      codicological unconscious of 154–6
      rubrication within 129–33
      table of contents 60–1
      for Scribe A 50–55
      for Scribe X 164–6
    Part II 10, 36, 39, 61, 84–5, 199
      quire ix of 91–2
      for Scribe B 42–4
      for Scribe C 44–6

GENERAL INDEX

for Scribe A 46–50
for Scribe X 55–60, 164–6
as type of compilation 190–91
Part III 36–7, 56, 57–8, 159, 164–6, 199
scribes 37–8, 6–7 (Table 1), 65–6 (Table 2)
Dodsthorpe 66–7, 199
Scribe A 28, 36, 40, 46–55, 64–5, 71–4 (Plates 2–5), 76–8 (Plates 7–9), 82 (Plate 13), 120, 128–32, 155–6
Scribe B 27, 42–4, 75–6 (Plates 6–7), 84–5, 91–6, 110, 115–17, 199
Scribe C 44–6, 49, 54, 76–7 (Plates 7–8)
Scribe X 27–9, 36, 38–9, 70–4 (Plates 1–5), 77–83 (Plates 8–14), 120
and *De nugis curialium* 128–32, 155–6
and John Wells 40
paleographic hand 56–8
and *Piers Plowman* 158–66, 179–180, 181, 190–5
relationship to *ex libris* 62–5
rubrication 59–61
scribal labor 55–65, 164–6
book history
bibliography 30–2
codicology 1–6, 9–13, 13–21, 30–3, 85–91, 190–1
analytical codicology 30–69, 91–2, 115–17, 128–33, 154–6, 162–6, 196–200
see also recomposition
booklet theory 16–18
paleography 37–8, 47, 56–8, 62–3
recomposition 42–65, 91–2, 115–17, 128–33, 154–6, 162–6, 196–200
see also analytical codicology
whole book 13–15, 36–42
see also codicological unconscious
Bridlington Prophecy 7 (Table 1), 8–9, 38, 47, 49–50, 58, 64–5, 65 (Table 2), 162, 181, 190, 192, 198
Britain 144
Brittany 144

Cambri carnaruan 7 (Table 1), 49, 64, 65 (Table 2)
Chaucer, Geoffrey 2–4, 85–7, 110, 116–17
codicological unconscious 5, 22–9, 91, 99, 116–17, 120, 129, 133, 154–6, 162–3, 180, 196–8
see also codicology *under* book history
codicology *see under* book history
Convocatio sacerdotum 6 (Table 1), 38, 66 (Table 2), 67, 199

De coniuge non ducenda 7 (Table 1), 27, 39, 64, 65 (Table 2), 75–6 (Plates 6–7), 84–5, 114–15
authorship and circulation 94–5
dating of 41–2
decoration of 60–1
embodiment 107–110
insatiability 100–3
misogamy 180–1
and *Piers Plowman* 28–9, 187–9, 191–4
reception 95–7
as satire 8, 10, 162–3
for Scribe A 53–5
for Scribe B 42–4, 91–2
for Scribe C 46
for Scribe X 67–8, 165–6
De mundi vanitate 43–4, 94
De nugis curialium 6 (Table 1), 22, 27–8, 36, 39, 47, 64, 65 (Table 2), 68, 71–4 (Plates 2–5), 82 (Plate 13)
chapter 2.4 (deformed foot) 123–4, 152–3
chapter 2.11 (Gwestin Gwestiniog, Triunein Vagelauc) 50–1, 119–20, 130 (Table 3), 131–33, 137–46, 148, 155–6
chapter 2.12 (Eadric Wilde, Alnoth the Pious) 50–1, 119–20, 130 (Table 3), 131–7, 139–46, 148, 150–2, 155–6
chapter 2.13 52, 119–20, 130 (Table 3), 131–3, 135–7, 139–54, 155–6
see also fantasm, fantasmata, fantasy
chapter 4.8 132, 139, 140–1, 143–4, 146
see also De nugis curialium 2.11
chapter 4.10 132, 139, 140–1, 142–3, 144–6
see also De nugis curialium 2.12

GENERAL INDEX

decoration 50–2, 58, 59–61, 62
Dissuasio Valerii ad Rufinum 10, 27, 28–9, 73 (Plate 4), 86–8, 111, 118–19, 123, 158, 163, 180–4, 189, 192–3
   material state 53–5
   organization 118–20, 128–32, 139–45
   reception 122–3, 141, 155–6
   as satire 8, 10–11
   for Scribe X 163, 164–6, 192–4
   style 123–5, 145–54
   textual criticism 121, 125–28
Debate between heart and eye 7 (Table 1), 11, 39, 45–6, 48, 53, 55–6, 60–1, 64, 65 (Table 2), 76 (Plate 7), 165–6
Dissuasio Valerii ad Rufinum see under De nugis curialium

Eadric Wilde *see* chapter 2.12, chapter 4.10 *under De nugis curialium*
editing *see* textual criticism
Epistola sathanae 6 (Table 1), 65 (Table 2), 55–6, 60 n.55, 162
eucharist 175–9
ex libris see components *under* Bodley 851
Execution of Archbishop Scrope (poem) 6 (Table 1), 38, 66 (Table 2), 67

fairy 119, 133–140, 142–5, 151–2, 157, 192–4
Fall of Carthage (poem) 6 (Table 1), 47, 50, 52, 56, 64, 65 (Table 2), 166
Fall of Troy (poem[s]) 7 (Table 1), 10–11, 46, 47, 49, 54, 60, 64, 65 (Table 2)
fantasm, fantasmata, fantasy 50–1, 119, 130 (Table 3), 132–3, 135–7, 139–154, 192–4
   see also chapter 2.13 *under De nugis curialium*
Four Evangelists 169–72

Gerald of Wales 121–2
Geta 7 (Table 1), 9–11, 66 (Table 2), 67
gluttony 99–100, 103, 171–9
goliard, goliardic 11–12, 42–3, 67–8, 92 n.20, 95–7, 151 n.80, 180–1, 192
Golias 8, 95–6
Gwestin Gwestiniog *see* chapter 2.11, chapter 4.8 *under De nugis curialium*

Henry of Avranches 9 n.8, 44–5
Hippolytus of Rome 112
Hundred Years War 41–2
   see also Battle of Crécy (poem), *Battle of Neville's Cross* (poem), *Bridlington Prophecy*

incubus *see* fairy
insatiability 27, 91, 98, 99–110, 115–17
intention 23–6, 51, 53, 64–5, 91–2, 125–8, 155–6
Invectives of Michael of Cornwall 7 (Table 1), 10–11, 37, 44–6, 46–9, 58–9, 64, 65 (Table 2), 76–7 (Plates 7–8), 190

Jerome, St 85–8, 99, 101–2, 107, 109, 110–13, 113, 116, 169–72, 184, 186
John of Bridlington *see Bridlington Prophecy*
John of Garland 10
John of Wales 86

Kempe, Margery 179

London 10, 40, 42, 63–4, 173–5

manuscript study *see* book history
Map, Walter 8–9, 22, 27–8, 30, 61–2, 92, 154–6, 187, 198
   influence on *Piers Plowman* 192–4
   pseudonymous authorship 86, 95–6, 157–9, 180
   for Scribe X 163–6
   style 118–29, 141, 144–5
   see also De nugis curialium
marriage *see* misogamy, misogyny
Mary, mother of Jesus 85, 93, 96–8, 103–10, 113–15, 185, 188–9
Maximos of Turin 111–13
Michael of Cornwall *see Invectives* of Michael of Cornwall
miracles 123–4, 132, 146–8, 152–4
misogamy 27, 28–9, 42–3, 84–91, 96–8, 110–17, 180–9
   see also antifeminism, misogyny
misogyny 27, 84–5, 88, 110–11, 116–17, 163, 181–3, 187
   see also antifeminism, misogamy

New Formalism 20–1
New Philology 19–20

Origen 112
Oxford 37, 39–40, 54, 63, 85, 95, 165, 181

Paul, St 97–8
phantasm, phantasmata *see* fantasm, fantasmata, fantasy
Piers Plowman 7 (Table 1), 8, 22, 28–9, 37, 39–41, 55, 56, 58, 59, 60, 62, 64–5, 65 (Table 2), 66–7, 81 (Plate 12), 83 (Plate 14), 157–195
　Conscience 182–7
　Holy Church 170, 182–9, 193–4
　Hunger 163, 166–80
　Meed 181–9
　Reason 183–4
　Z–redactor 161–2, 180, 193 n.71

Ramsey 37, 39–40, 54–5, 60
recomposition *see under* book history

satire 8, 28, 94–5, 167–8, 172, 187
　in compilations 10–11, 190
　Mappeana 121–3, 151 n.80, 178–9, 180–2, 187
　for Walter Map 136–9, 157–8
scholastics, scholasticism 149–50, 169–171
schools 10, 89, 158, 181–2
scribes *see under* Bodley 851
Speculum stultorum 7 (Table 1), 38, 39, 64, 65 (Table 2), 78 (Plate 9), 162

influence on *Piers Plowman* 190, 198
recension 61
rubrication 49–50
as satire 9–11, 162, 198
for Scribe A 46–7, 54–5
for Scribe X 55–6, 165, 181
St. Mary le Bow 190
succubus *see* fairy

textual criticism 18, 30–2, 66–7, 121–9, 155–6
textual unconscious 24, 99, 115–17, 129
Triunein Vagelauc *see* chapter 2.11, chapter 4.8 *under De nugis curialium*
Troilus and Criseyde 2–4
Troy 10
　see also Fall of Troy

vernacular 11 n.13, 11 n.14, 12, 15, 84, 96, 162, 199

Wales 122, 144
　see also chapter 2.11, chapter 2.12, 4,8, 5.10 *under De nugis curialium*
Walter of Wimborne 27, 43–4, 67–8, 84, 93–7, 107, 110, 165
　see also De coniuge non ducenda, De mundi vanitate
Wells, John 37, 39–41, 60, 62–4, 67

Z–redactor *see under Piers Plowman*